TWENTIETH CENTURY VIEWS

The aim of this series is to present the best in
contemporary critical opinion on major authors,
providing a twentieth century perspective on
their changing status in an era of profound
revaluation.

Maynard Mack, *Series Editor*
Yale University

SHAKESPEARE
THE COMEDIES

SHAKESPEARE THE COMEDIES

A COLLECTION OF CRITICAL ESSAYS

Edited by

Kenneth Muir

Prentice-Hall, Inc. *Englewood Cliffs, N.J.*

A SPECTRUM BOOK

Current printing (last digit):

11   10   9   8   7   6

Contents

Introduction

by Kenneth Muir

I

It is surprising that, in spite of the overproduction of books on Shake-speare, so few should have been devoted to the comedies. Between H. B. Charlton's book in 1938 and J. Dover Wilson's twenty-four years later, there have been only a handful of books concerned wholly with the comedies and none of them seems likely to achieve the authority of Bradley's book on the tragedies.

Charlton's book, though learned and full of useful information, is critically unsatisfactory. He tended to disparage those comedies which are least like the three masterpieces, *Much Ado about Nothing, As You Like It, Twelfth Night;* he had an unduly low opinion of *Love's Labour's Lost;* he argued that the plays of the last period showed a weakening of Shakespeare's power of imaginative vision, even though "poetically they are of great price"; and, determined to believe that Shakespeare went from strength to strength until the period of the great tragedies, he assumed that the problem plays preceded *Much Ado about Nothing.* The title of George Gordon's posthumous volume, *Shakespearian Comedy,* is misleading, for only a few of its amusing and charming essays are actually concerned with the comedies. E. C. Pettet gives a brief survey of the comedies in *Shakespeare and the Romance Tradition* and the book is valuable for its account of the poet's debt to his predecessors. S. C. Sen Gupta and T. M. Parrott have provided comprehensive accounts of Shake-speare's comedies, but these are descriptive rather than critical. John R. Brown's *Shakespeare and his Comedies* is a highly intelligent book in which "by following a few themes, or ideas, through all the early comedies," Brown "tries to discover the judgements which inform the individual plays"; but an excerpt from this book would give a misleading impression of it. Even more stimulating, though rather narrower in scope, is C. L. Barber's *Shake-peare's Festive Comedy.* Bertrand Evans deals effectively with one aspect of the comedies—the way in which Shakespeare keeps the audience informed of what is hidden from some or all of the characters on the stage. The audience knows all the time, for example, that Portia is disguised as a lawyer and that

Shylock will be foiled; that Ganymede is Rosalind; that Cesario is Viola and that because Sebastian has been saved Olivia will be provided with a husband; that the Friar in *Measure for Measure* is Vincentio and that he will intervene to save Isabella's chastity and Claudio's life. Almost the only exception is in *The Winter's Tale*, in which the audience is allowed to suppose that Hermione is dead. (Shakespeare would never have followed Jonson's practice in *The Silent Woman* of revealing the "woman's" sex only in the last act.) Evans throws a spotlight on one aspect of Shakespeare's method, but the illumination is limited in area. There is, finally, J. Dover Wilson's *Shakespeare's Happy Comedies*, written largely before the Second World War, and published some twenty-five years later. It reflects the gusto and enjoyment which forty-five years of editing has been unable to tarnish.

In addition to these general books, there are special studies of the problem plays (by W. W Lawrence and E. M. W. Tillyard) and of the last plays (by G. Wilson Knight, Derek Traversi, and Tillyard). There are even books on individual plays—J. W. Draper and Leslie Hotson on *Twelfth Night*, Frances Yates on *Love's Labour's Lost*, Mary Lascelles on *Measure for Measure*, S. L. Bethell on *The Winter's Tale*, C. T. Prouty on *Much Ado about Nothing*.

But although there is some good criticism in nearly all these books, some of the most satisfying criticism is to be found in uncollected essays and in general books on Shakespeare. The present selection is made from all these sources.

II

Some years ago, in *Shakespeare and the Tragic Pattern*, I tried to show that there was no such thing as Shakespearian Tragedy: that each tragedy from *Titus Andronicus* to *Coriolanus* must be considered as a unique work of art; and that it is almost as absurd to judge *Antony and Cleopatra* by "rules" evolved from a study of *Hamlet* and *King Lear*, as it would be to deplore Shakespeare's violation of the unities or Racine's failure to provide comic relief.

The same thing is surely true of Shakespeare's comedies: the differences between any one play and another are more significant than the resemblances. The only characteristic that all the comedies have in common is the use of disguise. In *The Two Gentlemen of Verona* Julia, disguised as a boy, is employed by the man she loves, as Viola is employed by Orsino. In *The Taming of the Shrew* Christopher Sly is disguised as a lord, Lucentio and Tranio exchange clothes, Lucentio is disguised as Cambio, and a Pedant is disguised as Vincentio. In *A Midsummer-Night's Dream* Bottom is translated into an ass; in *Love's Labour's Lost* the lords dress up as Muscovites; in *The Merchant of Venice* Jessica disguises herself in "the lovely garnish of a boy" and Portia and Nerissa likewise don masculine attire; in *Much Ado about Nothing*—apart from the masked ball—Margaret poses as Hero and Hero poses as her cousin; in *As You Like It* Rosalind and Celia become Ganymede and Aliena; in *The Merry Wives of Windsor* Ford disguises himself as Brook; in *All's Well that Ends Well* Helena passes herself off in bed as Diana, much as Mariana in *Measure for Measure* takes Isabella's place in her assignation with Angelo; in this same play the Duke is disguised as a friar, Polixenes attends the sheep-shearing feast in disguise in order to spy on his son, and Imogen disguises herself as Fidele; and in *The Tempest* Ariel appears as a nymph and a harpy. The only apparent exception is *The Comedy of Errors*. But even here Antipholus and Dromio of Syracuse are, in a sense, "disguised" as their Ephesian counterparts.

For women to disguise themselves as boys may have been suggested by the fact that there were no actresses on the Elizabethan stage; but Shakespeare does not appear to have used this device so frequently merely to simplify the task of his female impersonators. The boy who played Rosalind, for example, had to pretend to be a girl, disguised as a boy (Ganymede), acting the part of Rosalind; and whoever played Perdita had to pretend to be a princess, supposed to be a shepherdess, and playing the part of the mistress of the sheep-shearing feast. Such complications, disguises within disguises, must have required a great deal of skill and sophistication from the actors. More significantly, disguise enabled Shakespeare to symbolize one of his favorite themes, the contrast between appearance and reality. But although disguise and mistaken identity are prominent features of Shakespearian comedy, they do not seem to be its essence.

When Shakespeare began to write he had several possible models. He could attempt to write allegorical plays in euphuistic prose; but Lyly's plays were written to be performed by child actors before a specialized audience, and they would have been manifestly unsuitable for the popular theatre. Nevertheless their influence is discernible on Shakespeare's comedies, as G. K. Hunter and others have demonstrated. The witty exchanges between servants, pert pages, the sophisticated conversations of heroines, the use of song as an integral part of a play, the grouping of characters, and the tightening of prose rhythm are some of the techniques in which Shakespeare may have profited by Lyly's example.

So many plays have been lost—by Munday, for example—that we cannot be certain of Shakespeare's debts to plays which have survived. He could learn from Robert Greene in the interweaving of different plots. He could read Italian comedies and he probably knew something of the *commedia dell'arte*. He could, finally, go to the plays of Plautus and Terence, which were probably his first introduction to drama, and which had an unrivaled reputation in the sixteenth century. *The Comedy of Errors*, probably Shakespeare's first comedy, is clearly based on the *Menaechmi* of Plautus—one scene was obviously suggested by the famous episode in the *Amphitryon*, where the hero is shut out of his own house. Shakespeare outwent his models by providing the twins with twin servants; but he realized that Latin comedy could not merely be transplanted if it was to take root in English soil. He gave Adriana a sister to complicate the intrigue still further and to provide Antipholus of Syracuse with a fifth-act bride; Adriana's jealousy and her husband's roving eye enabled him to introduce some serious discussions of the marriage bond; and the Aegeon story, derived probably from the tale of Apollonius of Tyre, was used to frame the farcical scenes with a tragi-comic prologue and epilogue. Already, in his first comedy, Shakespeare was experimenting. Dissatisfied with mere farce, he humanized his material, so that the characters, although placed in farcical situations, are confronted with basic human problems.

In what was probably his next comedy, *The Two Gentlemen of Verona*, Shakespeare used as his source, directly or indirectly, the Spanish romance, Montemayor's *Diana*. His heroine, as in so many of his later comedies, is disguised as a page. His unheroic hero, Proteus, who betrays his friend, is permitted to soliloquize when confronted with temptation—a sign perhaps that the poet was dissatisfied with the stereotypes of farce. His two servants, Launce and Speed, are nicely differentiated, and they both speak in prose rather than in the doggerel verse of the Dromios. But the play (in the opinion of most critics), though it aims higher, is less successful than *The Comedy of Errors*, largely because of the absurd ending in which Valentine offers to resign Sylvia to a would-be rapist. This ending has been variously excused or explained by unintelligent cutting, by the unfortunate influence of the sonnets-situation on the play, and by uncertainty of touch in an attempt to satirize the conventional assumption that the true gentleman would sacrifice love to friendship. In no other comedy does Shakespeare so leave us in perplexity.

For his third comedy, *The Taming of the Shrew*, Shakespeare went to Gascoigne's *Supposes* (translated from Ariosto), but he combined this plot, very ingeniously, with the "taming" plot, and he set both in the framework of the gulling of Christopher Sly. The distancing of the play by the induction, the contrast between the levels of reality represented by the two main plots, and the sermon with which the play concludes—however unpalatable to modern tastes—prevent the comedy from being farcical.

The fourth comedy, *Love's Labour's Lost*, is almost the only one for which no source has been discovered, and it is the only one which depends for a great deal of its effect on satire of contemporary affectations and even of personalities. This is why many of the studies of the play (in books by Frances Yates, Muriel C. Bradbrook, and Robert Gittings) have been concerned primarily with the identification of the different characters. Is Armado meant to represent Raleigh or Perez? Is Holofernes supposed to be Florio or Harvey or merely a generic Pedant? Is Boyet Chapman? These are questions which are still in debate and it is not even certain that "The School of Night," discussed at length by Miss Yates, existed. Whatever the extent of contemporary satire, recent productions have shown that the play can still delight an ordinary audience. H. Granville-Barker began his preface to the play with the words: "Here is a fashionable play; now, by three hundred years, out of fashion. Nor did it ever, one supposes, make a very wide appeal." But this was written before the numerous successful productions at the Old Vic and Stratford-upon-Avon demonstrated the continued vitality and popularity of the play. The plot is of the flimsiest—its resolution is obvious from the start—but the poetry, the extraordinary verbal invention, and several of the characters are more successful than those of any previous play.

These first four comedies, then, have an astonishing variety, and no comic formula can be applied to them all. The same variety is apparent in the maturer comedies which followed.

III

The first comic masterpiece, *A Midsummer-Night's Dream*, was followed during the next five or six years by *The Merchant of Venice, Much Ado about Nothing, As You Like It, Twelfth Night*, and the less interesting *Merry Wives of Windsor*, in which Falstaff, deprived of most of his wit, is put into a contemporary comedy of intrigue. *A Midsummer-Night's Dream* seems, on internal evidence, to have been written for a wedding, though it was afterwards performed in the public theatre. In it Shakespeare combined a series of inter-related plots. The quartet of young lovers who change partners under the influence of Puck's magic juice, the quarrel between Oberon and Titania and her love for an ass, and the tragical mirth of Quince's play all exhibit the irrationality of romantic love; and even though the love of Theseus and Hippolyta is more mature and stable, we are reminded of earlier amorous episodes in Theseus' career. The speech on the resemblance between the lunatic, the lover, and the poet sums up ironically the necessary role of the imagination in human affairs. The play is the first in which Shakespeare used imagery to create a unified atmosphere.

One of two critics, notably Walter De la Mare and J. Dover Wilson, have argued that some of the verse is so bad that Shakespeare must have taken over lines from an earlier play; but there is no real evidence for this. The suspect passages are in rhymed verse, and Shakespeare was using more rhyme in 1595 than he had done earlier. He must have been as aware as his critics of the absurdities of the verse, and one can only suppose that he used them to point up the absurd behavior of the lovers.

In *The Merchant of Venice*, as G. Wilson Knight and C. S. Lewis have shown, we have two contrasted worlds of Venice and Belmont, a contrast between gold and blood, between the letter and the spirit. The two plots of the caskets and the pound of flesh, both concerned with metals, are structurally related. The stories are both incredible in themselves, but together they are symbolically acceptable—the caskets suggesting the contrast between appearance and reality, and the hazard of Antonio for his friend being contrasted with Shylock's usury and hatred. The play is rounded off with the light-hearted business of the rings and the music of Belmont. Shakespeare went some way to humanize his villain, but recent history has made it difficult for us to accept Shylock in the same way the original audience would have done. It would be wrong, nevertheless, to suppose that the humanizing of Shylock brings the play too close to tragedy. We know, all the time, that he will be foiled. It would be still more wrong to take the actions of the characters too literally and to suppose, with Sir Arthur Quiller-Couch and others, that Bassanio is a mere fortune-hunter, Lorenzo a cad, all the Christians morally deplorable, and Jessica a traitress. As J. Middleton Murry amply demonstrates, such an interpretation is totally at odds with the spirit of the play even when played in a modern theatre.

In one respect *The Merchant of Venice* resembles *Much Ado about Nothing*. In both, love and happiness are brought to the verge of disaster by the intrusion of evil. But the overall theme of *Much Ado*, apparent in the Dogberry scenes, as well as in the two main plots, is (as John Masefield observed) the power of report to alter human destiny, and the iterative imagery is concerned with clothing—an appropriate image for the contrast between appearance and reality. The play is also concerned with modes of love. The marriage of Hero and Claudio (which is hardly more than a marriage of convenience) is contrasted with the relationship between Benedick and Beatrice, whose wit-combats display a deeper love which they are both reluctant to admit, partly because they are in revolt against the inanities of romantic love. The play is written on several different levels. The tragicomedy of Hero and Claudio is largely in somewhat mannered and artificial verse; the comedy of manners of the other lovers is written in vigorous and witty prose which gives them a much greater vitality and reality.

It is significant that, in creating Shylock, Falstaff, Beatrice, Rosalind, and Malvolio, Shakespeare made considerable use of prose, as though he found it difficult, at this stage in his career, to write verse flexible enough to express the full individuality of his characters. He had succeeded with Berowne, with Juliet's Nurse, with Richard III, and with Bolingbroke; but it was not until the turn of the century that his verse found a flexibility and freedom to match the new vitality of his characters.

The next comedy, *As You Like It*, based on Lodge's pastoral romance, is itself concerned with different kinds of pastoral—the noble outlaws, the eclogue tradition represented by Phoebe and Silvius, the country bumpkin (the country seen through the eyes of the townsman), the genuine country-man (Corin), and the fine ladies posing as shepherd and shepherdess. Jaques acts as a satirical commentator on the outlaws but is himself criticized by the exiled Duke and by Rosalind; and Touchstone, a critic of the country and of love, is himself driven to marry a country wench whom he despises. But it is Rosalind herself who is the chief satirist of love. Her attack on the "cruel" shepherdess, Phoebe, makes short work of one conventional aber-ration of romantic love and her witty exchanges with Orlando are alike a satire on her own sex and on the foolishness of lovers.

It has often been said that *Twelfth Night* is a masterpiece of recapitulation. In other words, most of the dramatic devices used in the play are repeated from previous comedies. But this is rather misleading, for the total impression is quite different from anything previously written by Shakespeare. Although the main source is Barnaby Riche's tale of Apollonius and Silla, this is Shakespeare's one play which is modeled plainly on Italian comedy. It differs, however, from its Italian analogues in its lyrical atmosphere, in its use of music and song throughout, and its interweaving of different plots. Like its immediate predecessors, the play pokes fun at the absurdities of lovers. Orsino's affected love-melancholy, Olivia's affected love for her dead brother, Sir Andrew Aguecheek's delusions as a suitor, Malvolio's self-love (without which he would not be gulled) are all satirized by Feste, as many critics have pointed out. At the end, all the characters are brought to self-knowledge. Orsino is made to realize the difference between love and sentimentality; Olivia is cured by her passion for Cesario and her marriage to Sebastian; Sir Andrew realizes the brutal truth about his exploitation by Sir Toby; Malvolio is converted to an honest hatred.

It is characteristic of nearly all Shakespeare's comedies that the heroines should largely escape his satire and that it is their qualities (wit, humor, generosity, initiative, balance, courage) which bring about a satisfactory resolution of the plot. Portia, Rosalind, and Viola embody the values of the plays in which they appear; and the falsities of society and the corruption of sentimentality are revealed for what they are in the clear light of the comic spirit.

IV

The greatest change in critical opinion in the past sixty years relates to the so-called "problem" comedies. Most nineteenth century critics—Pater being the outstanding exception—regarded them with embarrassment and distaste, assuming that Shakespeare was passing through a period of sex-nausea as the result of some unfortunate experience in his private life. But in the present century these plays have attracted more attention than any of the other comedies. This is partly because in their treatment of sex they are closer in spirit to modern literature than to nineteenth century literature, and partly because their ambiguity makes them a more interesting topic for criticism than the earlier comedies, of which the meaning is not seriously in doubt.

The ending of *Measure for Measure*—the substitution of Mariana for Isabella in Angelo's bed, the Duke's pardon of Angelo, and Isabella's marriage—outraged Robert Bridges as it had Coleridge, because it ignored the claims of justice. It has been defended in the present century on two different levels: by W. W. Lawrence as a conventional conclusion which would be readily acceptable to the Jacobean audience, and by several later critics on theological grounds. G. Wilson Knight—in one of his earliest and best essays, published in 1930—stressed the scriptural affinities of the play; but he argued that Isabella, after failing to sacrifice her chastity to save her brother's life, was converted to a greater humanity by the example of Mariana. He was followed by J. Middleton Murry in his chapter on the play in *Shakespeare* (1936). These interpretations did not satisfy Una Ellis-Fermor, who regarded the play as cynical. R. W. Chambers (in the essay in this volume) regarded the play as an essentially Christian treatment of forgiveness, and he defended Isabella's refusal to sacrifice her chastity—Shakespeare departed from all his sources in making her a novice—and her subsequent forgiveness of her enemy, Angelo. Muriel C. Bradbrook discussed Shakespeare's use of morality techniques; and Roy Battenhouse went even further in treating the play as an allegory, in which even the names of the characters are significant—Lucio, for example, being Lucifer. To Elizabeth M. Pope (*Shakespeare Survey 2*) Shakespeare was clarifying the ordinary Christian doctrine of the Renaissance and making a deliberate effort to harmonize the "discrepancy between the conceptions of religious mercy and secular justice." To J. C. Maxwell *Measure for Measure* is one of Shakespeare's most perfect works of art, and F. R. Leavis has also written on the greatness of the play.

On the other hand, several recent critics have reverted to the view that the play is in some sense a failure. T. M. Parrott speaks of the "incongruity between the tragic theme, the tragi-comedy technique, and the realistic background." E. C. Pettet speaks of a "sour spirit of disillusionment and cynicism" in the play and a sense of strain in the artistry; E. M. W. Tillyard complains of "an artistic breach of internal harmony" in the contrast between the two halves of the play; and Clifford Leech (in an article in this volume) is clearly uneasy at the attempts to make the play a theological allegory. This continuing debate at least exemplifies the complexity and vitality of the play, and the fascination it holds for recent critics.

There is a greater measure of agreement on *All's Well that Ends Well*. The nineteenth century view that Helena was contaminated by the sordid means she employed to obtain a prize of doubtful worth has given place to a realization that Shakespeare was dramatizing a tale of a heroine who fulfilled

an apparently impossible task and that the Jacobean audience would cheerfully believe in Bertram's fifth-act repentance. To Bernard Shaw Helena was
a true Ibsenite character; to Wilson Knight she embodies qualities to be
found in no other Shakespearian heroine; and to Muriel C. Bradbrook she
exemplifies the theme that virtue is the true nobility.*

V

Victorian critics tended to sentimentalize the comedies of Shakespeare's
final period. They often assumed that the poet had emerged from the gloom
of his tragic period to reach an "ultimate mood of grave serenity," at peace
with the world, and expressing his hopes for its future in the young lovers
of the last plays. It was to counteract this sentimental attitude that Lytton
Strachey wrote his notorious essay on "Shakespeare's Final Period," in which
he called attention to the many evil characters to be found in these plays, and
argued that the poet at this time was bored with the theatre, bored with life,
and bored with everything except his poetical dreams. Strachey's views were
as absurd as the ones he sought to supersede, and critics of the past fifty years
have sought to show that he was misguided. Some have shown that the
existence of evil characters does not prove that Shakespeare was not concerned with reconciliation and forgiveness: it merely indicates that he was
not escaping into a poetical utopia, where forgiveness and reconciliation
would not be needed. Other critics have pointed to the theatrical mastery
displayed in the plays—e.g., in the extraordinary last act of *Cymbeline*—which
proves that he was still interested in the theatre. E. M. W. Tillyard argued
that Shakespeare was seeking to complete the tragic cycle and to juxtapose
"planes of reality," so that, for example, he could in a single play make use
of Holinshed's *Chronicles*, an Italian novel, a folk-tale, and the pastoral
tradition. T. S. Eliot once suggested that Shakespeare had gone "beyond the
dramatic," that he was no longer interested in character for its own sake.
Other critics have sought to explain the last plays by the changing fashions
of the time and by the influence of Beaumont and Fletcher and Heywood.

It should be emphasized, on the one hand, that the first play of the series,
Pericles, probably preceded the tragi-comedies of Beaumont and Fletcher,
and that the romances have links with Shakespeare's earlier comedies; and,
on the other hand, that he was trying to do something different from anything he had attempted before, devoting himself (in Keats's phrase) to
"other sensations." Although the four romances resemble each other in

* Although *Troilus and Cressida* is sometimes treated as a comedy or a "comical satire"—
notably by Oscar J. Campbell and Alice Walker—it seems more appropriate to regard
it as a tragedy or tragical satire. This is Nevill Coghill's view in his book, *Shakespeare's
Professional Skills* (1964).

several ways—they are all concerned, in one way or another, with reunion or reconciliation; they all impose a happy ending on a plot that could have ended in tragedy; three of them end with the reunion of parents, in two of them the reconciliation is cemented by the marriage of the children, and in three the sea plays a major role. Yet the plays also differ widely from each other: the hero of *Pericles* is unlucky; the hero of *The Tempest* is betrayed; the heroines of *The Winter's Tale* and *Cymbeline* are victims of jealousy; *The Tempest* obeys the unities of time and place, whereas *Pericles* and *The Winter's Tale* flagrantly disregard the unities to enable the daughters to grow to marriageable age; in two of the plays the hero repents and is forgiven by his wronged wife; and in *The Tempest* the wronged hero forgives his enemies.

In spite of the possibility of dividing the comedies into groups, therefore, it is more profitable to stress the differences between one comedy and another in the same group. Although all the comedies bear the mark of Shakespeare's hand, and although he repeated over and over again a number of favorite comic devices, each comedy was an attempt to do something different. Even the greatest is flawed, either by textual corruption or sheer carelessness, but each one is a unique experience.

VI

The present collection attempts to give a cross-section of twentieth century criticism of the comedies. It includes some essays which already seem rather old-fashioned and others, included for the sake of representativeness, with which the editor does not agree. There is nothing on the imagery (for little has been written on it) and nothing on the relationship between Shakespeare's comedies and those of his contemporaries. Nor is there anything on Shakespearian Comedy in general, for reasons stated earlier. But the reader will find essays, all good of their kind, on all the major comedies; and in the bibliography there is a list of books and articles from which the final selection was made.

Themes and Structure in
The Comedy of Errors

by Harold Brooks

Four of Shakespeare's comedies, there is little doubt, are earlier than the rest: *The Comedy of Errors*, *The Taming of the Shrew*, *The Two Gentlemen of Verona*, *Love's Labour's Lost*. Their chronological sequence is uncertain. I incline to think them all subsequent to *Richard III* (*c.* 1591) and conjecture *c.* 1592 for *The Comedy of Errors*. The neo-classical features in *Errors* and *The Shrew* may associate them with the Ovidian narrative poems, *Venus and Adonis* (1593) and *The Rape of Lucrece* (1594); though I should like to think also that behind them lie youthful experiments in school drama. For if, as Beeston related, Shakespeare was formerly a schoolmaster in the country, and if he had worked in Latin and neo-classical drama with the boys, this would admirably account for the command he shows, from the very outset of his career as a playwright, of the elements of dramatic construction.

No extant play of his, however early, lacks evidence of this command. It operates on the large scale and the small. *The Comedy of Errors* has its large dramatic design, but is no less remarkable for its controlled detail, unparalleled at this date, except in *The Spanish Tragedy*, outside Shakespeare's other plays. His handling of the lesser units of structure, from the scene downwards, is already sure, and indeed within its conventions brilliant. These units include the scene, a new one beginning whenever the stage is clear; the sub-scene, or *scène* as understood in French drama, a new one beginning whenever the group on stage is altered by anyone leaving or joining it; the passage of dialogue or the set speech, more than one, sometimes, going to make up the *scène*; besides every physical action, whether procession, brawl, or bit of minor business. Fully to appreciate the close bonding of such units in the structure one has to ask what is contributed by every passage as it occurs, and how it is interrelated with others throughout the play. Some illustration is possible, however, by taking a single scene.

"Themes and Structure in *The Comedy of Errors*." From *Early Shakespeare*, ed. J. R. Brown and B. Harris (London: Edward Arnold, 1961), pp. 55-71. Reprinted by permission of the author and publishers.

11

Act I, scene ii will serve, the better as it is not exceptionally highly wrought. Yet even a scene so expository (being the first of the main action) is not allowed to lack the immediate interest that holds an audience. Shakespeare has already the art of fulfilling, and with the economy that secures dramatic compression, three principal requirements of dramatic structure: retrospect, preparation, and immediate interest. By retrospect and preparation the play-wright keeps his action moving—the great virtue of dynamic or progressive structure—with the strongest continuity. Further, while he concerns himself with the matter of the present scene, he can add force and meaning to what has gone before, and pile them up for what is to come after, so that, in effect, he is building up several (perhaps widely separated) parts of his play at once. This can be of great value in what I will call the harmonic structure: the structure which by parallel, contrast, or cross-reference, independent perhaps of the cause-and-effect connections of the progressive action, makes us com-pare one passage or person of the play with another, and so find an enriched significance in both. As for immediate interest, that is indispensable: "What one requires in the theatre," wrote William Archer to Gilbert Murray, "is, so to speak, a certain pressure of pleasurable sensation to the square inch, or rather to the minute"; and "pleasurable" being taken in the right sense, this puts it admirably.

With the first entry and speech of our illustrative scene, there is interest in the appearance of three fresh persons, and some tension: Antipholus the alien is warned that he is in danger of the fate which overtook Ægeon in the scene before; a fate summarized in the natural course of the warning. This retro-spect, and parallel of situation, link the opening of the main action and that of the Ægeon action within which it is to be framed. The link is strengthened by reference to three themes already started in the Ægeon episode: risk (and in particular the hazards of Ephesus), wealth, and time. Ægeon, Antipholus is told:

> . . . not being able to buy out his life
> According to the statute of the town
> Dies ere the weary sun set in the west.

Since these themes will now be developed throughout the main action, the references to them are preparatory no less than retrospective. The theme of moneyed wealth is emphasized by stage "business": the merchant hands back to Antipholus

> . . . your money that I had to keep,

and Antipholus passes it on to his Dromio. The bag of money is to furnish one of the two subjects of the first comic misunderstanding, due to occur later in the scene, and therefore is implanted visually on the audience's mind beforehand; moreover, it will form a parallel with the gold chain and the purse, other concrete visible properties which carry on the theme and become foci of similar cross-purposes in subsequent acts. The second subject of the imminent misunderstanding, the summons to dinner by the Ephesian Dromio, is also prepared, and the time-theme touched, in Antipholus's observation:

> Within this hour it will be dinner-time.

Another chief theme of the play is introduced when he is warned to conceal his Syracusan origin; for this concerns his identity. Again, when he bids Dromio depart with the money, Dromio's exit lines:

> Many a man would take you at your word,
> And go indeed, having so good a mean,

foreshadow the suspicion that his master will shortly entertain, while preparing us to recognize it as groundless, a comic error. The rendezvous arranged, at the Centaur, leads to the reunion of master and servant in II. ii.

Dromio's jesting exit ends the first *scène*. It is Shakespeare's cue for underlining the promise of comedy: the note of tension at the start has now passed into the background. It is the cue also for Antipholus's direct comment upon Dromio's character, which adds to what has been gathered of his own and of the relations between the two of them. The audience's present curiosity about them is gratified, and its appetite whetted, both together; for the promise of comedy is contained in the informative comment itself:

> A trusty villain, sir, that very oft,
> When I am dull with care and melancholy,
> Lightens my humour with his merry jests,

jests, it is clear, which are very timely. Antipholus's experience of Dromio as a jester is needed to explain his coming assumption that the invitation to dinner is his servant's joke, and his slowly mounting surprise and anger when it is persisted in out of season. The rendezvous with the merchant, "at five-o-clock," like that arranged in *scène* I with Dromio, helps to establish the theme of timing, and the motifs of timely or untimely meetings or failures to meet. It points forward, moreover, to the hour (cf. v. i. 118) so fateful for Ægeon, the hour (though we do not yet know this) of the *dénouement*; somewhat as the mention of dinner-time in *scène* I began to make ready for the dinner episode (III. i), the play's central pivot.

The *scènes* of three, then two persons, are succeeded by Antipholus's first soliloquy. Here and in the two remaining *scènes*, the immediate interest for the audience strengthens. From the point of view of comedy and the intrigue, *scène* 4, the encounter with the wrong Dromio, is the climax of the whole scene. It is flanked, in the ABA form so frequent in Shakespeare, by Antipholus's soliloquies, which are the imaginative climaxes, and, together with the moment when he strikes (the Ephesian) Dromio, the emotional climaxes too, though there is contrast between his emotion as an exasperated and as a "melancholy" imaginative man. From the imaginative, introspective man he is, soliloquies (his brother has none) come naturally; his allusion to his "care and melancholy" has prepared the way for them.

The first of them explains both his special occasion of "care," and his arrival, contributing by a single stroke to the logic at once of the character and of the plot. He has an aim, fruitlessly pursued: "to find a mother and a brother." It is a dull member of the audience who does not refer this back to Ægeon's retrospect (narrating much of the dramatist's "fable," prior to the part enacted), and so conjecture who Antipholus must be. The audience is held, too, by the revelation of feeling. Antipholus's emotional reflections spring from the farewells just exchanged at the end of *scène* 2: "I will go lose myself," he said, and was commended by the Merchant to his "own content." This is the phrase which prompts his soliloquy, where he laments that what would content him is precisely what he cannot get. The idea of his "losing himself" is taken up in a profound sense, and couched in a fine image commensurate with its thematic importance. The theme of identity is here linked with those of relationship (dislocated or re-established), and of risk. To seek reunion with the lost members of the family, Antipholus is risking his identity; yet he must do so, for only if the full relationship is restored can he find content. And then, hints the image of one water drop seeking another, the present individual identity will be lost, or transformed, in another way. It is to claim a sinking of identity in the marriage-relation, with the emergence of a new identity, where each is also the other, that Adriana uses the closely similar image in II. ii. In the play's harmonic structure, while this soliloquy is thus recalled at that point, in its own place it recalls the situation of Ægeon, who on virtually the same quest as Antipholus, has so risked his mortal identity that it is forfeit to the executioner. Antipholus's fear that he is losing himself is full of comic irony. No sooner has he expressed it, than, with the entry of his brother's Dromio, he begins to be the victim of the successive mistakes of identity to which his words are designed by Shakespeare as a prelude, and in the course of which he will come to wonder whether he is beside himself, and has lost himself indeed. The often uproarious comedy arising from these and the other errors is not my immediate subject; and as regards the *scène* of cross-purposes, I shall make only a few observations, concerned with themes and structure. In the progressive structure of the play, it has two main functions. First, it interests us in Adriana, ready for her entrance in the next scene (II. i), and leads to her personal summoning of the alien Antipholus to dinner (II. ii). Second, it produces the comic dislocation of relationship between him and his own Dromio when they meet in II. ii and Dromio denies the offences he is supposed to have committed here. The present failure of communication and relationship between Antipholus and the other Dromio, resulting from the mistake of identities, is made visible, audible, and tangible by "business": the blow. Like the theme of relationship, the mistiming theme is brought into close connection with that of mistaken identity. Dromio's impatient mistress, when by strike of clock it was twelve, has "made it one" upon his cheek; and for him Antipholus is her husband, his master, late for dinner, while for Antipholus Dromio is his servant, returned too soon, and obstinate in ill-timed jest. By Dromio's entrance are initiated the enigmas that beset the characters, and Antipholus is given an aptly enigmatic comment upon it:

> Here comes the almanack of my true date.

The new arrival has the appearance of his Dromio, who constitutes a record of his span from the time of their simultaneous nativities; but by a comic irony, so does the Dromio who has really entered: the comment fits both the false inference from appearance, and the reality itself. Its enigmatic nature conceals, so one finds from the final speech of the Abbess after the *dénouement* (v. i. 401-7) a further meaning: what approaches with this Dromio is the occasion which will secure Antipholus his true identity through a new date of birth—his true birth into the restored family relationship. That is the metaphor the Abbess employs.

It is by mistaking appearance for reality that Antipholus and his brother's Dromio misidentify one another. The threat to the very self involved in the confusion of appearance and reality is the thought most vividly conveyed in Antipholus's second soliloquy. The soliloquy rounds off the scene, not without certain resemblances to the beginning. Then, the theme of moneyed wealth was given prominence; and there was tension because the Ephesian law spelled danger to Antipholus's goods or life. Now, he is keenly anxious about his money; indeed, that is the motive for his final exit to seek Dromio at the Centaur. And tension rises again with his anxiety; but still more with the profoundly disturbing fears into which it merges, of worse perils than the law's in Ephesus, suggested by its repute as a place of illusions and shapeshifting, of jugglers that deceive the eye, of mountebanks and disguised cheaters, of

> Dark-working sorcerers that change the mind:
> Soul-killing witches that deform the body.

The lines seize the imagination of the audience at the deep level where the ancient dread of losing the self or soul is very much alive. They are highly characteristic of the imaginative Antipholus, develop the idea in his first soliloquy that his self is at hazard, and set the pattern for his interpretations of the strange experiences that befall him henceforward. At present his sense of those reputed perils of Ephesus, awakened by what seems the extraordinary behaviour of Dromio, produces the provisional resolve:

> If it prove so, I will be gone the sooner;

the first sign of the recurrent danger that he will depart before recognition and family reunion, with the consequent saving of Ægeon's life, can come about. His fears are not cowardice; such a view of them has been guarded against in *scènes* 1 and 2, where despite the warning of Ægeon's fate, he was determined to explore the town. The spirit he showed there prepares us for his acceptance of what will seem to him the mysterious adventure offered him by Adriana and Luciana: in spite of his forebodings now, for a time he will be ready to believe that the mystifications and transmutations of Ephesus may not be all malevolent.

Every passage in our illustrative scene has thus its functions both in the scene itself, and in the wider dynamic, harmonic, thematic, comic structure of the play. Besides this close, economical texture, there are of course other proofs of Shakespeare's early command of construction in the dramatic medium. He constructs in terms of theatre: he knows, for instance, the value of business and of devices and episodes which belong peculiarly to the stage. A famous example is the serenade scene in *Two Gentlemen*, with its music, its distancing of Sylvia at her window, and its eavesdroppers—the Host appreciative or drowsing to sleep, Julia (in male costume) painfully intent. In *The Comedy of Errors*, the gold chain seen, the blows seen and heard, make double the effect they would in narrative. The asides or semi-asides of the alien Antipholus and Dromio in II. ii, by a sound use of dramatic convention, mark the dichotomy between their mental worlds and that of Adriana and Luciana with whom they are in converse. The hilarious and crucial episode of the rightful husband and his party shut out from dinner depends for its full impact upon the stage-arrangement: the parties in altercation are both plainly visible to the audience though not to each other. But the supreme power manifest in Shakespeare's art of dramatic construction is the combinative power well indicated by Hardin Craig, who writes of "his unequalled [skill] in fitting parts together so that they [reinforce] one another," and notes that in working upon materials which often gave him much of his fable ready-made, his "originality seems to have consisted in the selection of great significant patterns." Of such patterns and such combining of parts, *The Shrew*, among the first four comedies, offers in the manifold relationships between its Induction and the main play perhaps the finest illustration.

In *The Comedy of Errors*, the combinative power is exercised in drawing upon diverse sources to compose a play of diverse yet cooperating strands and tones, a play which ranges from the averted-tragical, in prologue and *dénouement*, to low comedy, as in the drubbings and the account of Luce; while the middle comedy of the Antipholi provides its central substance. The adventures of the alien Antipholus, particularly his falling in love with Luciana, have emotional chords that relate them to the tone of the Ægeon story; the marital conflict of Antipholus the husband and his Adriana is bourgeois comedy, informed by intellectual and emotional discussion. Both Antipholi, through the association of master and man, take part with the Dromios in the lower comedy, which besides knockabout farce includes burlesque of academical logic and rhetoric, a comic parallel to the more serious concern with ideas at other levels of the action.

The play appealed at once to the taste for neo-Plautine intrigue comedy, and to what may be regarded as the four great interests traditionally supplied by romance. It is based on Plautus's *Menaechmi*. There Shakespeare found twin brothers, the traveler in search of the denizen, lost since childhood. The traveler is mistaken for his brother by all the important characters in turn, except the doctor, and his own servant, who once mistakes the brother for him. The second great source of complications is likewise the same as in Shakespeare: when characters have met the twin they do not know, and taken him for the one they do, they then meet the one they really do know, and debit or credit him with what in fact took place between them and the other. Such a misunderstanding occurs once between the traveler and his servant; and it is through errors of this kind that the denizen is brought into trouble. From his parasite (incensed at the traveler) his wife learns that he has given her cloak to a courtesan he frequents; she turns him out of doors to recover it. The courtesan has entrusted the cloak and her own gold chain to his twin, whom by mistake for him she has had to dinner; and shuts him out when he denies having received them. At the climax just before the final recognition, the traveler, accused of marital injustice by the wife and her father, replies, as they think, like a madman: a doctor is summoned, and catechizes the real husband, who is shortly seized at his orders. Here are the originals of the Antipholi, Adriana, the Courtesan, Dr. Pinch, and the alien Dromio. The other Dromio, as the servant who begins the train of errors by bringing to the wrong twin the summons to dinner afterwards seconded by his mistress, to that extent plays the same part as the courtesan's cook in Plautus. The courtesan has a maid as well as a cook; Adriana has Luce as well as a Dromio. There are minor hints in the dialogue for the personage of the goldsmith, the rope's end, and the alien twin's anxiety about the money handed for safe keeping to his servant. The father reproves the supposed husband for his treatment of the wife, as Luciana does in Shakespeare; but he first reproved the wife, like Luciana again (and like the Abbess later). Shakespeare has gone far to exonerate the husband. For the cloak, the wife's property, the gold chain is substituted as a gift only promised her (its place in the courtesan's plaints is supplied by her ring); and he does not propose to bestow it upon the courtesan until provoked by his wife's barring him out, and that in the face of the guests he had invited. Moreover, he has not frequented the courtesan; and his visit now is suggested by his wife's baseless jealousy of her. Had the wife barred out *this* husband because of her sense of grievance, it would have been hard to believe in her love of him, which is vital to Shakespeare's play; but she does not—she acts under a delusion, without recognizing him.

Even within the ambit of intrigue comedy, the *Menaechmi* did not furnish enough for Shakespeare. He shared the Renaissance and English desire for "copy" or copiousness, and he required an action long enough for the Elizabethan stage. Accordingly, he crossed what he took from the *Menaechmi* with the celebrated situation from Plautus's *Amphitruo*. There, the husband is shut out while Jupiter in his likeness seduces his wife within; the husband's slave, too, Sosia, is impersonated and excluded by Jupiter's henchman, Mercury. The consequences of the cross have been analysed closely by T. W. Baldwin. We may note that it gives Shakespeare one of his far-reaching changes from the plot of the *Menaechmi*, the matching of the twin masters by twin servants; goes with a second, the transfer of the dinner from the courtesan's to the wife's, and helps to prompt a third, the invention of Luciana. With love and marriage conceived in the human terms they are in Shakespeare's comedy, a seduced Adriana would be tragic not comic; chaste, like Lucrece, in mind but not in body. The supposed husband therefore must be in no serious danger of succumbing to her importunities, and partly for this reason, partly for the sake of love-interest and comic effect, Luciana is introduced to be the object of his devout and legitimate passion, that will seem to her and her sister doubly illegitimate. Naturally Shakespeare's changes interlock: thus, as opposite number to the alien servant, the second servant now belongs to the husband and wife not to the courtesan, and so it is from the wife he brings his summons. Since there is no seduction, the summons from the wife is requisite to bring the supposed husband to her house. Above all, the shutting-out of the real husband by the wife in *Menaechmi*, is transformed into the much stronger situation derived from *Amphitruo*, and the shutting-out by the courtesan is dropped: hence yet again it is at the wife's, as part of the strong situation there, that the dinner needs to be located. The shift contributes, in keeping with Shakespeare's treatment of the marital conflict and of love, to lay emphasis on the wife, the husband, and the true lover at the center, and to make the courtesan's part no less subordinate than the goldsmith's, which Shakespeare invents. The shift also obviates the necessity for the husband to order the dinner beforehand, as he does in Act I of *Menaechmi*, where the errors do not begin till Act II. Except for a hint of provocation offered by the wife, and her desire to oversee the husband's comings and goings, Shakespeare jettisons this first Act, getting the errors started in the first scene of his main action with Dromio of Ephesus's mistake, which likewise ensures that Dromio's master will be involved more quickly than the denizen in Plautus. Finally, to have two pairs of twins instead of one, multiplies and makes more complex the errors available for plot and comedy.

Among the more important neo-Plautine or neo-Terentian features of the play is its observance of the unity of time: Shakespeare advertises the limit of a few hours within which his action is to be, and is, compressed. Other such features are the unity of place, and the setting, with its three houses—and (as Peter Alexander points out) the Harbor imagined "off" on the one side, the Mart or Town on the other: a conception originally from Athens, where it corresponded with fact. The first scene performs the function of a classical prologue: there is Seneca as well as Plautus in its ancestry. The Terentian five-act structure expounded by T. W. Baldwin we shall notice shortly. The contrasts of prose and various sorts of verse, including rhyme, to suit the changing character of the episodes, is compared by Cornelia Coulter to the similar use of lyric measures and the lower-toned senarii in Latin comedy. For other similarities, her article should be consulted; but one has to bear in mind that one and the same feature commonly has antecedents in more than one tradition. Shakespeare's comic servants inherit from Cain's Garcio and the rest in the miracle cycles, and from the native Vice, as well as from the Latin Servus, and Lyly's pert lads like the Dromio in *Mother Bombie*. The love of balance seen in the doubling of the twins and the invention of a sister and confidante for Adriana, a prospective wife for the bachelor Antipholus—if we are to seek the sources of it further than in Shakespeare's own artistic sense—is not to be traced only to Terence, Plautus, and Lyly: balanced grouping of personages is characteristic of moralities and Tudor interludes. Men of the Renaissance read Latin comedy in the light of their own predilections, formed to a considerable extent by the tradition that had come down from medieval romances and had branched into the novelle. Consequently, as Madeleine Doran has shown, they gave to the motifs of recognition, shipwreck, long lost children and the like, when they met them in Terence and Plautus, far more than the value they had originally had there as romance. To a lesser degree, what love-interest Terence in particular afforded was similarly magnified.

Hence, when through his neo-Plautine warp Shakespeare ran a weft dyed in colours of romance, he was making no extreme change from the Latin genre as then frequently understood. Rather, he was overgoing Plautus, and Terence, on their supposed romantic side, as well as on that of comic intrigue. For this purpose, and for "copiousness," he drew on additional sources. The leading interests of romance—as one might exemplify from Arthurian romances, from *The Squire's Tale*, or, coming to the period of our play, from the romance aspects of *Arcadia* and *The Faerie Queene*—were adventure; marvel, especially enchantment; the high sentiment of love; and *sens*, the implications brought out in the *matière*, the meaning the reader takes away with him, as a result of the author's treatment. Shakespeare develops into an adventure story, that of Ægeon, the successful quest for the long-lost child which in

Menaechmi is hardly more than a presupposition of the plot. For the initial peril demanded by a plot of this kind, he provides by translating from hoax into fact the situation of the Sienese merchant in Gascoigne's *Supposes*, where it was already part of a drama of mistaken identities; and by heightening it from a potential threat to goods into a provisional sentence of death. The shipwreck and intervention of piratical fishermen, whereby, Ægeon narrates, the family was first divided, have a probable source in Greene's *Menaphon*, and form a link with the source of the happy ending, the adventures of Apollonius of Tyre, related by Gower and Twine. After vicissitudes including shipwreck, succor from a fisherman, loss of his wife at sea, and the kidnapping of his daughter by pirates, Apollonius's reunion with his family is completed at Ephesus. There he discovers his wife in the Priestess of Diana's Temple, as the Abbess is discovered to be Ægeon's. The interest of adventure is not confined to the *dénouement* and the opening scene; through the alien Antipholus it is carried into the main action. To him it seems that he has a series of adventures with the supernatural. His thoughts and feelings about them, like the providential coincidences that have brought all the members of the family to Ephesus, speak to our sense of marvel. His illusion of supernatural menace in these experiences is set against the real peril of Ægeon, and against the truth of his love, even though his love adventure, which brings the loftiest of love-sentiment into the comedy, seems to him supernatural and at least equivocally perilous too. In the idea of the town as a home of supernatural delusion, Shakespeare is again combining sources. The Epidamnum of *Menaechmi* (II. i) is notorious for cheats. The denizen's house there is associated by Shakespeare with Amphitruo's, a scene of supernatural shapeshifting. Epidamnum itself he has changed to Ephesus, no doubt as the site of Diana's Temple in the Apollonius story, which becomes his Abbey. Diana of the Ephesians inevitably recalls Acts XIX, whence Shakespeare would remember, besides the uproar on her account, the references to curious (that is, black) arts practised in Ephesus, and to the exorcists, with whom Dr. Pinch (founded on the Medicus in *Menaechmi*) has something in common. The Ephesians are warned against supernatural foes in St. Paul's Epistle, which also exhorts them, Geoffrey Bullough reminds us, to domestic unity, dwelling on the right relationships of husbands and wives, parents and children, masters and servants. With the father's rebuke to the wife in *Menaechmi*, and the long tradition of marital debate in medieval and Tudor literature, it thus contributed, no doubt, to the *sens* of the play.

To consider the *sens* is to consider the themes. However they are deepened and interconnected by Shakespeare's treatment, they are not recondite: for the audience, they are the general ideas arising most naturally from the motives and development of the plot, and the response of the characters. The play begins and ends with relationship: a family torn asunder and reunited. Relationship is the motive that has brought Ægeon, and the alien

Antipholus and Dromio, to the hazards of Ephesus; relationship is threatened
by the tensions in the marriage of Antipholus the denizen. The chief entangle-
ments spring from mistaken identity and mistiming:

> I see we still did meet each other's man,
> And I was ta'en for him, and he for me,
> And thereupon these ERRORS are arose.

The twins appear the same, but in reality are different; those who meet them
are led by appearance into illusion. Repeatedly one of the persons assumes
that he shared an experience with another, when in reality he shared it with
a different one. In consequence, the persons cease to be able to follow each
other's assumptions, and become isolated in more or less private worlds.
Mistakes of identity all but destroy relationship, and loss of relationship calls
true identity yet more in question; the chief persons suspect themselves or
are suspected of insanity, or of being possessed, surrounded, or assailed by
supernatural powers—madness or demoniac possession would be the eclipse
of the true self, and sorcery might overwhelm it. The alien Antipholus and
Dromio fear Circean metamorphosis; Ægeon, that he has been deformed out
of recognition by time. Yet the hazard of metamorphosis and of the loss of
present identity is also the way to fresh or restored relationship. Antipholus
the bachelor desires that Luciana will transform him and create him new;
and Adriana's belief that in marriage the former identities coalesce and
emerge identified with each other, is true if rightly interpreted. How the
possessive interpretation, not relinquished by Adriana till almost the end, is
at odds with the free giving and hazarding in which the wealth and debts of
love differ from those of commerce, is another central theme, well traced by
J. R. Brown. Adriana's envy of a husband's status contravenes principles of
order that for Shakespeare and orthodox Elizabethans extended through the
whole cosmos. The status of husband, and of wife, Kate's lines in *The Shrew*
imply, are related to their places in this hierarchical order:

> Such duty as the subject owes the prince
> Even such a woman oweth to her husband.

Adriana comes to style her husband lord, and they each lay their case, as each
has come to see it, before the Duke, reminding themselves and him that the
match was first made by his authority. By this point, disorder from the
various disruptions of relationship has gone so far in the community, that
only the appeals for justice addressed to the Abbess and to him, God's
viceroys spiritual and temporal, are capable, the time now being ripe, of
leading to a solution.

Not only are the themes organically developed in the action; they are
organically connected in themselves. At the center is relationship: relationship between human beings, depending on their right relationship to truth

and universal law: to the cosmic reality behind appearance, and the cosmic order. Trust in mere appearance results in illusion and mistakes of identity, thus dislocating relationship, and so disrupting order: blind conflict and disorder are inevitable when men misconceive true identity and become isolated in private worlds. Besides illusion, there are other factors of disorder: revolt against a wife's place in the cosmic hierarchy is the original source of discord in Adriana's marriage: order is broken, too, by everything untimely. As Ovid's *Tempus edax rerum*, time opposes mutability to the creative cosmic order. By that mutability, identity itself may be threatened: *"Nec species sua cuique manet . . ."*—the link of time-theme and appearance-theme is present in Ovid, and particularly clear in the apostrophe to Time wrung from Ægeon when he finds himself unrecognized. Here, and in the dread of Circean transformation into beasts, metamorphosis is seen in its hostile aspect; but, as we have observed, it can also transform for the better: time, too, when it is ripe, brings a new order. Till then, patience would mitigate disorder, which cannot be ended till the claims for justice, distorted by the claimants' assumption that their private worlds are real, are laid before those who in the hierarchy of order are founts of justice upon earth. More than justice is needed: without mercy, the godly prince is not himself; and amid the demonstrations of love's wealth, lacking which there would be little of the genial warmth that glows in the conclusion, Solinus is inspired to what he had declared impossible, and freely remits the debt Ægeon owes the law. In this organic structure, of the two themes which next to relationship are the most inclusive, the first, cosmic order, presides in Shakespeare's early Histories; its importance in his drama is well recognized, and the importance of the second, appearance and reality, is becoming so. The first is a familiar part of "the Elizabethan world-picture"; the second, presumably, has affiliations with Renaissance neo-Platonism.

The themes are given prominence in several ways. They are voiced by the speakers, who often relate one theme to another: the examples in our analysis of I. ii are characteristic. The dominant imagery, of man as beast, reflects the ideas of illusory appearance and malign metamorphosis; above all, it mirrors the threats to identity and to status in the cosmic order. Appropriately, it stops on the brink of the *dénouement*, with the Duke's explicit formulation:

> I think you all have drunk of Circe's cup.

Thematic, likewise, are the two images of the water drop, its identity lost for relationship's sake. The whole harmonic structure, of which the correspondence of images forms part, is a vehicle of the themes. How generosity and two degrees of possessiveness in love are defined by juxtaposition of *scènes* in III. ii, with reference back to Adriana's attitude in Act II, has been shown by J. R. Brown. The supreme instance is the parallel between the "gossips' feast" to which everyone is going at the end, and the dinner from which the husband and his guests were shut out. The gossips' or baptismal feast affirms relationship and identity: the kin are united, the Duke is patron, all are friends and godparents, witnesses to the identities now truly established and christened into the family and the community; long travail is rewarded, and increase (the progressive aspect of cosmic order) which, despite the double birth of twins, was mocked by the intervention of mutable fortune, is now truly realized. It is not only as a sensational error of identity that the exclusion from dinner contrasts with this: balked or broken feasts (G. Wilson Knight has made us aware) are recurrent symbols in Shakespeare of the breakdown of human fellowship and its pieties. Both this motif, and the extravagant comedy of the barring-out, are worked up by the burlesque Lylyan or Erasmian colloquy on whether good cheer or welcome makes the feast. The burlesque "turns" for the clowns belong to the harmonic structure in much the same way. The theme of time's depredations, for instance, is the text of the mock disputation on Time and Hair. In iv. ii, iii, the clown's interlocutors are bamboozled by the spate of mock rhetorical similitudes in which he drowns the identity of his subject, the Sergeant, who is verbally transmogrified into devil, wolf, perverse hound, evil angel, and so forth; and whose function, arrest for debt (to be compared with the love claims of Adriana) is the pith of the jests. To these themes, thus linked, of debt, identity, metamorphosis, and supernatural malice, the further comic fancy of debtor Time turning back an hour when he meets with a Sergeant, links those of untimeliness and reversal of cosmic order.

The *Comedy* appeals first and foremost to laughter, as is obvious at any performance. I have dwelt on its serious themes and strands of romance, because it is these that student and producer are prone to discount. In his famous Stratford production (1938), Komisarjevsky guyed Ægeon, Emilia, and the wooing scene: he could not present them "straight" and still keep them in key with the rest, which he was evidently determined to exploit for all it was worth as farce, thereby turning Shakespeare's comedy with its several finely balanced tones into his own scintillating single-toned vaudeville. Among dramas of recognition, *The Comedy* is not a superior *Supposes*, without much in it (that signifies) beyond lively intrigue and farcical situations. On the contrary, it resembles the *Ion* and *The Confidential Clerk* in matching a mystification about identity, at the level of intrigue, with an exploration of serious issues appropriate to such a plot. Less than half the total number of lines (some 750, I estimate, out of some 1750) are mainly devoted to the essentials of the intrigue comedy. About 300 are elaborations of comic rhetoric; the remainder develop the romance interests, and, with the comic rhetoric, point the themes. Even so rough a criterion confirms that the play is not to be regarded as a farcical intrigue comedy and little more.

To recognize this is not to undervalue the intrigue, so brilliantly contrived to make the most of all the opportunities for comic error. The progressive action, in which the intrigue is one factor, develops the comedy and themes of the play along with the fortunes of its persons; and is organized no less firmly on the large scale than the single scenes are on the small. So far as the plot is concerned, this organization corresponds, T. W. Baldwin has shown, to the five-act structure Renaissance and earlier critics found in Terence; particularly the form found in the *Andria*. How far it depends upon neo-classical theory is perhaps a question: among the features Baldwin indicates, those of most consequence for dramatic effect can be paralleled in a medieval drama like *The Castle of Perseverance*, and to a playwright well endowed with structural sense might seem natural, theory or no theory, in plays with a central crisis and a final solution. However this may be, the comedy begins *in medias res*, with the partial exposition of what has happened already, and the immediate occasions of the subsidiary and main actions: the suspended sentence on Ægeon and the summons to the wrong Antipholus. Act II completes the exposition and *protasis* by introducing the sisters and their motivation, especially Adriana's; and ends, when the same Antipholus accedes to her summons, with the beginning of the *epitasis* or entanglement proper. This leads to the central crisis in III. i: locked out, the husband is brought into the entanglement, and narrowly fails to meet his twin: despite the Dromios' scolding-match, recognition is missed. By the last words of Act IV, with the firm resolve of the alien to depart, there is imminent danger it will be missed forever; and there follows in the supposed madness of the twins and the expiration of Ægeon's respite, the climax of distresses that precipitates the *dénouement*. There, meeting and recognition are combined with the completion and correction of Ægeon's retrospect:

> Why here begins his morning story right.

The development of the action is supported by the use made of the stage set. Acts II and III are focused upon the Phoenix, scene of the central crisis. Act IV brings into play the second *domus*, the Porpentine, and in accord with the fast-extending complications has no one focal point: the action is related by turns to the Phoenix, the Porpentine, and neither. The third *domus*, the Abbey, is kept in reserve as the appropriate focus for the *dénouement*. Dynamic progress is strongly felt in the mounting violence, from the first mere thwack to the drawing of swords, thrashing with a rope's end, overpowering of "madmen," and elaborate (narrated) vengeance upon Pinch; in the spreading of error beyond the family to courtesan, goldsmith, and merchant, until the whole town, at least in Adriana's fevered fancy, seems involved; and in the darkening conviction of the imaginative Antipholus that his supernatural experiences are from the devil. With this explanation, natural to his melancholy temperament, he has positively encased himself in error, for it is as coherent as it is fallacious. In like fashion his choleric brother comes to attribute all his sufferings to a conspiracy instigated by his wife: both the Antipholi reach the verge of persecution-mania. Since Adriana also is given her point of view, which alters before the end, one can say of the three main persons that although they do not develop in the sense of being felt to change in character as a result of the action, their attitudes of mind develop, so that each is felt to have an inner self. That is, they are not wholly flat characters, such as might be fitting protagonists of pure farce. They are simple, but have just enough depth for the play, which Shakespeare, as we have seen, has deepened considerably beyond the expected limitations of neo-classical comedy.

Even so, in depth and scope he was, of course, far to surpass it. None the less, it is in its own kind an extraordinarily finished work. The kind being one that not even Shakespeare could extend beyond somewhat narrow limits, a less tight form, exemplified in *The Two Gentlemen*, held more promise of *Twelfth Night*. Yet in recognizing this, one ought also to recognize how much, in *The Comedy*, he has in fact found room for. Like the other early plays, it will always be judged by two standards. One, quite properly, is the standard set later by Shakespeare himself. But the play should also be appreciated for what it is in its own right: still actable as a hilarious yet balanced comedy, more pregnant than has perhaps been supposed with Shakespearian ideas.

A Midsummer-Night's Dream

by Ernest Schanzer

"I know not why Shakespeare calls this play a Midsummer-Night's Dream, when he so carefully informs us that it happened on the night preceding *May* day," wrote Dr. Johnson almost two hundred years ago.[1] There have been surprisingly few attempts in the interval to supply an answer. Most of them came from Johnson's contemporaries. "I imagine that the title of this play was suggested by the time it was first introduced on the stage, which was probably at *Midsummer*. 'A Dream for the entertainment of a Midsummernight.' *Twelfth Night* and *The Winter's Tale* had probably their title from a similar circumstance," wrote Malone.[2] And Steevens: "In *Twelfth Night*, Act III, scene iv, Olivia observes of Malvolio's seeming frenzy, that 'it is a very *Midsummer* madness.' That time of the year we may therefore suppose was anciently thought productive of mental vagaries resembling the scheme of Shakespeare's play. To this circumstance it might have owed its title."[3] In the nineteenth century we have to look to Germany for a discussion of the problem. Tieck, after giving Malone's explanation, adds that *"viele Kräuter und Blumen sollten nur in dieser Nacht ihre vollkommene Kraft, oder irgend etwas Zauberisches erhalten"* [4] [it is only during this night that many plants and flowers attain their full strength and any magical powers—ED.'s TRANS.]. Simrock declared that *A Midsummer-Night's Dream* was a title which cannot have come from Shakespeare, and defiantly entitled his translation of the play *Walpurgisnachtstraum*. In our own century several more explanations have been offered. Sir Edmund Chambers finds the significance of the title in Puck's invitation to the audience to regard the whole play as a dream. "It is life seen through a glass darkly; such a vision of life as a man might have on Midsummer Night, the one season of the year around which

"*A Midsummer-Night's Dream.*" Printed by permission of the author. (A longer and translated version of this essay appeared in *Œvres Complètes de Shakespeare,* ed. Pierre Leyris and Henri Evans [Paris, 1958].)

[1] Boswell's Variorum edition (1821), vol. 5, p. 296, n. 3.

[2] *Ibid.*

[3] *Ibid.*

[4] Notes to Schlegel's Translation, vol. 3, p. 352.

Elizabethan superstition gathered most closely, when herbs were believed
to have their especial virtues, and strange beings to be abroad." [5] Walter
De la Mare completes the range of conjectures by surmising that the title
may be due to the fact "that 'on such a night' the happy notion of it stole
into Shakespeare's mind," [6] thus making the dreamer the poet himself.

None of these explanations are mutually exclusive. But most of them
merely shift the problem. For we are now left to explain why Shakespeare
should have chosen the eve of Mayday for the action of most of his play,
rather than Midsummer Night. Both nights are well fitted to provide the
time-setting for the supernatural events in the wood, for they are the two
nights of the year when fairies were thought to be particularly powerful and
when magic and every form of witchcraft was believed to be practised. But
there are three associations which the eve of Mayday did not share with
Midsummer Night: that of flower magic, the notion being that certain herbs
and flowers gathered on that night possessed various wonder-working powers;
that of lovers' dreams; and that of madness. The explanations, therefore,
which seem to me most plausible are those of Steevens, Tieck, and Chambers.
Of these Steevens's seems the most important. For love-madness is the central
theme of A Midsummer-Night's Dream. It is this which ties together various
sections of the play, from Demetrius's transfer of affection from Helena to
Hermia and then back to Helena, to Titania's temporary love for Bottom.
The theme has both a prologue and an epilogue, in each of which it receives a
generalized formulation. The prologue is found in Helena's soliloquy in
Act I, the epilogue in Theseus's speech on the lunatic, the lover, and the
poet in Act V.

> Now happy some o'er other some can be!
> Through Athens I am thought as fair as she,
> But what of that? Demetrius thinks not so:
> He will not know what all but he do know.
> And as he errs, doting on Hermia's eyes,
> So I, admiring of his qualities . . .
> Things base and vile, holding no quantity,
> Love can transpose to form and dignity.
> Love looks not with the eyes, but with the mind:
> And therefore is winged Cupid painted blind.
> Nor hath Love's mind of any judgement taste:
> Wings and no eyes figure unheedy haste.
> And therefore is Love said to be a child:
> Because in choice he is so oft beguiled.   (I. i. 226 ff.)

[5] Shakespeare: A Survey (1935), p. 83.
[6] Pleasures and Speculations (1940), p. 275.

The love described here is cut off both from the evidence of the senses, which it belies, and from the corrective power of judgment. It is purely a creature of the imagination, of "seething brains," a kind of madness, in which the victim may be intellectually aware of his illusion but unable to resist it:

> And as he errs, doting on Hermia's eyes,
> So I, admiring of his qualities.

It is a love which has no basis in reality, which creates a phantom, a mere shadow of the beloved person; it is a dream. Though it is entirely devoid of judgment the victim is, ironically, under the delusion that he is following reason in his choice. When Lysander, under the power of the love-philter, has been made to transfer his love from Hermia to Helena, he exclaims:

> The will of man is by his reason swayed;
> And reason says you are the worthier maid.
> Things growing are not ripe until their season:
> So I, being young, till now ripe not to reason—
> And touching now the point of human skill,
> Reason becomes the marshal to my will,
> And leads me to your eyes; where I o'erlook
> Love's stories, written in love's richest book.   (II. ii. 123 ff.)

This love is wholly due to the whims of Cupid.

> Cupid is a knavish lad,
> Thus to make poor females mad,

exclaims Puck when moved to pity by the sufferings of the two maidens (III. ii. 440-1). Oberon, in his use of the love-philter, merely usurps the function of Cupid, but instead of the love-god's aimless and wilful exercise of his power turns them towards beneficent as well as selfish ends. It is a controlled exercise of Cupid's power but its effects are exactly the same, whether produced by love-juice or golden arrow: the eyes are blinded, the judgment is disabled, and reason is put to flight. Former love is turned to loathing, former loathing to love.

Shakespeare next shows us the *reductio ad absurdum* of this love-madness in the Bottom-Titania love scenes. Here, in the infatuation of the Queen of fairies for a weaver metamorphosed into an ass, we have displayed the full absurdity of the kind of love which is engendered in the imagination only, uncorrected by judgment and the senses. Bottom himself points the moral of the situation. To Titania's impassioned declaration of love,

> I pray thee, gentle mortal, sing again!
> Mine ear is much enamoured of thy note . . .
> So is mine eye enthralled to thy shape,

> And thy fair virtue's force—perforce—doth move me,
> On the first view, to say, to swear, I love thee,   (III. i. 130 ff.)

he replies:

> Methinks, mistress, you should have little reason for that.
> And yet, to say the truth, reason and love keep little
> company together now-a-days. The more the pity, that some
> honest neighbors will not make them friends. Nay, I can
> gleek upon occasion.

In the relationship of Theseus and Hippolyta reason and love have been made friends and keep company together. Hence it is fitting that the final summing up of the theme of love-madness should be entrusted to Theseus in his famous speech about the lunatic, the lover, and the poet. The lines on the poet, as Professor Dover Wilson was the first to point out,[7] appear to have been added by Shakespeare as an afterthought. But while they are for us the most interesting part of the speech and also contain the best verse, they do obscure its original purpose. For we are left chiefly with the impression of the poet as a madman, while Shakespeare's earlier intention was to make us see the lover in this role, clinching the identification of love and madness which has been suggested throughout the play.

While the theme of love-madness weaves together various apparently unrelated portions of *A Midsummer-Night's Dream*, Shakespeare creates unity of atmosphere chiefly by flooding the play with moonlight. There is only one daylight scene in the entire play, part of the first scene of Act IV, where we watch the coming of dawn and with it the arrival of Theseus's hunting party. And here the coming of daylight and the sounding of the hunting horns announce the return of sanity, the dispersal of magic and illusion, the end of the dream. Theseus and Hippolyta are both daylight characters. Neither of them is unimaginative, and Theseus, at least, is depicted as an ardent lover. But he has wooed Hippolyta with his sword, in a fashion very different from Lysander's wooing of Hermia, of which Egeus tells him:

> Thou hast by moonlight at her window sung,
> With feigning voice, verses of feigning love.   (I. i. 30)

And the Duke's cool reason and good sense throw into relief the lovers' absurdities. They have their natural existence by moonlight, which propagates phantoms and illusions, the world of dreams.

In this play we are given three wholly distinct kinds of fairies, provided we can speak of Puck as a fairy at all. He was not considered so in popular

---

[7] New Shakespeare ed. *A Midsummer-Night's Dream*, pp. 80 ff.

superstition, but was thought of as a spirit of another sort, whose merry pranks made him the favorite among all the sprites that haunted the English countryside. In our play he considers himself to be a fairy, as his "And we fairies, that do run By the triple Hecate's team" (v. i. 381) shows. He is the complete opposite of the tiny fairies with whom Shakespeare fills Titania's train, being gross and earthy, boisterous, rough, and boyish, where the tiny fairies are aerial, timid, and courteous. Nothing could be more misleading than to speak of them as irresponsible children, as some critics do. They are conscientious and very much overworked servants of the queen, with little time for idle gossiping. In their encounters with Bottom the tiny fairies, so far from being like children, show themselves accomplished and ceremonious courtiers. To see them otherwise robs the scene of much of its humor. For Bottom, with his customary adaptability to any part he is called upon to play, at once fits himself to his new role of Prince Consort, and proceeds to hold a levee. As we would expect, he plays the part to perfection. He is courteous without condescension, well informed about each fairy's family, genuinely interested in their affairs. In his second encounter with them we find the same qualities, mingled with greater familiarity. Now we have, "Scratch my head, Peaseblossom," but also, "Give me your neaf, Monsieur Mustardseed. Pray you, leave your curtsy, good monsieur" (iv. i. 6 ff.).

Oberon and Titania, though very different from the attendant fairies, are no more childlike or irresponsible than they. When commentators speak of "little Titania," or when one critic, lamenting the undomesticated life led by Oberon and Titania, tells us that "acorn-cups impose no fellowship," [8] it is evident that they take the King and Queen of fairyland to be of the same miniature brand as their attendant spirits. That Shakespeare did not think of them in that way is plain enough. Not only would it be unactable to have a tiny Titania make love to Bottom, but it would also be unthinkable. For much of the humor of their love scenes depends on our realization that it is a supremely beautiful woman who is enamored of this weaver turned ass. (Had Shakespeare thought of the fairy queen as diminutive, "Titania" would have been a most unhappy choice of name for her.) Shakespeare clearly thinks of Titania and Oberon as of the same stature as the traditional English fairies, who were believed to be of normal human height or slightly below it. Nor are they depicted as ethereal, mere gossamer and moonlight. Not only Titania's "Sleep thou, and I will wind thee in my arms" (iv. i. 39), but also Oberon's

> Come, my queen, take hands with me,
> And rock the ground whereon these sleepers be   (iv. i. 84)

make against this impression.

[8] H. B. Charlton, *Shakespearean Comedy* (1938), p. 117.

But more harmful than the notion of Oberon's and Titania's diminutive size is the notion of their childlikeness and irresponsibility. Of this I can find no trace in the play. They are the counterpart in the spirit-world of Theseus and Hippolyta, like them full of stateliness, but more ceremonious and distant. Their quarrel is not a children's squabble, no sooner engaged in than forgotten, as Sir Edmund Chambers would have us believe,[9] but a quarrel which has been in progress for many months, disrupting the whole body politic of fairyland. Only thus can we understand Titania's speech about the chaos in nature, which has arisen out of their quarrel (II. i. 82 ff.). It is more than merely a topical allusion to an unusually bad English summer. It rather portrays the disorder in the macrocosm which, in so many of Shakespeare's plays, accompanies disorder in the body politic, here the state of fairydom.

Shakespeare has sometimes been reproached with having gelded the English fairy, with having robbed it of its fearfulness and hence its reality, and turned it into a trifle light as air, the mere plaything of the imagination. We can see why he should have done so for the purposes of this play. He probably felt that the traditional English fairy was too uncanny and fearful a creature to be accommodated in this scene of tragical mirth. And so, in creating the attendant faries in this play, he drew on a *jeu d'esprit* written probably a few months earlier, Mercutio's Queen Mab speech in *Romeo and Juliet*. But the miniature and flower-like fairies had been created for a special purpose in a particular play and in no way ousted the traditional English fairy from the poet's imagination. Not until *The Tempest* does he return to the "Shakespearian" fairy; all the references in the intervening plays are to the conventional fairies of English folklore.

[9] *op. cit.*, p. 85.

Shakespeare's Method:
The Merchant of Venice

by J. Middleton Murry

The Merchant of Venice probably shares with *Hamlet* the distinction of being the most popular of all Shakespeare's plays. It was not always so. After the Restoration, *The Merchant of Venice* suffered eclipse. When it was at last revived (in a drastic adaptation) at the beginning of the eighteenth century, Shylock was played as a purely comic part. Not until 1741, when Macklin played Shylock at Drury Lane, did something near to Shakespeare's text come back to the stage. The return was triumphant. "Macklin made Shylock malevolent," says Mr. Harold Child, "and of a forcible and terrifying ferocity." Macklin's Shylock, which Pope accepted as Shakespeare's, dominated the stage for nearly fifty years; and it imposed the conception described by Hazlitt:

> When we first went to see Mr. Kean in Shylock, we expected to see, what we had been used to see, a decrepit old man, bent with age and ugly with mental deformity, grinning with deadly malice, with the venom of his heart congealed in the expression of his countenance, sullen, morose, gloomy, inflexible, brooding over one idea, that of his hatred, and fixed on one unalterable purpose, that of his revenge.

With this conception of Shylock *The Merchant of Venice* became truly popular. Garrick chose it for the opening performance of Drury Lane under his management in 1747, and in it Kean made his triumphant first appearance at the same theatre in 1814. It was Kean's Shylock, as Hazlitt makes plain, which caused a revolution in the attitude of criticism towards the character. "In proportion as Shylock has ceased to be a popular bugbear, 'baited with the rabble's curse,' " wrote Hazlitt, "he becomes a half-favorite with the philosophical part of the audience, who are disposed to think that Jewish revenge is at least as good as Christian injuries."

"Shakespeare's Method: *The Merchant of Venice*." From *Shakespeare* (London: Jonathan Cape, Ltd., 1936), pp. 188-211. Reprinted by permission of the author's executors and the publishers.

That is a singular and significant stage-history. For both these popular Shylocks are Shakespeare's: or rather both are to be found in Shakespeare. As the attitude to the Jew became more civilized, at the beginning of the nineteenth century, so it was discovered that the new attitude also was prophetically contained in Shakespeare's Jew.

But *The Merchant of Venice* is more than Shylock. It is, more even than *Hamlet*, more than any other of Shakespeare's plays, a matter-of-fact fairy tale: a true folk story, made drama; and it makes its secular appeal to that primitive substance of the human consciousness whence folk tales took their origin. Or, without reaching back to these dark and dubious beginnings, we may say that it is, as nearly as possible, a pure melodrama or tragi-comedy, an almost perfect example of the art-form which being prior to art itself, most evidently and completely satisfies the primitive man in us all. If the English theatre be considered as a place of popular entertainment, strictly on a level with the football field, the prize ring and the racecourse, then *The Merchant of Venice* is the type of entertainment the theatre should supply—villain discomfited, virtue rescued, happy marriages, clowning, thrills, and a modest satisfaction of the general appetite for naughtiness.

The Merchant of Venice happens to be Shakespeare's; but Shakespeare has not much to do with its popularity. True, *The Merchant of Venice* almost *is* Shakespeare in the popular mind. But this popular Shakespeare, who wrote *The Merchant of Venice* and *Richard III*, is scarcely a person. He is rather a name which gives to these satisfactions of our elementary appetites for melodrama the prestige of art. This impersonal "Shakespeare" is a great stumbling block to criticism, which is forever engaged, consciously and unconsciously, in the effort to dissolve him out of existence. But he did most certainly exist: he is the Shakespeare who, in his own day as in ours, was veritably popular, who tickled the groundlings because his living lay that way (and surely it was a better way than being hand-fed by the aristocracy, gratification for dedication), who did what he could to season his caviar to the general appetite, and made not a virtue of his necessity—that was hardly his nature—but the best of it.

It is the more striking, therefore, that of all the plays of this period *The Merchant of Venice* is the most typical of Shakespeare—the most expressive of what Coleridge once called his "omni-humanity." It contains tragedy, comedy high and low, love lyricism; and, notably, it does not contain any "Shakespearian" character. The Berowne-Mercutio-Benedick figure, witty, debonair, natural, is diffused into a group of young Venetian noblemen, all credible and substantial, but none possessing the inimitable individuality of their progenitor. Antonio, who stands apart from them, and was (if my judgment of the various verse-styles of the play is to be trusted) the last figure in it to have been elaborated, is a singular character. He supplies a background of sadness to the whole drama. He seems to be older than the friends who surround him, and detached from their thoughtless extravagance. Actually, in his final elaboration, by reason of the quality and color given to him by Shakespeare's rewriting of Act i, scene i, he becomes, as a character, slightly inconsistent with the contemptuous opponent of Shylock of later scenes; but it is not the function of Antonio to be primarily a dramatic "character." In that capacity, he is negative; he is a shadow beside Shylock and Portia, and unsubstantial even in comparison with his Venetian entourage. But as the vehicle of an atmosphere, he is one of the most important elements in the play. He provides, for the beginning of the play, what the lyrical antiphony of Lorenzo and Jessica supplies for the end of it—a kind of musical overtone which sets the spiritual proportions of the drama. He shades into the Duke of *Twelfth Night*.

The analogue between *The Merchant of Venice* and a musical composition is significant, I think, when taken in conjunction with the basic popularity of the play and the probability that its origin is to be sought in a play of many years before called *The Jew*, which Stephen Gosson exempted from abuse in 1579 because it displayed "the greediness of worldly chusers and the bloody mind of usurers." That is too apt a summary of the purely dramatic content of *The Merchant of Venice* to be accidental, and it fits too well with our impression of the play as the product of much rewriting to be ignored. Whether or not *The Merchant* is, as Malone suggested, the "Venetian Comedy" mentioned by Henslowe in 1594—a date which would suit very well for Shakespeare's first drafting of *his* play—may be left undecided. The important fact is that in *The Merchant* we have, almost certainly, Shakespeare's treatment of a dramatic plot which came to him, substantially, as a datum.

Out of this substance Shakespeare wrought a miracle. He transformed it, and yet he left the popular substance essentially the same. What he did not, could not, and, so far as we can see or guess, would not do, was to attempt to make it an intellectually coherent whole. That seems to have been no part of his purpose; he did not entertain the idea because he knew it was impossible. The coherence of *The Merchant of Venice* is not intellectual or psychological; and there has been much beating of brains in the vain effort to discover in it a kind of coherence which it was never meant to possess.

As an example of what I believe to be a radical misunderstanding of the nature of *The Merchant of Venice*, we may take the edition of the play in the *New Cambridge Shakespeare*. It will serve as a typical example of a mistaken approach to Shakespeare, for *The Merchant* in its origins, its methods of composition, and its final splendor, is typical of Shakespeare's achievement. The very stubbornness of his material compelled, I believe, a more or less complete abeyance of Shakespeare's personality. In his work upon this play he was pre-eminently the "artist," but not in the modern and largely romantic sense of the word.

When the news of the disaster to Antonio's ventures comes to Belmont, in the very ecstasy of happiness there, Jessica adds her witness to Salerio's report of Shylock's implacability:

> When I was with him, I have heard him swear
> To Tubal and to Chus, his countrymen,
> That he would rather have Antonio's flesh
> Than twenty times the value of the sum
> That he did owe him: and I know, my lord,
> If law, authority and power deny not,
> It will go hard with poor Antonio.   (iii. ii. 285-91)

On this passage, the New Cambridge editors have the following note:

> We are tempted to put this speech into square brackets as one from the old play which Shakespeare inadvertently left undeleted in the manuscript. Note (1) it jars upon a nerve which Shakespeare of all writers was generally most careful to avoid: that a daughter should thus volunteer evidence against her father is hideous . . .

This fits, precisely, with the description of Jessica given in the essay of general introduction to the play:

> Jessica is bad and disloyal, unfilial, a thief; frivolous, greedy, without any more conscience than a cat, and without even a cat's redeeming love of home. Quite without heart, on worse than an animal instinct—pilfering to be carnal— she betrays her father to be a light-of-lucre carefully weighted with her father's ducats.

This is, indeed, to break a butterfly upon a wheel. But more alarming than the severity of the sentence is its irrelevance. *The Merchant of Venice* is not a realistic drama; and its characters simply cannot be judged by realistic moral standards. Jessica, taken out of the play, and exposed to the cold light of moral analysis, may be a wicked little thing; but in the play, wherein alone she has her being, she is nothing of the kind—she is charming. She runs away from her father because she is white and he is black; she is much rather a princess held captive by an ogre than the unfilial daughter of a persecuted Jew. Whether or not it is true that Shakespeare "of all writers" was most careful to avoid representing unfilial behavior without condemning it—and the proposition becomes doubtful when we think of *Romeo and Juliet* and *Othello*—it is almost certainly true that he did not himself conceive, or imagine that others would conceive, that Jessica's behavior was unfilial.

The relations between the wicked father and the lovely daughter are governed by laws nearly as old as the hills.

Yet even so, in rejecting Jessica's words as un-Shakespearian because morally hideous, the *New Cambridge Shakespeare* is not consistent; for the introductory essay discusses the problem how it is that Shylock is made "sympathetic" to us, and argues that it is because he is deserted by his bad and disloyal daughter: "he is intolerably wronged," and we feel for him accordingly. We cannot have it both ways; we cannot argue that Shakespeare deliberately made Jessica unfilial in order to gain our sympathy for the Jew, and at the same time reject a passage as un-Shakespearian because in it Jessica reveals herself unfilial. The dilemma is absolute, but it is of the modern critic's making, not Shakespeare's. It is the direct result of applying to *The Merchant of Venice* a kind of criticism which it was never meant to satisfy.

Criticism of this kind seeks for psychological motives where none were intended or given. Shylock's hatred of Antonio is, in origin, a fairy-tale hatred, of the bad for the good. And perhaps this fairy-tale hatred is more significant than a hatred which can (if any hatred can) be justified to the consciousness. At any rate Shakespeare was at all times content to accept this antagonism of the evil and the good as self-explanatory. Not to speak of Iago, or Goneril, or Edmund, in the very next play in the Folio, *As You Like It*, which was probably written at about the same time as *The Merchant of Venice*, Oliver, in plotting Orlando's death, similarly confesses his elemental hatred of his brother: "I hope I shall see an end of him; for my soul, yet I know not why, hates nothing more than he." Some would explain these simple assertions of a primal antagonism as compelled by the conditions of the Elizabethan theatre, which required the characters clearly to label themselves as villains or heroes; but it is quite as likely that Shakespeare accepted the sheer opposition of good and evil as an ultimate fact of the moral universe. Assuredly, if it was a necessary convention of the Elizabethan theatre, it was a convention which Shakespeare found it easy to use for his own purposes. For the hatred of his villains always lies deeper than their consciousness.

Thus Shylock at one moment declares that he hates Antonio "for he is a Christian"; at another, because he is a trade rival: "I will have the heart of him if he forfeit, for were he out of Venice, I can make what merchandise I will." If we take the psychological point of view, the contradiction should not trouble us. We may say that Shylock is trying, as later Iago will try, to rationalize his hatred of Antonio: that he contradicts himself in so doing, is in accord with everyday experience. Or, on a different level, we may say that Shakespeare himself is trying to rationalize his elemental story. Unlike Oliver, who appears only at the beginning and the end of *As You Like It*, unlike the unsubstantial Don John in *Much Ado*, Shylock is the main figure of the play. What is in reality the simple fact of his hatred has to be motivated. Oliver and Don John are not required to be credible; Shylock is.

But these two kinds of explanation are not contradictory, as some critics think they are. They are two modes, two levels, of the operation of the same necessity: the "psychologization" of a story that is a datum. In the process, Antonio's character suffers some slight damage. He spits upon Shylock's Jewish gaberdine. If we reflect in cold blood on Antonio's reported behavior to Shylock, we are in danger of thinking that Shylock's intended revenge was not excessive. But we are not meant or allowed to reflect upon it. We are not made to *see* this behavior. It is a sudden shifting of the values in order to make Shylock sympathetic to us at the moment he is proposing the bond. This is a dramatic device of which Shakespeare was always a master. But because Shakespeare was Shakespeare it is something more than a dramatic device.

Shylock undoubtedly is, to a certain degree, made sympathetic to us; and it is important to discover how it is done. For this, almost certainly, was a radical change wrought by Shakespeare in the crude substance of the old play. But the effect was certainly not achieved by Shakespeare's representing Shylock as the victim of Jessica's ingratitude. On the contrary, Shakespeare is most careful to prevent any such impression from taking lodgment in our minds. At the moment when we might feel a little uneasy about Jessica's treatment of her father, any nascent misgiving is stifled by Salerio's description of Shylock's outcry at the discovery:

> My daughter! O my ducats! O my daughter!
> Fled with a Christian! O my Christian ducats!
> Justice! the law! my ducats, and my daughter!
> A sealed bag, two sealed bags of ducats,
> Of double ducats, stolen from me by my daughter!
> And jewels, two stones, two rich and precious stones,
> Stolen by my daughter! Justice! find the girl;
> She hath the stones upon her, and the ducats.   (II. viii. 14-22)

It is not the loss of his daughter that moves Shylock, but only the loss of his money. Shylock, at this moment, is presented as an ignoble being whom Jessica does well to escape and despoil.

Shylock is deliberately made unsympathetic when it is required to cover Jessica. He is made sympathetic when Shakespeare feels the need, or welcomes the opportunity of making a truly dramatic contrast between Shylock and Antonio. At critical moments he is given dignity and passion of speech and argument to plead his cause to us and to himself. His hatred then is represented as deep, irrational and implacable, but not as mean and mercenary. It is then a force of nature—something greater than himself:

> So can I give no reason, nor I will not,
> More than a lodged hate and a certain loathing
> I bear Antonio, that I follow thus
> A losing suit against him.   (IV. i. 59-62)

"A losing suit," because he, who grieves more for his ducats than his daughter, refuses many times the value of his debt to have his bond of Antonio; and his implacability is supplied with excuses enough to more than half persuade us—Antonio's expressed contempt for him, and the magnificent speech, which may have been hardly less magnificent in the verse from which Shakespeare seems to have changed it.

> And if you wrong us, shall we not revenge?
> If we are like you in the rest, we will
> Resemble you in that. If a Jew wrong
> A Christian, what is his humility?
> Revenge! And if a Christian wrong a Jew
> What should his sufferance be?
> By Christian example, why, revenge!
> The villainy you teach me
> I will execute: and it shall go hard
> But I will better the instruction.   (III. i. 71 *sq.*)

Not content with that, Shakespeare in the trial scene gives Shylock a truly tremendous argument:

> *Duke.* How shalt thou hope for mercy, rendering none?
> *Shy.*   What judgment shall I dread, doing no wrong?
>   You have among you many a purchased slave,
>   Which, like your asses and your dogs and mules,
>   You use in abject and in slavish parts,
>   Because you bought them: shall I say to you,
>   Let them be free, marry them to your heirs?
>   Why sweat they under burthens? let their beds
>   Be made as soft as yours, and let their palates
>   Be seasoned with such viands? You will answer
>   "The slaves are ours": so do I answer you:
>   The pound of flesh, which I demand of him,
>   Is dearly bought: 'tis mine and I will have it.
>   If you deny me, fie upon your law!
>   There is no force in the decrees of Venice.
>   I stand for judgment: answer, shall I have it?   (IV. i. 87-103)

Shall I not do as I will with mine own? It is the morality of a whole society, to which Antonio and his friends belong no less than Shylock, which Shylock challenges here, and by anticipation blunts the edge of Portia's great plea for mercy. As Hazlitt put it, in his tempestuous way, "the appeal to the Jew's mercy, as if there were any common principle of right and wrong between them, is the rankest hypocrisy, the blindest prejudice." The world where mercy prevails is not the world of the play. That is a world where justice is the bulwark of injustice.

This is much more than a dramatic device to gain a momentary sympathy for Shylock; yet it is less, or at least other, than a deliberate posing of a profound moral problem. *The Merchant of Venice* is not a problem play; it is a fairy story, within the framework of which Shakespeare allowed free working to the thoughts of his mind and the feelings of his heart. What an unfettered Shylock might say, this fettered Shylock does say.

In other words, Shylock is both the embodiment of an irrational hatred, and a credible human being. He is neither of these things to the exclusion of the other. And if we ask how can that be? the only answer is that it is so. This was Shakespeare's way of working. If we choose, we may say that there are in the story primitive elements which he could not wholly assimilate to his own conception; but such an explanation, in *The Merchant of Venice* as in *Hamlet,* brings us against the fact that the dramatic impression made by these plays is the impression of an artistic whole. And, indeed, it seems more probable that Shakespeare did not deal in "conceptions" of the kind that are often attributed to him. He set himself in successive attempts to infuse a general impression of credibility into an old story, and to secure from his audience no more, and no less, than "that willing suspension of disbelief which constitutes poetic faith."

One cannot too often emphasize the nature of Shakespeare's dramatic "method." It was not chosen by him, neither was it imposed upon his reluctant genius; it was simply the condition of the work he had chosen to do. The situation was given; necessarily, therefore, the "characters" in a certain primitive sense—much the same sense in which we can speak of "characters" in a nursery-story like Cinderella or Robin Hood or a Punch and Judy show. They are simply the necessary agents for that situation or that story. Shakespeare proceeded to endow them with poetic utterance, and with character in a quite different sense. He did what he could to make them credible human beings to himself. He gave them, so far as was possible, humanly plausible motives for their acts and situations, although these were often in fact prior to humane psychology. In a word, the method of Shakespeare's drama consists, essentially, in the humanization of melodrama. And each of those terms must have real validity for the Shakespeare critic who is to avoid ascending or descending into some private universe of his own and calling it Shakespeare.

This Shakespeare, who strove to humanize melodrama, and yet was perforce content with the immediate dramatic impression—an "essential Shakespeare," if ever there was one—is apparently very difficult for modern criticism to grasp. There is something monstrous about him which must be brought to order. The methods of disciplining him are various. In their extreme form they were practised by the late Mr. J. M. Robertson, and consisted in assigning to somebody else, on "stylistic" grounds, nearly all that was unpalatable in Shakespeare. In the more circumspect form, practised by the New Cambridge editors, they are a combination of discovering "old-play-fossils," which generally contain the parts of Shakespeare which are held to be morally or aesthetically reprehensible, and downright charges of bad workmanship, by standards which are irrelevant. Thus, the New Cambridge edition argues that, since "everyone of the Venetian *dramatis personae* is either a 'waster' or a 'rotter' or both, and cold-hearted at that," the true dramatic contrast between Shylock and Antonio and his friends is blurred.

> For the evil opposed against these curious Christians is specific; it is Cruelty; and yet again specifically, the peculiar cruelty of a Jew. To this cruelty an artist at the top of his art would surely have opposed mansuetude, clemency, charity and specifically Christian charity. Shakespeare misses more than half the point when he makes his intended victims, as a class and by habit, just as heartless as Shylock without any of Shylock's passionate excuse.

The basis of this argument is surely mistaken. To supply the true dramatic contrast to Shylock's insistence upon his bond, not rare Christian charity, but ordinary human decency is enough. The contrast would not be heightened, but made intolerable, if Antonio and his friends were represented as uncanonized saints. Deliberate and conscious cruelty is an outrage upon ordinary human nature. And the careless paganism of Antonio's friends— ordinary "decent" young aristocrats—is the proper foil to it.

Antonio and his friends are unconscious. They do not realize any more than did the average decent man of Shakespeare's day, that their morality is essentially no finer than Shylock's, or rather that Shylock's is the logical consequence of their own. Because they are unconscious, they are forgiven; where Shylock, being conscious, cannot be. And that is true to life. Logic in morality is intolerable and inhuman, and Antonio's escape from Shylock's revenge by a legal quibble is poetic justice. The impediment of logic and law is broken down by logic and law, and the stream of human life—ordinary, approximate, unconscious, instinctive human life—can flow on. The decency of an age and an average prevails over the design of an isolated bitterness.

There is a morality in *The Merchant of Venice,* though it is not of the formulable kind; nor is it a morality on the level of the deepest insights expressed in the play. Shylock's incrimination of "Christian" society, Portia's appeal to Christian mercy—these are overtones, as it were caught from the celestial spheres.

> Sit Jessica. Look how the floor of heaven
> Is thick inlaid with patines of bright gold:
> There's not the smallest orb which thou beholdest
> But in his motion like an angel sings
> Still quiring to the young-eyed cherubins;
> Such harmony is in immortal souls;
> But whilst this muddy vesture of decay
> Doth grossly close us in, we cannot hear it.   (v. i. 58-65)

No one distinctly hears that harmony in the play: and it would be fatal if they did. For this play was never intended to vex us with thoughts beyond the reaches of our souls, but "to give some shadow of satisfaction to the mind of man in these points where the nature of things doth deny it."

That axiom of Bacon's may be applied not merely to *The Merchant of Venice* as a whole, but to Shakespeare's work upon the story. If we try to make the play as a whole consistent with the points in which Shakespeare gave satisfaction to his own mind, we retire discomfited. If we persist, we are landed in critical extravagance. Thus one of the New Cambridge editors (who is in general a very fine critic) condemns Shakespeare as a bad workman because he did not attune all the Venetian gallants to the key of Portia's appeal for mercy. He dismisses the rest of Antonio's friends as beneath contempt, and concentrates his indignation upon Bassanio.

> When we first meet him, he is in debt, a condition on which—having to confess it because he wants to borrow more money—he expends some very choice diction.

> > 'Tis not unknown to you, Antonio,
> > [No, it certainly was not!]
> > How much I have disabled mine estate,
> > By something showing a more swelling port
> > Than my faint means would grant continuance.

> That may be a mighty fine way of saying you have chosen to live beyond your income; but Shakespeare or no Shakespeare, if Shakespeare means us to hold Bassanio for an honest fellow, it is mighty poor poetry. For poetry, like honest men, looks things in the face and does not ransack its wardrobe to clothe what is naturally unpoetical.

Moral indignation runs floodgate here: for the consequences of this statement are, first, that it is "naturally unpoetical" to live beyond your income, and second that poetry should look such a condition "in the face." What the effect of this contemplation would be we cannot surmise—perhaps a naturally unpoetical poetry. At all events it is clear that Sir Arthur Quiller-Couch has for the moment become unmindful of the very nature of poetic drama; he would banish the generous spendthrift from it for ever.

Even so Bassanio is not done with. He crowns his unmitigated offences by paying suit among the rivals to Portia's hand.

> O my Antonio, had I but the means
> To hold a rival place with one of them,
> I have a mind presages me such thrift,
> That I should questionless be fortunate.

Now this (says his stern mentor) is bad workmanship and dishonoring to Bassanio . . . But he gets the money of course, equips himself lavishly, arrives at Belmont; and here comes in worse workmanship. For I suppose that, while character weighs in drama, if one thing more than another is certain, it is that a predatory young gentleman such as Bassanio would *not* have chosen the leaden casket.

To all which the only reply is that every ordinary reader of the play, so far from considering Bassanio predatory, hopes, expects, is certain, that so debonair a gentleman will choose the right box. The lapse is not in Shakespeare's workmanship, but in his editor's judgment. Shakespeare remembered what he was doing, his editor has forgotten. *The Merchant of Venice* is not, and was never intended to be, a realistic problem-play. It is possible not to like what it is; but the first duty of a critic is to see it as what it is, and not as something quite different. No one would hold up tragi-comedy as the highest form of poetic drama; but it is a separate form, with a quality and flavor all its own. *The Merchant of Venice* is the finest example of it that we possess.

Dr. Dover Wilson's method of dealing with the baffling substance of *The Merchant of Venice* is different. He does not accuse Shakespeare of being a bad workman. He convinces himself that there are substantial elements of a pre-Shakespearian play in Shakespeare's text. He reaches this conviction, in fact, on *a priori* grounds, for his bibliographical evidence points merely to the probability of revision, which any careful reader of the play will admit; it supplies no ground for supposing that the original text, which Shakespeare revised and revised again, was not Shakespeare's own. But for some cause Dr. Dover Wilson is anxious to prove that there is non-Shakespearian matter in the play. There is—and it hardly needs proving. The bare plot is, almost certainly, not Shakespeare's own. But Dr. Dover Wilson wants to prove much more than this: namely, that substantial elements of the writing are not Shakespeare's. And the cause of this anxiety, we believe, is that he is perplexed by the substance of the play. At all events, the anxiety must needs be devouring to enable him to imagine that there is any validity in the argument he uses. "Mere surmise is not enough," he truly says. "What we need is proof, and proof of such a kind as will leave no doubt that two distinct dramatists have been at work on the structure of the play." The sentiment is admirable. But Dr. Wilson thus continues:

> The divergent conceptions of the Venetian polity evident in the play, though hitherto unnoticed by critics, furnish, we think, the proof required. Consider these three passages:

>> He plies the duke at morning and at night,
>> And doth impeach the freedom of the state,
>> If they deny him justice.   (III. ii. 278-80)

>> The duke cannot deny the course of law:
>> For the commodity that strangers have
>> With us in Venice, if it be denied,
>> Will much impeach the justice of the state,
>> Since that the trade and profit of the city
>> Consisteth of all nations.   (III. iii. 26-31)

>> I have possessed your grace of what I purpose,
>> And by our holy Sabbath have I sworn
>> To have the due and forfeit of my bond:
>> If you deny it, let the danger light
>> Upon your charter and the city's freedom.   (IV. i. 35-9)

In the second we recognize the historical Venetian republic, the independent state, the great world port and world market, whose trade and confidence were only secured by the city's even-handed and rigorous enforcement of the law of contract. In the third passage the constitution has completely changed; Venice has now become a city, like London or many other English townships, enjoying privileges under a royal charter, privileges liable to suspension if the city misbehaved itself. As for the first of the three passages, it must remain uncertain what type of constitution it has in view, seeing that "freedom" may refer either to "the commodity (i.e. privileges) that strangers have" in the port of Venice, or to the freedom of the city itself from royal or baronial interference. Indeed, one may hazard the guess that it was just the ambiguity of this word "freedom" which gave rise to the contradiction in the other two passages. In any case, it can hardly be denied that the contradiction is there and that its presence makes it absolutely certain that two different dramatists have been at work upon the text. Nor, we think, should there be any doubt which of the two was Shakespeare. The historically accurate lines from III., iii. give us pedestrian and unskilful verse, witness the awkwardness of "since that," the ugly repetition in "deny . . . denied," and the muddled construction of the whole sentence which no commentator has quite succeeded in unravelling. On the other hand, the lines which inaccurately credit Venice with a royal charter come not only from the trial scene, but from the mouth of one of Shakespeare's supreme creations at his most characteristic moment.

We have quoted the argument entire, because it shows very plainly the process by which non-literary theory can tamper with literary judgment. No one reading those three passages without prepossession would be inclined to deny any one of them to Shakespeare. To adduce the "muddled construction" of the second as evidence that it is not Shakespeare's is perverse. Compressed and pregnant syntax of precisely that kind (where the main drift is plain) is pre-eminently Shakespearian.[1] Further, if the passages came before us simply as anonymous fragments, we should naturally conclude that the second was from the same hand as the first: the phrases, "impeach the freedom of the state," "impeach the justice of the state," would certainly be attributed by the ordinary literary critic to the same pen. Dr. Wilson, however, requires us to believe that each is the work of a different hand, simply because the conceptions of Venetian polity in two of them are inconsistent. Since when is Shakespeare required to be rigidly consistent in such matters? Shall we conclude that two distinct dramatists had a hand in *Othello* because the members of the Council are in one place called "senators" and in another "consuls," and a third where Iago says that Brabantio is twice as powerful as the Duke and has power of his own motion to divorce Desdemona from the Moor. Every reader of Shakespeare knows that he was quite careless of consistency in such matters. Dr. Wilson himself knows this far better than most of us, but he has managed to persuade himself, and would persuade us, that the negligible inconsistency "makes it absolutely certain" that in *The Merchant of Venice* two different dramatists have been at work upon the text of yet a third.

We believe that these are aberrations of criticism, and that they ultimately derive from the peculiarity of Shakespeare's methods, which are perhaps exceptionally prominent in *The Merchant of Venice*. The unity of a Shakespeare play (if we may generalize) is seldom what would be described today as a unity of conception. That was precluded, save in rare cases, by the necessities of Shakespeare's peculiar craft. The axiom, which has long been current in Shakespeare criticism, that the situation derives from the character is, in the main, a mistaken one. The reverse is nearer to the truth; for the situations are generally prior to the characters. But that does not mean, as some modern critics assert, that the reverse *is* the truth, and that the characters derive from the situations. They do not. They are largely epiphenomenal to the situations.

This is difficult to grasp, because it is so simple. There is an element in a

---

[1] For a parallel, see the Bastard's speech on Commodity, above: p. 159 [in the original text—ED.].

Shakespeare character which derives from the situation; but that element is relatively small compared to the element which floats as it were free of the situation. On this element Shakespeare lavished himself, because here he was, within limits, a free agent. A simple example is Antonio's motiveless melancholy at the opening of *The Merchant.* It is motiveless: because it is motiveless, modern "scientific" criticism explains it away by a "cut." "We have here," says Dr. Dover Wilson, "a dramatic motive deliberately suppressed at the time of a revision, and the broken line 'I am to learn' shows us where one of the 'cuts' involved in this suppression took place." On the contrary, I am persuaded that Shakespeare intended Antonio's melancholy to be motiveless and that the half-line was deliberate. Shakespeare was taking advantage of that part of Antonio's character which was free to introduce a depth into his character, and still more a feeling-tone into the play, which he felt the play could bear, and which would enrich it. That Antonio's character, as fixed by the situation, does not fully square with this; that he has subsequently to be one who "rails upon" the Jews, and spits upon a Jewish gaberdine, did not trouble Shakespeare. He had had to learn not to be troubled by such necessities. Antonio would remain a presence in the responsive imagination, a character whose nature was not wholly expressed in the acts required of him. It is not otherwise with Shylock. Shylock's "free" character is created of sentiments and thoughts which are, on any cool analysis, incompatible with the acts required of him. The "bloody-minded usurer" is the mouthpiece of an oppressed nation and the impassioned critic of current Christian morality; yet he is, because he has to be, "the bloody-minded usurer" as well. And Shakespeare, as we have seen, will exalt and degrade him at need, either to make uncouthness in the action more plausible, or to wring every atom of imaginative and dramatic possibility out of the central situation. As Dr. Bridges wrote, "He had, as it were, a balance to maintain, and a fine sense of its equipoise: if one scale descends, he immediately throws something into the other, and though he may appear to be careless as to what he throws in, he only throws in such things as he knows he may be careless about. But an examination of those matters would tend to prove that he did not regard the reader as well as the audience of his plays."

Coherent, in the modern sense of the word, such characters are not. Nor are they even consistent among themselves, so to speak. At their best, which is often, they create the inimitable Shakespearian impression of being imagined "in the round" and exhibiting in action only one aspect of their rich substance to us; at the worst, which is rare, they are puzzling and demand from the reader more than the normal effort towards the willing suspension of disbelief which constitutes poetic faith. Such a method of character-creation could arise (I think) only out of a sort of consubstantiality of the poet with the theatre. It was imposed by the practice of rewriting time-honored and time-proven theatrical material: and it is notable that where Shakespeare had a relatively free hand this imaginative ambiguity is much less frequent. For in this order we should need to make a distinction between story-material which was familiar to Shakespeare's audience, and story-material which, though not of Shakespeare's invention, was not familiar to them. The degree of Shakespeare's liberty to adjust his dramatic action to his imaginative need must have varied greatly according to the definiteness of popular expectation.

To determine that variation is, perhaps fortunately, beyond our power. We lack the knowledge, and it is unlikely that we shall ever attain it. But it is worthy of more than passing notice that the two perennially popular plays of Shakespeare—*The Merchant of Venice* and *Hamlet*—are the two of which we can say, most definitely, that his freedom to alter the action was most limited; and that they are also the plays in which the nature of the chief character is most disputed.

Much Ado About Nothing

by A. P. Rossiter

Deception by appearances in *love* is patently what most of *Much Ado* is "about." As Hero puts it:

> Of this matter
> Is little Cupid's crafty arrow made,
> That only wounds by hearsay . . .   (III. i. 21-3)

Cupid is not responsible for calumny; but "hearsay" is a main force in both love-plots: each is about its effects on proud, self-willed, self-centered and self-admiring creatures, whose comedy is at bottom that of imperfect self-knowledge, which leads them on to fool themselves. Is it exaggeration to bring even Dogberry into this pattern? to point to his manifest self-admiration ("a fellow that hath had losses; and one that hath two gowns, and everything handsome about him"), and to hint that the little arrow that wounds *him* "by hearsay" is magnificent language and "wit"? Are not words and wisdom his Cupids? No doubt that stretches "love" too far. But self-love is a common term to all three of the splendid comedians of the piece.

The play's wit has been justly praised and is worth some examination in detail. It is of several distinguishable sorts: the simpler important only in so far as contributing to the cumulative effect, one of impetuous exuberance, a kind of competitive vitality, expressing itself in quick manipulations of language. The Messinans have dancing minds, and make words dance or caper to their unpremeditated tunes. At its simplest level, it is mere quibble: where A has used a word capable of two meanings in different contexts, and B shows his awareness of both, by displacing it. This may be no more than a conventional game, "comic wit degenerating into clenches";[1] and though editors explain them, "the mind," as Johnson says, "is refrigerated by

"*Much Ado About Nothing.*" From *Angel With Horns*, by A. P. Rossiter (London: Longmans, Green & Co., Ltd., 1961), pp. 67-81. Reprinted by permission of the author's executor, Longmans, Green & Co., Ltd., and Theatre Arts Books. Copyright © 1961 Longmans, Green & Co., Ltd.

[1] Dryden: *Essay of Dramatic Poesy.*

interruption." *Much Ado* suffers but little from this. It may, again, be an
elaboration of that: when A and B are the same person, as when Beatrice
"takes herself up" on Claudio: "The Count is neither sad, nor sick, nor
merry, nor well; but civil count—civil as an orange, and something of that
jealous complexion" (II. i. 262–4). That is exactly at the point where mere
verbal cleverness, non-significant quibble, passes over into relevant wit:
evocative here either of Beatrice's vitality (the "character" view), or of the
exuberant quality of lively minds which strike fire by scoring off each other:
the quality I called *competitive* vitality, as of a "college of wit-crackers."

In the wit-game Benedick and Beatrice rightly regard themselves as
"seeded" players. Beatrice makes this clear in the scene in Hero's apartment
before the wedding (III. iv.), when Margaret scores off her for once. Shown
Hero's new gloves, she is not interested (her mind is bothered with Benedick),
and unguardedly pretends to have a cold:

> I am stuff'd, cousin, I cannot smell.
> *Margaret.* A maid and stuff'd! There's goodly catching of cold.
> *Beatrice.* O, God help me! God help me! How long have you profess'd
> apprehension?

("Since when have you been a wit-cracker in this line?"—which Beatrice
regards, with good reason, as her own.) Beatrice gets more of her own
medicine later, over the prescription of "Carduus Benedictus": here the wit
is both verbal and something more—we might call it the wit of situation.
No precise *double-entendre* is made; but Beatrice's state of mind is such that she
feels (like Benedick before her) "there's a double meaning in that"; and she
lays herself open to another laugh by again using the wrong word:

> Benedictus! why Benedictus? You have some moral in this
> "Benedictus."
> *Margaret.* Moral? No, by my troth, I have no moral meaning.

It is a notable point in Shakespeare's contrivance that he gives both wits
their off-day, as soon as love has disturbed their freedom.

As a rule, bawdy quibble outlives its contemporaries—simply because of
"human nature"; or because the fundamental situation is practically constant. In this play, jesting about sex is apposite: its subjects are sex-opposition,
wooing, wedding, wiving (with due attention to the dangers of the last in
making sport of a man). The audience certainly laughed at Benedick's
"Well, a horn for my money, when all's done" (II. iii. 56), the *second* time
they saw the play. It becomes comic dramatic irony, if you read Elizabe-
thanly. Yet, quite often, I see no great gain by doing so. There is something
pathetic in the detailed scholarship which laboriously strives to conjure from

its grave every ghost of an expired laugh.[2] "Lighthearted bawdry" has its point in *Much Ado* (as in Mercutio); but only the best of points can stand heavy-handed annotation. Much of it turns on obsolete phrases: the fuse of the whole firework has to be replaced with a dry note; and the verbal transaction, by losing all its speed, loses nearly all its crack. Quibble in slow-motion ceases to be witty. None the less, by noticing or examining the dexterities of verbal switch required, we are speeded up to a better awareness of the Elizabethan manipulations of language; and, at the same time, made more conscious of the vitality evoked individually by characters, and cumulatively by quibble, pun, and jest together.

Shakespeare's wit in devising the linguistic mishaps and semantic excesses of Dogberry is the other side to the flat and despised "mere quibble." Dogberry exaggerates, by accident and in self-satisfied ignorance, the processes by which the true wits divert the meanings of words deliberately, knowingly, and with pride in their craft. But the one is the antithesis to the other; and both sides could be told, "Thou hast frighted the word out of his right sense, so forcible is thy wit" (Benedick to Beatrice, v. ii. 48). Wit and nitwit share a common obsessive delight in the wonders of words. This is largely what makes Dogberry the apposite farce-fool for a play in which all three plots turn on understandings and misunderstandings: quite apart from his being a marvel of the official numbskull's capacity to make extreme ado about genuine nothing.

But has the "Malaprop" had its day? It took the stage in *Woodstock* (? 1594), was cornered by Sheridan, survived to Dickens. It is perhaps funniest in hierarchical societies, where clever and witty management (or mismanagement) of language distinguishes the *élite*; and aping this makes the linguistic lower orders flatteringly absurd. My impression is that Malaprops are only comic nowadays to over-language-conscious schoolmasters; or, of course, when bawdily Dogburian: when the right idea comes out in very much the wrong word. But, unless I mistake, Dogberry's skids are never improper. Impropriety in this play is the privilege of the educated.

The wit that does *not* turn on word-play is best shown by examples. Essentially it is the exuberance which leaps beyond expectation in "improving the occasion." Not only Benedick and Beatrice have this hyperbolic comic inventiveness: the former his strokes of Falstaffian invention, the latter her alarming opportunism (she is likely to score suddenly off anyone, at any time). The qualities of swiftness and unexpectedness are just as neatly shown by old Leonato's perfectly timed shot at Benedick. Don Pedro asks if Hero is Leonato's daughter. "Her mother hath many times told me so,"

---

[2] The smutty puns, for example, humorlessly expounded by Kökeritz in *Shakespeare's Pronunciation*, are often so farfetched as to be linguistically dubious and not worth the carriage.

is the conventional formula in reply. "Were you in doubt, sir, that you ask'd her?" asks Benedick. "Signior Benedick, no; for then were you a child" (a palpable hit). They appear equally in Beatrice's magnificent impertinence to Don Pedro. She must cry "Heigh ho for a husband!"—

> *Don Pedro.* Lady Beatrice, I will get you one.
> *Beatrice.*   I would rather have one of your father's getting. . . .

And the quality of "comic inventiveness" is shown immediately after, when he teasingly offers himself, and she says she will not have him unless she can have another for working days: he is so costly she would have to keep him for best.

Both quickness of repartee and comic inventiveness (hyperbolic feats of exaggeration and elaboration) are intrinsic to the attitudes of self-dramatization upon which the comedy of character depends. Energy is delight and accomplished dexterity a pleasure to watch. Benedick and Beatrice have both: all the more because they are playing a part before themselves, and playing it high in an infectious sort of daring: figures of pride, which is at once humanly splendid, and "goes before a fall." There is no need to repeat what others have said of their proud hearts as a source of misogamy, because marriage means submission and commonplaceness. Benedick shows a more delicately amusing self-conceit than this in, for example, the admirable lines (v. ii. 63 ff.), where the two mock-solemnly agree (*a*) that they are too wise to woo peaceably, and (*b*) that not one wise man among twenty will praise himself. Benedick then hits the high note impeccably with "Therefore is it most expedient for the wise, if Don Worm, his conscience, find no impediment to the contrary, to be the trumpet of his own virtues, as I am to myself"—a pause, to let the conceit of it shock all modest minds; then he goes one better—"So much for praising myself, who, I myself will bear witness, is praiseworthy." Here he is playing the Falstaffian game of carrying outrageousness as far as it will go. The *other* side of this self-conceit is in ii. iii. 200 ff., his solemn resolutions to profit morally by what he has overheard on his character: "I must not seem proud; happy are they that hear their detractions and can put them to mending"; and the heroic resolve to make the supreme sacrifice: "No; the world must be peopled." There, he is magnificently *absurd*, and totally unaware of himself. I stress the point to bring out the unappreciated fact that the common distinction between persons we laugh *at* and those we laugh *with* is too naïve and crude, at any rate for Shakespeare. Benedick's subsequent efforts to extract a double meaning from two snubbing sentences of Beatrice's repeat this vista of ingenious absurdity. Besides being excellent comedy of mistaken meanings, the last speech in ii. iii. is a perfect miniature sample of the love-humor racing a man past himself: "I will go get her picture (*Exit*)."

It may seem a wantonly paradoxical view, in so verbally brilliant a piece, but I would contend that some of the wittiest work is to be found in the interrelations and inter-inanimations of the plots. Of the three, the one that takes attention foremost is technically a subplot. We hardly notice that it gets going before the "main" plot, but Beatrice is "at" Benedick before Claudio appears; and this sex-antagonism in a fencing match between experts with sharp words is musically "the first subject." The comedy of this Benedick and Beatrice plot is not the simple, sentimental indulgence of the "boy meets girl" pattern, although that is included; rather it lies in the entertaining, good-natured, critically aware contemplation of the bents in human nature shown in (a) their antagonism (their incapacity to leave one another alone); (b) their deception by contrived intrigue; (c) the revelations which spring from this, under the pressure of circumstances (that arise from the main plot): leading to (d) reversal of all their first positions. The audience is always in a slightly superior position, *not* identifying itself with either of them, though sympathetic. When all the analysers have anatomized, and perhaps reconstructed Benedick and Beatrice, they remain "just representations of general nature," and hence, as Johnson says, "please many and please long."

If I were to answer in a word what the Benedick and Beatrice plot turns on, I should say *misprision*. Benedick and Beatrice misapprehend both each other *and* themselves: each misprizes the other sex, and misapprehends the possibility of a complete agreement between them, as individuals, on what causes that misprision: love of freedom and a superior conceit of themselves as "wise" where others are fools; as "free" and untied; and as having a right to enjoy kicking over other people's traces. They fancy they are quite different *from*, and quite indifferent *to* each other. Indifferent they are not; and the audience is "superior" in seeing their humors *as* humors; and in being aware that the opposite to love (as passionate, obsessive interest) is not hate (another passionate interest), but cool or unnoting indifference. How little Beatrice's "disdain" for Benedick is truly disdainful is shown in her immediately thinking of him as a measure for Don John (II. i. 6 ff.).

Because the mind of each runs on the other, they can both be simply gulled by hearsay; provided that it is overheard and includes the sort of freedom of comment we all use on absent friends: mildly malicious in tone, unspiteful in intent, and near enough true on their recognizable oddities and shortcomings. The overhearers, for all their sharpness of wit, know that the *comments* have some truth, and naturally accept the rest as also true.[3] Thus the introduction of love-thoughts into both results from a species of misapprehension. They take the *sense* of the words, but totally fail to apprehend their *intention*. The two gulling scenes belong to the comedy of advertisement. Even the advertisers' nice touches of flattery are not lacking. The criticism is spiced with proper appreciation, as when Don Pedro hints—

[3] Cf. Aristotle on lying, *Poetics*, 24.9: "Homer more than any other has taught the rest of us the art of telling lies in the right way. I mean the use of a fallacy," *et seq*.

a very subtle inducement—that he would quite like to have Beatrice himself.

That the "main" plot of Hero and Claudio turns on misapprehension leading to the misprision of violent disprizing, is too obvious to need commentary: but much of the play's total effect hangs on the structural mainness of this plot being displaced. As sometimes in Mannerist pictures, the emphasis is made to fall on what appears structurally to be a corner. This displaced emphasis helps to maintain the sense that the "Ado" is about "Nothing" (it is only through the distortion that reading gives, that much attention is given to the "character" of Claudio).

But though the misapprehension from judging by appearances is quite obvious, it is easy to overlook the incidental touches by which the theme of false report, misunderstanding, and jumping to conclusions is strengthened. Not logically strengthened: the "incidents" are not necessary to the *story*; but the whole sub-episode of the proxy wooing does chime in cleverly with what is to follow. Don Pedro agrees to woo Hero; *immediately* Leonato's 'good sharp fellow' overhears and misreports (I. ii. 5 ff.); the correct report gets into the wrong ears, Borachio's; he tells Don John, who straightaway uses it maliciously on Claudio (pretending to think him Benedick behind the masque-vizor). And Claudio at once anticipates his later violent and self-regarding impetuosity by assuming that Don Pedro *has* cheated him of Hero. Call this "atmosphere," if you like; say, perhaps, that Messina is no place to trust any man's word; whatever you say, it strengthens the theme; and the ready *and perhaps drastic* misapprehensions of quick and apprehensive minds appear as of major importance in the play, as a play and not as a merely logical story.

I say "perhaps drastic" to suggest how the matter of this part is balanced neatly on a tonal frontier: not between comedy and tragedy, but between comedy and tragi-comedy. Hence the "limited" of my description of the play at the beginning: the drastic possibilities are so lightly touched that there is a sense of withholding—as if the author, in another mood, could give these incidents quite another tone: but not now; not yet. This feeling is most evident in the Church scene, which is *not* tragic. T. W. Craik's line[4] here is mainly sound; and his interpretation that *all* the passions are presented to be viewed with comic detachment is preferable to the conventional explanation, that "the audience is throughout in the know," etc.[5]

Without striving to make too much of it, the dance in II. i. is beautifully apposite. The couples walk their round, two by two, all masked; and all are using words to back the disguise of false faces with trivial deceit. The play-acted defamation of Hero, by means of a false dress on the wrong woman and names used falsely, is exactly parallel. In both, the truth is *behind* the

---

[4] In *Scrutiny*, xix (1953).
[5] So is the audience in *Othello*, for what that is worth!

looks and words. The *bal masqué* is only a game of seeming; yet it is a most apt symbol of the whole. The vizor is half deceit, half no deceit: you can never be sure. Believe it, and you make ado about what is nothing. And in the social order and shared delight of the dance—all moving to the controlling rhythm, in their appointed patterns—there is too the emblem of the harmony in which all will conclude: as the play does, with another dance, all the vizors laid aside. The real play is not ended with "Strike up, pipers." The very movement of II. i., where all the main misapprehensions started, is repeated and completed; and even the professed misogamists are dancing to the same tune. It is as neat and pretty as "Sigh no more, ladies, sigh no more."

The third plot—Dogberry, Verges, the Watch—though mainly Dogberry, is not a mere farcical variety-turn: there *is* a thread of connected episode. The Watch overhear Borachio's scheme and hear it correctly enough (their invention of a thief named "Deformed" is a nice touch: he has arrived at official constabulary existence by the end). They only overhear because they carry out Dogberry's ridiculous orders and make the policeman's lot a not-unhappy one by, as far as possible, doing nothing whatever. Despite their superb stupidity they do disentangle the plot: though only because, Don John having fled, Borachio tells everything, and gives them the game hands down. This is very natural and well-managed. For had Borachio set out to bluff, the Watch would have been utterly bamboozled in no time. *Superb* stupidity, however, belongs more rightly to Dogberry alone. One side of him is his art of "comprehending vagrom" *words*: there a more "senseless and fit man" could not be found. But this is not the whole of him; though a part entirely harmonious with the whole. Dogberry is a perfect instance of the comic mirth which Plato explained in *Philebus*: "mirth," he says, "is generally evoked by the sight of self-ignorance or self-conceit, as when a man fancies himself richer, more handsome, more virtuous or wiser than he really is; and this mirth must be present in one who is powerless to inflict hurt on others, otherwise he would cease to be a source of mirth and become a source of danger instead."[6] As a *real* official Dogberry would be a terror. Conceited ignorance and vast self-importance in local government officers is—and was, in the time of Elizabeth—as good a joke in fiction as a very bad joke in fact.

But misprision and misapprehension are present here too, in a different guise. The incomprehension of the stupid ass is a limiting case of failure to apprehend; and over and above his miscomprehensions of language, Dogberry's own view of Dogberry is a vast misprision. To himself a superb creature, a wise fellow, as pretty a piece of flesh as any in Messina, he is superbly asinine in the Messina of wit and word-play. Yet, while apparently an *opposite* to the wit-crackers, he is also a parallel: in that pride of self-opinion

[6] *Philebus*, 48-9 (summarized).

and a nice appreciation of one's own wisdom and cleverness is as much theirs as his. There is no caustic correction of self-love in Benedick or Beatrice. But the parallel gives another common term, showing on analysis how the three plots have their implicit correspondences, how they genuinely belong together.

"Nothing can permanently please, which does not contain in itself the reason why it is so, and not otherwise." I have been trying to probe down to the nervous system of those interrelations which *Much Ado* contains within itself, and which give it, as comedy, the poetic unity Coleridge there demands. I find a complex harmony of interdependent themes, some parallels, some direct oppositions; and it seems to me that misapprehensions, misprisions, misunderstandings, misinterpretations and misapplications are the best names for what the comedy *as a whole* is "about". The misapprehensions of language are one side of the play; those of human beings and states of affairs the other. At root the two are one; and both you can regard with Dogberry's formula for obdurate drunks: "You may say they are not the men you took them for." A step or stage beyond this, and what a different pattern of seemings might result: where neither looks nor words are to be trusted, but everything distrusted. . . . But *Much Ado* touches that for only a moment, and that unsymptomatic of the whole: for a few lines of Claudio's in the Church scene. They only point to what *might* be thought and felt: in the real tragi-comedies it *will* be. Yet even in *Much Ado*, all appearances *are* equivocal.

Before leaving the plots, mark how deftly they are intertwined. Benedick and Beatrice misapprehend themselves and misprize each other. Claudio's contrived misprision of Hero, the result of intrigue, is finally dissipated by the *coup* of the Watch, which reduces all the ado to nothing. But at its zenith this same disprizing is the catalyst which liquidates the mutual misprisions of Benedick and Beatrice in the Church scene. But the reactions to that scene (the confessions of love and Beatrice's implicit admission that she needs a man—to "kill Claudio") only occur because Benedick and Beatrice have been prepared to "apprehend": prepared by intrigue, which, like Don John's, is dependent on hearsay and overhearing, taking appearances at their face value, and being led or misled by words.[7]

Words I must stress, because Dogberry is no essential part of this intertwining as I have summarized it. I suppose you could formulate it all again by saying that the controlling theme might be styled "mistaken identities"; for, in their pride or conceit, all the principals in some degree mistake themselves: as they mistake or wrongly take situations, and mistake or wrongly take words, on purpose and wittily or accidentally and absurdly. Leonato and Antonio, the two old men lashing themselves back into a youth-

[7] Cf. the fusing of plot with plot in *The Miller's Tale*.

ful fury, and threatening duels, equally mistake themselves: they are pathetic and laughable at once. And, in a way, they reflect on Benedick's sternly assuming the role of truculent executioner to Claudio—and having a comical difficulty in maintaining the part. This is a good example of Shakespeare's detachment in this play: of the amused distance at which his creations should be held, if we are to take *Much Ado* as an artistic whole.

Despite Coleridge's too often quoted comment, "The interest in the plot is always in fact on account of the characters, not vice versa, as in almost all other writers; the plot is a mere canvas and no more,"[8] I still think that plot (in a deeper sense than "story") is here even more important. His implied contention that the "interest" in the main plot is "on account of the characters" (Hero and Claudio, chiefly; and I suppose Don John) seems to me simply untrue. Against Coleridge and his echoers we might set Jonson, putting Aristotelian principle in his own words, and answering the question "What is a Poet?": "A poet . . . is a maker, or a feigner: his art, an art of imitation or feigning; expressing the life of man in fit measure, numbers, and harmony. . . . Hence he is called a poet, not he which writeth in measure only, but that feigneth and formeth a fable, and writes things like the truth. For the fable and fiction is, as it were, the form and soul of any poetical work or poem.[9] In a later note, "the very fiction itself," he says, is "the reason or form of the work" (cxxx). "Reason" and "form" are abstractions from the apprehended, "felt" interrelations between distinguishable parts of a whole. Such interrelations I have made the central matter of my examination, attempting to resolve the theme to which the three "plots" are subservient.

Much Ado is not a "serious" play: it is "limited" in managing potentially serious matters with a deft nonchalance which passes by the possibility of some being sharp things that might cut. At the same time, it is a play full of themes which are to have sufficiently serious explorations and consequences in Shakespeare's later work. Othello's situation, for example, is a variant of Claudio's; just as Claudio's behavior to Hero is a sketch of Bertram's (hurt pride turned spiteful: providing we do not see Claudio as only "mechanical"). Deceit by words (especially words of great meaning) is a constant in the tragi-comedies; and the comedy or farce of crediting too much of what is heard, or thought to be heard, is only the other side to "O love's best habit is in seeming trust," and the self-imposed deception by seeming and fair words which are found in the Sonnets.

Seeming and being in the later plays have a quite different seriousness. But such a theme exists here, as it does in *1 Henry IV*; and if we say that the one is on *love* (and sex), the other on *honor*, then, looking ahead, the change in Shakespeare's playwriting is partially represented by *Much Ado* leading

---

[8] *Lectures on Shakespeare*, 1818.
[9] *Timber, or Discoveries*, cxxviii.

to *Measure for Measure;* and *1 Henry IV* leading to *Troilus and Cressida.* By this I suggest that potentially serious and distressing human situations (involving love and honor) are in *Much Ado* and *1 Henry IV* handled "lightly", as we say: contrived so as to keep them amusing, diverting, stimulating; but also so as to hold them more or less insulated from the deeper and more trenchant inquisitions into values of the tragi-comedies.

The place where we can hardly not notice little *points* of contact with the tragi-comedy outlook is the Church scene. "Seeming" is harshly emphasized; Claudio seems on the edge of playing a part that would make it quite another *sort* of play; and the Friar's moral lines on lost affections—sad, uncomfortable thoughts—are echoed by the King in *All's Well That Ends Well.* But those points mark the real insulation of *Much Ado.* The disturbed feeling of *Measure for Measure*—its troubled thinking—is not here. We can hardly speak of "lack of feeling" in so bright, lively, glittering a piece: but is there not a certain *hard* quality, as with the bright colors of some Italian painting?

It is a *Decameron*-like story (barring the Watch), with some of the *Decameron* qualities of volatility in the persons, no wasting of sympathy on victims of jests, and the expectation of swift, unreflecting volte-faces of attitudes and emotions at the call of Fortune's pipe. That usually leaves an impression of shallowness, of a lack of *depth* of emotion, in northern European minds. The people seem rather heartless, while not in the least "cold"; and the stories are apt to leave us thinking more about "Now what did X really feel when . . . ?" than we know we *should.* In *Much Ado,* the brushing aside of the tone of calamity, the expectations of volatile changes of feeling in Claudio, the jocular (for so it is) "Think not on him till to-morrow. I'll devise thee brave punishments for him. Strike up, pipers," only catch up a bright hardness (the result of a *deliberate* limitation of sympathies in the author?) which runs through the play.

Much Ado is a fantasy of equivocal appearances in a glittering world of amiable fools of all sorts. As naturally as Italians talk Italian, the Messinans talk "equivocal"; but their "double tongues" are as harmless as those of the "spotted snakes" in *A Midsummer-Night's Dream.* This equivocal quality, moreover, is deftly restricted to appearances: there are only the slightest touches of suggestion of any intrinsic equivocation in things themselves (in love, for example). Ambivalence is not a term to apply here.

These qualities urge me to "place" the play in the course of Shakespeare's writing as follows. In the breaking down of sensitive endurance, and of mental resistance to the revelation of the unfairness of human nature, there is a point where a sense of humor *fails;* where to see life and the world in humorous proportions is no longer possible: it cannot be assumed by an act of will, or, if so, the assumption cannot be maintained. At this point distresses distress, and cannot be accepted tolerantly as the world's way, muffled by an easy "they soon get over it" and by the cant of time. (I think of John Keats, of course; but without "Keatsifying" Shakespeare. In the *later* plays the "miseries of the world/Are misery"; but not here in *Much Ado*). Immediately *before* that point, the besieged mind and invaded heart may defend themselves by the assumption of a certain hardness: assume the *Decameron virtu*—the trappings and the suits of *joy*—though they hath it not within. They may also find a certain high-flown gaiety—not hysterical, but making the best, and most, of the farce of human misunderstanding, deception, misprision—in the comedy of language (devised, so one may suppose, to communicate: but often used for just the reverse, either in game or in earnest). It is as if the sensitive mind and heart sought to persuade themselves by demonstration that life is a jest, and that the wider the comic net the likelier it is to resolve all the unmentioned but implied and subjective troubles in one great humorous or laughable plan, in which Fortune favors the laughers. This is the point at which great clowns who are melancholic— Chaplin, Raimu, Jouvet, Fernandel—stand and abide. One step from that strange equilibrium may turn to "cynicism" (especially in England): the cynicism where the attitudes I called "hardness" (self-defensive) and "farce" (offensive, debunking) combine to "place" love, honor, truth, only to devalue them. *Much Ado* stands in the Shakespearian canon just at that point.

As You Like It

by Helen Gardner

As its title declares, this is a play to please all tastes. It is the last play
in the world to be solemn over, and there is more than a touch of absurdity
in delivering a lecture, particularly on a lovely summer morning, on this
radiant blend of fantasy, romance, wit and humor. The play itself provides
its own ironic comment on anyone who attempts to speak about it: "You
have said; but whether wisely or no, let the forest judge."

For the simple, it provides the stock ingredients of romance: a handsome,
well-mannered young hero, the youngest of three brothers, two disguised
princesses to be wooed and wed, and a banished, virtuous Duke to be
restored to his rightful throne. For the more sophisticated, it propounds, in
the manner of the old courtly literary form of the *débat*, a question which is
left to us to answer: Is it better to live in the court or the country? "How like
you this shepherd's life, Master Touchstone?," asks Corin, and receives a
fool's answer: "Truly, shepherd, in respect of itself, it is a good life; but in
respect that it is a shepherd's life, it is naught. In respect that it is solitary,
I like it very well; but in respect that it is private, it is a very vile life."
Whose society would you prefer, Le Beau's or Audrey's? Would you rather
be gossiped at in the court or gawped at in the country? The play has also
the age-old appeal of the pastoral, and in different forms. The pastoral
romance of princesses playing at being a shepherd boy and his sister is
combined with the pastoral love-eclogue in the wooing of Phoebe, with the
burlesque of this in the wooing of Audrey, and with the tradition of the moral
eclogue, in which the shepherd is the wise man, in Corin. For the learned
and literary this is one of Shakespeare's most allusive plays, uniting old
traditions and playing with them lightly. Then there are the songs—the
forest is full of music—and there is spectacle: a wrestling match to delight
lovers of sport, the procession with the deer, which goes back to old country
rituals and folk plays, and finally the masque of Hymen, to end the whole

"*As You Like It.*" From *More Talking of Shakespeare*, ed. John Garrett (London: Longmans,
Green & Co., Ltd., 1959), pp. 17-32. Reprinted by permission of the author, Longmans,
Green & Co., Ltd., and Theatre Arts Books, Copyright © 1959 Longmans, Green & Co.,
Ltd. and Contributors.

with courtly grace and dignity. This is an image of civility and true society, for Hymen is a god of cities, as Milton knew:

> There let *Hymen* oft appear
> In Saffron robe, with Taper clear,
> And pomp, and feast, and revelry,
> With mask, and antique Pageantry.

The only thing the play may be said to lack, when compared with Shakespeare's other comedies, is broad humor, the humor of gross clowns. William makes only a brief appearance. The absence of clowning may be due to an historic reason, the loss of Kempe, the company's funny man. But if this was the original reason for the absence of pure clowning, Shakespeare has turned necessity to glorious gain and made a play in which cruder humors would be out of place. *As You Like It* is the most refined and exquisite of the comedies, the one which is most consistently played over by a delighted intelligence. It is Shakespeare's most Mozartian comedy.

The basic story is a folk tale. The ultimate sources for the plots of Shakespeare's greatest tragedy and his most unflawed comedy are stories of the same kind. The tale of the old king who had three daughters, of whom the elder two were wicked and the youngest was good, belongs to the same primitive world of the imagination as the tale of the knight who had three sons, the eldest of whom was wicked and robbed the youngest, who was gallant and good, of his inheritance. The youngest son triumphed, like Jack the Giant Killer, over a strong man, a wrestler, joined a band of outlaws in the forest, became their king, and with the aid of an old servant of his father, the wily Adam Spencer, in the end had his revenge on his brother and got his rights. Lodge retained some traces of the boisterous elements of this old story; but Shakespeare omitted them. His Orlando is no bully, threatening and blustering and breaking down the doors to feast with his boon companions in his brother's house. He is brave enough and quick-tempered; but he is above all gentle. On this simple story Lodge grafted a pastoral romance in his *Rosalynde*. He made the leader of the outlaws a banished Duke, and gave both exiled Duke and tyrant usurper only daughters, as fast friends as their fathers are sworn enemies. The wrestling match takes place at the tyrant's court and is followed by the banishment of Rosalynde and the flight of the two girls to the forest, disguised as shepherd and shepherdess. There the shepherd boy is wooed by the gallant hero, and arouses a passion of love sickness in a shepherdess who scorns her faithful lover. The repentance of the wicked brother and his flight to the forest provide the necessary partner for the tyrant's good daughter, and all ends happily with marriages and the restoration of the good Duke. Shakespeare added virtually nothing to the plot of Lodge's novel. There is no comedy in which, in one sense, he invents so little. He made the two Dukes into brothers.

Just as in *King Lear* he put together two stories of good and unkind children, so here he gives us two examples of a brother's unkindness. This adds to the fairy-tale flavor of the plot, because it turns the usurping Duke into a wicked uncle. But if he invents no incidents, he leaves out a good deal. Besides omitting the blusterings of Rosader (Orlando), he leaves out a final battle and the death in battle of the usurping Duke, preferring to have him converted off-stage by a chance meeting with a convenient and persuasive hermit. In the same way he handles very cursorily the repentance of the wicked brother and his good fortune in love. In Lodge's story, the villain is cast into prison by the tyrant who covets his estates. In prison he repents, and it is as a penitent that he arrives in the forest. Shakespeare also omits the incident of the attack on Ganymede and Aliena by robbers, in which Rosader in overpowered and wounded and Saladyne (Oliver) comes to the rescue and drives off the assailants. As has often been pointed out, this is both a proof of the genuineness of his repentance and a reason, which many critics of the play have felt the want of, for Celia's falling in love. Maidens naturally fall in love with brave young men who rescue them. But Shakespeare needs to find no "reasons for loving" in this play in which a dead shepherd's saw is quoted as a word of truth: "Whoever lov'd that lov'd not at first sight." He has far too much other business in hand at the center and heart of his play to find time for mere exciting incidents. He stripped Lodge's plot down to the bare bones, using it as a kind of frame, and created no subplot of his own. But he added four characters. Jaques, the philosopher, bears the same name as the middle son of Sir Rowland de Boys—the one whom Oliver kept at his books—who does not appear in the play until he turns up casually at the end as a messenger. It seems possible that the melancholy Jaques began as this middle son and that his melancholy was in origin a scholar's melancholy. If so, the character changed as it developed, and by the time that Shakespeare had fully conceived his cynical spectator he must have realized that he could not be kin to Oliver and Orlando. The born solitary must have no family: Jaques seems the quintessential only child. To balance Jaques, as another kind of commentator, we are given Touchstone, critic and parodist of love and lovers and of court and courtiers. And, to make up the full consort of pairs to be mated, Shakespeare invented two rustic lovers, William and Audrey, dumb yokel and sluttish goat-girl. These additional characters add nothing at all to the story. If you were to tell it you would leave them out. They show us that story was not Shakespeare's concern in this play; its soul is not to be looked for there. If you were to go to *As You Like It* for the story you would, in Johnson's phrase, "hang yourself."

In an essay called "The Basis of Shakespearian Comedy"[1] Professor Nevill

---

[1] *Essays and Studies* (English Association: John Murray, 1950).

Coghill attempted to "establish certain things concerning the nature of comic form, as it was understood at Shakespeare's time." He pointed out that there were two conceptions of comedy current in the sixteenth century, both going back to grammarians of the fourth century, but radically opposed to each other. By the one definition a comedy was a story beginning in sadness and ending in happiness. By the other it was, in Sidney's words, "an imitation of the common errors of our life" represented "in the most ridiculous and scornefull sort that may be; so that it is impossible that any beholder can be content to be such a one." Shakespeare, he declared, accepted the first; Jonson, the second. But although *As You Like It*, like *A Midsummer-Night's Dream*, certainly begins in sadness and ends with happiness, I do not feel, when we have said this, that we have gone very far towards defining the play's nature, and I do not think that the plot in either of these two lovely plays, or in the enchanting early comedy *Love's Labour's Lost*, which indeed has hardly any plot at all, can be regarded as the "soul" or animating force of Shakespeare's most original and characteristic comedies. Professor Coghill's formula fits plays which we feel rather uneasy about, *The Merchant of Venice* and *Measure for Measure*. It is precisely the stress on the plot which makes us think of these as being more properly described as tragi-comedies than comedies. Neither of them is a play which we would choose as a norm of Shakespeare's genius in comedy. In *As You Like It* the plot is handled in the most perfunctory way. Shakespeare crams his first act with incident in order to get everyone to the forest as soon as he possibly can and, when he is ready, he ends it all as quickly as possible. A few lines dispose of Duke Frederick, and leave the road back to his throne empty for Duke Senior. As for the other victim of a wicked brother, it is far more important that Orlando should marry Rosalind than that he should be restored to his rights.

Mrs. Suzanne Langer, in her brilliant and suggestive book *Feeling and Form*,[2] has called comedy an image of life triumphing over chance. She declares that the essence of comedy is that it embodies in symbolic form our sense of happiness in feeling that we can meet and master the changes and chances of life as it confronts us. This seems to me to provide a good description of what we mean by "pure comedy," as distinct from the corrective or satirical comedy of Jonson. The great symbol of pure comedy is marriage by which the world is renewed, and its endings are always instinct with a sense of fresh beginnings. Its rhythm is the rhythm of the life of mankind, which goes on and renews itself as the life of nature does. The rhythm of tragedy, on the other hand, is the rhythm of the individual life which comes to a close, and its great symbol is death. The one inescapable fact about every human being is that he must die. No skill in living, no sense of life, no inborn grace or acquired wisdom can avert this individual doom.

[2] Routledge, 1953.

A tragedy, which is played out under the shadow of an inevitable end, is an image of the life pattern of every one of us. A comedy, which contrives an end which is not implicit in its beginning, and which is, in itself, a fresh beginning, is an image of the flow of human life. The young wed, so that they may become in turn the older generation, whose children will wed, and so on, as long as the world lasts. Comedy pictures what Rosalind calls "the full stream of the world." At the close of a tragedy we look back over a course which has been run: "the rest is silence." The end of a comedy declares that life goes on: "Here we are all over again." Tragic plots must have a logic which leads to an inescapable conclusion. Comic plots are made up of changes, chances and surprises. Coincidences can destroy tragic feeling: they heighten comic feeling. It is absurd to complain in poetic comedy of improbable encounters and characters arriving pat on their cue, of sudden changes of mind and mood by which an enemy becomes a friend. Puck, who creates and presides over the central comedy of *A Midsummer-Night's Dream*, speaks for all comic writers and lovers of true comedy when he says:

> And those things do best please me
> That befall preposterously.

This aspect of life, as continually changing and presenting fresh opportunities for happiness and laughter, poetic comedy idealizes and presents to us by means of fantasy. Fantasy is the natural instrument of comedy, in which plot, which is the "soul" of tragedy, is of secondary importance, an excuse for something else. After viewing a tragedy we have an "acquist of true experience" from a "great event." There are no "events" in comedy; there are only "happenings." Events are irreversible and comedy is not concerned with the irreversible, which is why it must always shun the presentation of death. In adapting Lodge's story Shakespeare did not allow Charles the wrestler to kill the Franklin's sons. Although they are expected to die, we may hope they will recover from their broken ribs. And he rejected also Lodge's ending in which the wicked Duke was killed in battle, preferring his improbable conversion by a hermit. But why should we complain of its improbability? It is only in tragedy that second chances are not given. Comedy is full of purposes mistook, not "falling on the inventor's head" but luckily misfiring altogether. In comedy, as often happens in life, people are mercifully saved from being as wicked as they meant to be.

Generalization about the essential distinctions between tragedy and comedy is called in question, when we turn to Shakespeare, by the inclusiveness of his vision of life. In the great majority of his plays the elements are mixed. But just as he wrote one masterpiece which is purely tragic, dominated by the conception of Fate, in *Macbeth*, so he wrote some plays which embody a purely comic vision. Within the general formula that "a comedy is a play with a happy ending," which can, of course, include tragi-comedies, he wrote some plays in which the story is a mere frame and the essence of the play lies in the presentation of an image of human life, not as an arena for heroic endeavor but as a place of encounters.

Tragedy is presided over by time, which urges the hero onwards to fulfil his destiny. In Shakespeare's comedies time goes by fits and starts. It is not so much a movement onwards as a space in which to work things out: a midsummer night, a space too short for us to feel time's movement, or the unmeasured time of *As You Like It* or *Twelfth Night*. The comedies are dominated by a sense of place rather than of time. In Shakespeare's earliest comedy it is not a very romantic place: the city of Ephesus. Still, it is a place where two pairs of twins are accidentally reunited, and their old father, in danger of death at the beginning, is united to his long-lost wife at the close. The substance of the play is the comic plot of mistakings, played out in a single place on a single day. The tragi-comic story of original loss and final restoration provides a frame. In what is probably his second comedy, *The Two Gentlemen of Verona*, Shakespeare tried a quite different method. The play is a dramatization of a *novella*, and it contains no comic place of encounters where time seems to stand still. The story begins in Verona, passes to Milan, and ends in a forest between the two cities. None of these places exerts any hold upon our imaginations. The story simply moves forward through them. In *Love's Labour's Lost*, by contrast, Shakespeare went as far as possible in the other direction. The whole play is a kind of ballet of lovers and fantastics, danced out in the King of Navarre's park. Nearby is a village where Holofernes is the schoolmaster, Nathaniel the curate, and Dull the constable. In this play we are given, as a foil to the lords and ladies, not comic servants, parasitic on their masters, but a little comic world, society in miniature, going about its daily business while the lovers are engaged in the discovery of theirs. Shakespeare dispensed with the tragi-comic frame altogether here. There is no sorrow at the beginning, only youthful male fatuity; and the "putting right" at the close lies in the chastening of the lords by the ladies. The picture of the course of life as it appears to the comic vision, with young men falling in love and young women testing their suitors, and other men "laboring in their vocations" to keep the world turning and to impress their fellows, is the whole matter of the play. Much more magical than the sunlit park of the King of Navarre is the wood near Athens where Puck plays the part of chance. Shakespeare reverted here to the structural pattern of his earliest comedy, beginning with the cruel fury of Egeus against his daughter, the rivalry of Lysander and Demetrius and the unhappiness of the scorned Helena, and ending with Theseus's overriding of the father's will and the proper pairing of the four lovers. But here he not only set his comic plot of mistakings within a frame of sorrow turning to joy, he also set his comic place of encounters apart from the real world, the palace where the play begins and ends. All the center of the play takes place in the moonlit wood where lovers immortal and mortal quarrel, change partners, are blinded, and have their eyes purged.

Having created a masterpiece, Shakespeare, who never repeated a success, went back in his next play to tragi-comedy, allowing the threat of terrible disaster to grow through the play up to a great dramatic fourth act. *The Merchant of Venice* has what *The Two Gentlemen of Verona* lacks, an enchanted place. Belmont, where Bassanio goes to find his bride, and where Lorenzo flees with Jessica, and from which Portia descends like a goddess to solve the troubles of Venice, is a place apart, "above the smoke and stir." But it is not, like the wood near Athens, a place where the changes and chances of our mortal life are seen mirrored. It stands too sharply over against Venice, a place of refuge rather than a place of discovery. *Much Ado about Nothing* reverts to the single place of *The Comedy of Errors* and *Love's Labour's Lost;* and its tragi-comic plot, which also comes to a climax in a dramatic scene in the fourth act, is lightened not by a shift of scene but by its interweaving with a brilliant comic plot, and by all kinds of indications that all will soon be well again. The trouble comes in the middle of this play: at the beginning, as at the end, all is revelry and happiness. A sense of holiday, of time off from the world's business, reigns in Messina. The wars are over, peace has broken out, and Don Pedro and the gentlemen have returned to where the ladies are waiting for them to take up again the game of love and wit. In the atmosphere created by the first act Don John's malice is a cloud no bigger than a man's hand. And although it grows as the play proceeds, the crisis of the fourth act is like a heavy summer thundershower which darkens the sky for a time but will, we know, soon pass. The brilliant lively city of Messina is a true place of mistakings and discoveries, like the park of the King of Navarre; but, also like the park of the King of Navarre, it lacks enchantment. It is too near the ordinary world to seem more than a partial image of human life. In *As You Like It* Shakespeare returned to the pattern of *A Midsummer-Night's Dream*, beginning his play in sorrow and ending it with joy, and making his place of comic encounters a place set apart from the ordinary world.

The Forest of Arden ranks with the wood near Athens and Prospero's island as a place set apart, even though, unlike them, it is not ruled by magic. It is set over against the envious court ruled by a tyrant, and a home which is no home because it harbors hatred, not love. Seen from the court it appears untouched by the discontents of life, a place where "they fleet the time carelessly, as they did in the golden age," the gay greenwood of Robin Hood. But, of course, it is no such Elysium. It contains some unamiable characters. Corin's master is churlish and Sir Oliver Martext is hardly sweet-natured; William is a dolt and Audrey graceless. Its weather, too, is by no means always sunny. It has a bitter winter. To Orlando, famished with

hunger and supporting the fainting Adam, it is "an uncouth forest" and a
desert where the air is bleak. He is astonished to find civility among men who

> in this desert inaccessible,
> Under the shade of melancholy boughs,
> Lose and neglect the creeping hours of time.

In fact Arden does not seem very attractive at first sight to the weary escapers
from the tyranny of the world. Rosalind's "Well, this is the forest of Arden"
does not suggest any very great enthusiasm; and to Touchstone's "Ay, now
I am in Arden; the more fool I: when I was at home, I was in a better place:
but travellers must be content," she can only reply "Ay, be so, good Touchstone." It is as if they all have to wake up after a good night's rest to find
what a pleasant place they have come to. Arden is not a place for the young
only. Silvius, for ever young and for ever loving, is balanced by Corin, the
old shepherd, who reminds us of that other "penalty of Adam" beside "the
seasons' difference": that man must labor to get himself food and clothing.
Still, the labor is pleasant and a source of pride: "I am a true laborer: I earn
that I eat, get that I wear, owe no man hate, envy no man's happiness, glad
of other men's good, content with my harm; and the greatest of my pride
is to see my ewes graze and my lambs suck." Arden is not a place where the
laws of nature are abrogated and roses are without their thorns. If, in the
world, Duke Frederick has usurped on Duke Senior, Duke Senior is aware
that he has in his turn usurped upon the deer, the native burghers of the
forest. If man does not slay and kill man, he kills the poor beasts. Life preys
on life. Jaques, who can suck melancholy out of anything, points to the
callousness that runs through nature itself as a mirror of the callousness of
men. The herd abandons the wounded deer, as prosperous citizens pass with
disdain the poor bankrupt, the failure. The race is to the swift. But this is
Jaques's view. Orlando, demanding help for Adam, finds another image from
nature:

> Then but forbear your food a little while,
> Whiles, like a doe, I go to find my fawn
> And give it food. There is a poor old man,
> Who after me hath many a weary step
> Limp'd in pure love: till he be first suffic'd,
> Oppress'd with two weak evils, age and hunger,
> I will not touch a bit.

The fact that they are both derived ultimately from folk tale is not the
only thing that relates *As You Like It* to *King Lear*. Adam's sombre line,
"And unregarded age in corners thrown," which Quiller-Couch said might
have come out of one of the greater sonnets, sums up the fate of Lear:

> Dear daughter, I confess that I am old;
> Age is unnecessary: on my knees I beg
> That you'll vouchsafe me raiment, bed, and food.

At times Arden seems a place where the same bitter lessons can be learnt as Lear has to learn in his place of exile, the blasted heath. Corin's natural philosophy, which includes the knowledge that "the property of rain is to wet," is something which Lear has painfully to acquire:

> When the rain came to wet me once and the wind to make me chatter, when the thunder would not peace at my bidding, there I found 'em, there I smelt 'em out. Go to, they are not men o' their words: they told me I was everything; 'tis a lie, I am not ague-proof.

He is echoing Duke Senior, who smiles at the "icy fang and churlish chiding of the winter's wind," saying:

> This is no flattery: these are counselors
> That feelingly persuade me what I am.

Amiens's lovely melancholy song:

> Blow, blow, thou winter wind,
> Thou are not so unkind
>   As man's ingratitude. . . .

> Freeze, freeze, thou bitter sky,
> That dost not bite so nigh
>   As benefits forgot. . . ,

is terribly echoed in Lear's outburst:

> Blow, winds, and crack your cheeks! rage! blow!
>   .   .   .   .   .   .
> Rumble thy bellyful! Spit, fire! spout, rain!
> Nor rain, wind, thunder, fire, are my daughters:
> I tax not you, you elements, with unkindness;
> I never gave you kingdom, call'd you children. . . .

And Jaques's reflection that "All the world's a stage" becomes in Lear's mouth a cry of anguish:

> When we are born, we cry that we are come
> To this great stage of fools.

It is in Arden that Jaques presents his joyless picture of human life, passing from futility to futility and culminating in the nothingness of senility—"sans everything"; and in Arden also a bitter judgment on human relations is lightly passed in the twice repeated "Most friendship is feigning, most loving mere folly." But then one must add that hard on the heels of Jaques's melancholy conclusion Orlando enters with Adam in his arms, who, although he may be "sans teeth" and at the end of his usefulness as a servant, has, beside his store of virtue and his peace of conscience, the love of his master. And the play is full of signal instances of persons who do not forget benefits: Adam, Celia, Touchstone—not to mention the lords who chose to leave the court and follow their banished master to the forest. In a recent number of the *Shakespeare Survey* Professor Harold Jenkins has pointed out how points of view put forward by one character find contradiction or correction by another, so that the whole play is a balance of sweet against sour, of the cynical against the idealistic, and life is shown as a mingling of hard fortune and good hap. The lords who have "turned ass," "leaving their wealth and ease a stubborn will to please," are happy in their gross folly, as Orlando is in a lovesickness which he does not wish to be cured of. What Jaques has left out of his picture of man's strange eventful pilgrimage is love and companionship, sweet society, the banquet under the boughs to which Duke Senior welcomes Orlando and Adam. Although life in Arden is not wholly idyllic, and this place set apart from the world is yet touched by the world's sorrows and can be mocked at by the worldly wise, the image of life which the forest presents is irradiated by the conviction that the gay and the gentle can endure the rubs of fortune and that this earth is a place where men can find happiness in themselves and in others.

The Forest of Arden is, as has often been pointed out, a place which all the exiles from the court, except one, are only too ready to leave at the close. As, when the short midsummer night is over, the lovers emerge from the wood, in their right minds and correctly paired, and return to the palace of Theseus; and, when Prospero's magic has worked the cure, the enchanted island is left to Caliban and Ariel, and its human visitors return to Naples and Milan; so the time of holiday comes to an end in Arden. The stately masque of Hymen marks the end of this interlude in the greenwood, and announces the return to a court purged of envy and baseness. Like other comic places, Arden is a place of discovery where the truth becomes clear and where each man finds himself and his true way. This discovery of truth in comedy is made through errors and mistakings. The trial and error by which we come to knowledge of ourselves and of our world is symbolized by the disguisings which are a recurrent element in all comedy, but are particularly common in Shakespeare's. Things have, as it were, to become worse before they become better, more confused and farther from the proper pattern. By misunderstandings men come to understand, and by lies and feignings they discover truth. If Rosalind, the princess, had attempted to "cure" her lover Orlando, she might have succeeded. As Ganymede, playing Rosalind, she can try him to the limit in perfect safety, and discover that she cannot mock or flout him out of his "mad humor of love to a living humor of madness," and drive him "to forswear the full stream of the world, and to live in a nook merely monastic." By playing with him in the disguise of a boy, she discovers when she can play no more. By love of a shadow, the mere image of a charming youth, Phoebe discovers that it is better to love than to be loved and scorn one's lover. This discovery of truth by feigning, and of what is wisdom and what folly by debate, is the center of *As You Like It*. It is a play of meetings and encounters, of conversations and sets of wit: Orlando versus Jaques, Touchstone versus Corin, Rosalind versus Jaques, Rosalind versus Phoebe, and above all Rosalind versus Orlando. The truth discovered is, at one level, a very "earthy truth": Benedick's discovery that "the world must be peopled." The honest toil of Corin, the wise man of the forest, is mocked at by Touchstone as "simple sin." He brings "the ewes and the rams together" and gets his living "by the copulation of cattle." The goddess Fortune seems similarly occupied in this play: "As the ox hath his bow, the horse his curb, and the falcon her bells, so man hath his desires; and as pigeons bill, so wedlock would be nibbling." Fortune acts the role of a kindly bawd. Touchstone's marriage to Audrey is a mere coupling. Rosalind's advice to Phoebe is brutally frank: "Sell when you can, you are not for all markets." The words she uses to describe Oliver and Celia "in the very wrath of love" are hardly delicate, and after her first meeting with Orlando she confesses to her cousin that her sighs are for her "child's father." Against the natural background of the life of the forest there can be no pretence that the love of men and women can "forget the He and She." But Rosalind's behavior is at variance with her bold words. Orlando has to prove that he truly is, as he seems at first, the right husband for her, and show himself gentle, courteous, generous and brave, and a match for her in wit, though a poor poet. In this, the great coupling of the play, there is a marriage of true minds. The other couplings run the gamut downwards from it, until we reach Touchstone's image of "a she-lamb of a twelvemonth" and "a crooked-pated, old, cuckoldy ram," right at the bottom of the scale. As for the debate as to where happiness is to be found, the conclusion come to is again, like all wisdom, not very startling or original: that "minds innocent and quiet" can find happiness in court or country:

> Happy is your Grace,
> That can translate the stubbornness of fortune
> Into so quiet and so sweet a style.

And, on the contrary, those who wish to can "suck melancholy" out of anything, "as a weasel sucks eggs."

In the pairing one figure is left out. "I am for other than for dancing measures," says Jaques. Leaving the hateful sight of revelling and pastime, he betakes himself to the Duke's abandoned cave, on his way to the house of penitents where Duke Frederick has gone. The two commentators of the play are nicely contrasted. Touchstone is the parodist, Jaques the cynic. The parodist must love what he parodies. We know this from literary parody. All the best parodies are written by those who understand, because they love, the thing they mock. Only poets who love and revere the epic can write mock-heroic and the finest parody of classical tragedy comes from Housman, a great scholar. In everything that Touchstone says and does gusto, high spirits, and a zest for life ring out. Essentially comic, he can adapt himself to any situation in which he may find himself. Never at a loss, he is life's master. The essence of clowning is adaptability and improvisation. The clown is never baffled and is marked by his ability to place himself at once *en rapport* with his audience, to be all things to all men, to perform the part which is required at the moment. Touchstone sustains many different roles. After hearing Silvius's lament and Rosalind's echo of it, he becomes the maudlin lover of Jane Smile; with the simple shepherd Corin he becomes the cynical and wordly-wise man of the court; with Jaques he is a melancholy moralist, musing on the power of time and the decay of all things; with the pages he acts the lordly amateur of the arts, patronising his musicians. It is right that he should parody the rest of the cast, and join the procession into Noah's ark with his Audrey. Jaques is his opposite. He is the cynic, the person who prefers the pleasures of superiority, cold-eyed and cold-hearted. The tyrannical Duke Frederick and the cruel Oliver can be converted; but not Jaques. He likes himself as he is. He does not wish to plunge into the stream, but prefers to stand on the bank and "fish for fancies as they pass." Sir Thomas Elyot said that dancing was an image of matrimony: "In every daunse, of a most auncient custome, there daunseth together a man and a woman, holding eche other by the hande or the arme, which betokeneth concorde." There are some who will not dance, however much they are piped to, any more than they will weep when there is mourning. "In this theatre of man's life," wrote Bacon, "it is reserved only for God and angels to be lookers on." Jaques arrogates to himself the divine role. He has opted out from the human condition.

It is characteristic of Shakespeare's comedies to include an element that is irreconcilable, which strikes a lightly discordant note, casts a slight shadow, and by its presence questions the completeness of the comic vision of life. In *Love's Labour's Lost* he dared to allow the news of a death to cloud the scene of revels at the close, and, through Rosalind's rebuke to Berowne, called up the image of a whole world of pain and weary suffering where "Mirth cannot move a soul in agony." The two comedies whose main action is motivated by hatred end with malice thwarted but not removed. In *The Merchant of Venice* and *Much Ado about Nothing*, Shakespeare asks us to accept the fact that the human race includes not only a good many fools and rogues but also some persons who are positively wicked, a fact which

comedy usually ignores. They are prevented from doing the harm they wish
to do. They are not cured of wishing to do harm. Shylock's baffled exit and
Don John's flight to Messina leave the stage clear for lovers and well-wishers.
The villains have to be left out of the party at the close. At the end of *Twelfth
Night* the person who is left out is present. The impotent misery and fury of
the humiliated Malvolio's last words, "I'll be reveng'd on the whole pack
of you," call in question the whole comic scheme by which, through misunderstandings and mistakes, people come to terms with themselves and
their fellows. There are some who cannot be "taught a lesson." In Malvolio
pride is not purged; it is fatally wounded and embittered. It is characteristic
of the delicacy of temper of *As You Like It* that its solitary figure, its outsider,
Jaques, does nothing whatever to harm anyone, and is perfectly satisfied with
himself and happy in his melancholy. Even more, his melancholy is a source
of pleasure and amusement to others. The Duke treats him as virtually a
court entertainer, and he is a natural butt for Orlando and Rosalind.
Anyone in the play can put him down and feel the better for doing so. All
the same his presence casts a faint shadow. His criticism of the world has its
sting drawn very early by the Duke's rebuke to him as a former libertine,
discharging his filth upon the world, and he is to some extent discredited
before he opens his mouth by the unpleasant implication of his name. But
he cannot be wholly dismissed. A certain sour distaste for life is voided
through him, something most of us feel at some time or other. If he were not
there to give expression to it, we might be tempted to find the picture of life
in the forest too sweet. His only action is to interfere in the marriage of
Touchstone and Audrey; and this he merely postpones. His effect, whenever
he appears, is to deflate: the effect does not last and cheerfulness soon breaks
in again. Yet as there is a scale of love, so there is a scale of sadness in the
play. It runs down from the Duke's compassionate words:

> Thou seest we are not all alone unhappy:
> This wide and universal theatre
> Presents more woeful pageants than the scene
> Wherein we play in,

through Rosalind's complaint "O, how full of briers is this working-day
world," to Jaques's studied refusal to find anything worthy of admiration
or love.

One further element in the play I would not wish to stress, because though
it is pervasive it is unobtrusive: the constant, natural and easy reference to
the Christian ideal of loving-kindness, gentleness, pity and humility and to
the sanctions which that ideal finds in the commands and promises of
religion. In this fantasy world, in which the world of our experience is
imaged, this element in experience finds a place with others, and the world
is shown not only as a place where we may find happiness, but as a place

where both happiness and sorrow may be hallowed. The number of religious references in *As You Like It* has often been commented on, and it is striking when we consider the play's main theme. Many are of little significance and it would be humorless to enlarge upon the significance of the "old religious man" who converted Duke Frederick, or of Ganymede's "old religious uncle." But some are explicit and have a serious, unforced beauty: Orlando's appeal to outlawed men,

> If ever you have look'd on better days,
> If ever been where bells have knoll'd to church. . . ;

Adam's prayer,

> He that doth the ravens feed,
> Yea, providently caters for the sparrow,
> Be comfort to my age!

and Corin's recognition, from St. Paul, that we have to find the way to heaven by doing deeds of hospitality. These are all in character. But the God of Marriage, Hymen, speaks more solemnly than we expect and his opening words with their New Testament echo are more than conventional:

> Then is there mirth in heaven,
> When earthly things made even
> Atone together.

The appearance of the god to present daughter to father and to bless the brides and grooms turns the close into a solemnity, an image of the concord which reigns in Heaven and which Heaven blesses on earth. But this, like much else in the play, may be taken as you like it. There is no need to see any more in the god's appearance with the brides than a piece of pageantry which concludes the action with a graceful spectacle and sends the audience home contented with a very pretty play.

Shakespeare's *Twelfth Night*

by Harold Jenkins

What I shall try to do in this lecture is to examine some features of Shakespeare's comic art in one particular example. It may seem temerity enough to have chosen *Twelfth Night;* but since a dramatist, after all, even Shakespeare, is made as well as born, and it is interesting to see, if indeed one ever can, how his art perfects itself, I shall also venture from time to time some comparison between *Twelfth Night* and one of the earlier comedies of Shakespeare which led up to it.

In a book on *Twelfth Night* published four years ago Dr. Leslie Hotson suggested that the play was written to compliment an Italian nobleman, Virginio Orsino, Duke of Bracciano, in a court entertainment given for him on Twelfth Night, 1601, and that it was after this Orsino that one of the principal characters was named. I am not sure that the Italian Orsino would have felt complimented by seeing himself portrayed as a handsome and poetical but ineffective lover, and I do not think that Queen Elizabeth would have witnessed the play with delight if she had agreed with Dr. Hotson that the lady Olivia in the play was intended to represent her. But even if *Twelfth Night* were the play with which the Queen entertained the Italian Duke, it would not be necessary to suppose with Dr. Hotson that Shakespeare wrote it in ten or eleven days.[1] It is true that the Lord Chamberlain made a memorandum to arrange with the players "to make choice of" a play that would be "most pleasing to her Majesty" on this occasion,[2] but "to make choice of a play" is not quite the same thing as instructing the players to get up a new one.

The most interesting thing of course is that in however short a time Shakespeare ultimately wrote this play, he had in a sense been composing it during most of the previous decade. It was several years before the Twelfth Night entertainment of 1601—certainly not later than 1594—that Shakespeare first wrote a play about identical twins who were separated from one

---

"Shakespeare's *Twelfth Night*." From Rice Institute Pamphlet XLV (1959). Reprinted by permission of the author and Rice University.

[1] *The First Night of "Twelfth Night,"* 1954, p. 97.

[2] *Ibid.*, p. 15.

another in a shipwreck and afterwards mistaken for one another even by the wife of one of them; and it was at a similarly early stage in his career that Shakespeare wrote another play about a woman who served her lover as a page, and who in her page's disguise carried messages of love from her lover to another woman. When Shakespeare makes these things happen in *Twelfth Night* he is, in fact, combining the plots of *The Comedy of Errors* and *The Two Gentlemen of Verona*. He does not, however, combine them in equal degree. The heartsick heroine who in page's disguise takes messages of love to another woman provided little more than an episode in the complicated relations of the two gentlemen of Verona; but in *Twelfth Night* this episode has grown into the central situation from which the play draws its life. On the other hand, the confusion of twins which entertained us for five acts of *The Comedy of Errors* appears now as little more than an adroit device to bring about a happy ending. These shifts of emphasis show clearly enough the direction that Shakespeare's art of comedy has taken. When Sebastian appears in *Twelfth Night* we see that Shakespeare can still delight in the jolly mix-up of mistaken identities, not to mention their consequence of broken pates, but his plot now gives chief attention to the delineation of romantic love. This is more than just a preference for one situation rather than another: it means that a plot which turns on external appearances—a resemblance between men's faces—gives way to an action which involves their feelings. In *The Comedy of Errors*, though the physical resemblance between twins is no doubt a fact of nature, the confusion is really the result of accidental circumstances and is as accidentally cleared up. But in *Twelfth Night* the confusion is in the emotions and no *dénouement* is possible until the characters have grown in insight to the point where they can acknowledge the feelings that nature has planted in them. Thus *Twelfth Night* exhibits in its action one of the fundamental motifs of comedy: the education of a man or woman. For a comedy, as everyone knows, is a play in which the situation holds some threat of disaster but issues in the achievement of happiness; and those comedies may satisfy us most deeply in which danger is averted and happiness achieved through something that takes place within the characters. Orsino and Olivia come to their happy ending when they have learnt a new attitude to others and to themselves.

This, I take it, is what is also meant to happen in *The Two Gentlemen of Verona* in the much misunderstood conclusion of that play. Proteus, significantly named for his fickle nature, has vexed the critics by coming into a happiness he seems to have done nothing to deserve. But the point is that when his best friend has denounced him as a "treacherous man" and his mistress has rebuked him for his changeableness, he can penitently say, "O heaven, were man but constant he were perfect." This has struck some as complacent; but it is not to be taken lightly. For it means that Proteus has now learned the value of constancy, the very virtue he conspicuously lacked. This is what the play set out to teach him and it is only when he has learned it that he can say, "Bear witness, Heaven, I have my wish for ever," expressing simultaneously a sense of the happiness he is granted and a vow of constancy in future. It is true that in *The Two Gentlemen of Verona* Shakespeare did not allow himself scope to develop all the implications of Proteus's fickleness and reform; but such a story of treachery, if fully explored, might strike too deep for comedy. *Twelfth Night* has no unfaithful lover. But it cannot escape notice that Orsino's love is repeatedly compared to the sea— vast, hungry, but unstable, while his mind appears to Feste like an opal, a jewel of magical but ever-changing colors. The changeable man is there, but he has undergone a subtle transformation, and to notice this is, I think, of far more importance than to object, as Charlotte Lennox did in the eighteenth century, that Shakespeare in *Twelfth Night* has ruined the story of Bandello which she regarded as "undoubtedly" Shakespeare's source.[3] Shakespeare, she objects, deprives the story of probability because he neglects to provide his characters with acceptable motives. Viola, she says, "all of a sudden takes up an unaccountable resolution to serve the young bachelor-duke in the habit of a man." And since Viola has not even the excuse of being in love with the duke to start with, this goes "greatly beyond the bounds of decency." But if Shakespeare had wanted to make Viola assume her man's disguise because she was already in love with Orsino, he did not need Bandello to teach him; he had already tried that situation with Julia and Proteus, and it had necessarily involved Proteus in that heartless infidelity from which Orsino is to be spared. The emotional situation of *Twelfth Night* is of a much less obvious kind.

The most important source for *Twelfth Night*, one might therefore say, is *The Two Gentlemen of Verona*. For it is only by a paradox of scholarship that the word *source* is usually restricted to material that an author draws on from someone else's work. But that there were other sources for *Twelfth Night* I readily admit.[4] Charlotte Lennox knew of one in Bandello. And long before that one of Shakespeare's own contemporaries had pointed to another. When John Manningham saw *Twelfth Night* in 1602, he said in his Diary that it reminded him of an Italian play called *Gl'Inganni* (or *The Mistakes*). There were at least two plays of this title that Shakespeare might have used, and in one of them the heroine, on disguising herself as a page, assumed the name Cesare, which may well be why Shakespeare's Viola elects to call herself Cesario. There was also another Italian play called *Gl'Ingannati* (or *The Mistaken*), in which the master told the page, "You are a child, you do

[3] *Shakespear Illustrated*, 1753, I, 237 ff.
[4] For a survey and discussion of them, see Kenneth Muir, *Shakespeare's Sources*, 1957, pp. 66 ff. The more important ones are now assembled in *Narrative and Dramatic Sources of Shakespeare*, ed. Geoffrey Bullough, Vol. 2, 1958.

not know the force of love," and Shakespeare's Orsino of course is always similarly reminding Cesario of his uninitiated youth. So the nineteenth-century scholar, Joseph Hunter, perhaps influenced by the fact that he discovered it, found in this play *Gl' Ingannati* "the true origin" of Shake-speare's. Collier, however, asserted that it was from an English tale by Barnabe Riche, called *Apolonius and Silla*, that Shakespeare drew his plot. Furness was equally certain that he did not, but as he hoped that Shakespeare had never looked into Riche's "coarse, repulsive novel,"[5] perhaps this also was not quite an impartial judgment.

For my part I find no difficulty in agreeing with those modern scholars who assume that Shakespeare was familiar with all these versions of a story in which a woman disguised as a page pleads her lover's suit with another woman, who then falls in love with the page. But that Shakespeare read up these plays and novels for the express purpose of writing his own play is perhaps another matter. The similarities between Shakespeare and these others are certainly interesting; yet to point out similarities will usually end in drawing attention to their difference. For instance, *Twelfth Night* seems to echo Riche's tale when Olivia, declaring her unrequited love for Cesario, says she has "laid" her "honor too unchary out."[6] But in Riche the lady said that she had "charity preserved" her "honor." The phrasing is reminiscent; but Riche's lady boasts of her honor after she has sacrificed her chastity, while Shakespeare's Olivia reproaches herself for being careless of her honor when her chastity of course is not in question. Riche's lady is anxious lest she has lost her reputation in the eyes of the world, Olivia lest she has fallen from her own high ideal of conduct. Without accepting Furness's view that any reference to the act of sex is coarse and repulsive, we may easily find it significant that Shakespeare leaves it out. His delineation of Olivia's love for the page, in contrast to most of the earlier versions, omits all the physical demonstrations. The usual way when the lady falls in love with the page is for her to astonish him by falling on his neck and kissing him. In Secchi's play of *Gl'Inganni* the relations between them reach the point where the woman page is expected to play the man's part in an actual assignation and she gets out of it by the cunning substitution of her brother. In the play of *Gl'Ingannati*, which comes closer to Shakespeare, the lady takes the brother by mistake, but he goes to bed with her just the same. In Riche's story this incident has consequences, which force the lady so chary of her honor to demand marriage of the page, who can only establish innocence by the disclosure of *her* sex. Shakespeare appropriates this convenient brother as a husband for Olivia, but since he could easily have invented Viola's twin, and in *The Comedy of Errors* had, one might say, already tried him out, this

---

[5] *Twelfth Night*, Variorum Edition, p. xvii.
[6] I follow the emendation of Theobald, adopted by most editors, for the Folio *on't.*

debt is not a profound one. What is more remarkable, the similarity as usual embracing a contrast, is that when Olivia mistakes Sebastian for Cesario she takes him not to bed but to a priest. Olivia no less than Orsino is kept free of moral taint. And this is no mere matter of prudishness. The reckless abandonment of scruple shown by all these earlier lovers—both by the gentlemen who desert their mistresses and the ladies who fling themselves upon the page-boys—cannot coexist with the more delicate sentiment which gives *Twelfth Night* its character. In Shakespeare, even the twin brother, prop to the plot as he may be, shares in this refinement. When Olivia takes charge of Sebastian's person, what he gives her is less his body than his imagination. He is enwrapped, he says in "wonder." And it is his capacity to experience this wonder that lifts him to the level of the other lovers in the play, so that he becomes a worthy partner for Orsino's adored one and Viola's adorer.

Now if *Twelfth Night* is the greatest of Shakespeare's romantic comedies, it is partly because of its success in embodying these feelings of wonder in the principal persons of the play. Stories of romantic love owe something of their perennial appeal, we need not be ashamed to admit, to the taste for tales of pursuit and mysterious adventure, as well as to what psychologists no doubt explain as the sublimation of the natural impulses of sex. But the devotion which the romantic lover bestows upon a woman as pure as she is unattainable may also symbolize the mind's aspiration towards some ever alluring but ever elusive ideal. In the traditional romantic stories the course of true love does not run smooth because of obstacles presented by refractory parents or inconvenient rivals, who have to be overcome or made to change. This is the case in *A Midsummer-Night's Dream*. There are perhaps subtler situations, where the obstacles exist in the very nature of the protagonists, who must themselves be made to change. This is variously the case in *The Taming of the Shrew* and *Love's Labour's Lost*, where in their very different ways Katherina and the young gentlemen of Navarre are, to begin with, recalcitrant to love. But a still subtler situation may arise with characters who are from the beginning full of devotion to an ideal of love while mistaking the direction in which it should be sought. This, I take it, is the case with Orsino and Olivia. Orsino, with whom *Twelfth Night* begins and who draws us from the start into the aura of his imagination, is in some ways the most perfect of Shakespeare's romantic lovers simply because he is so much more. This is easily appreciated if we compare him with his earlier prototypes in *The Two Gentlemen of Verona*. He is, as I have suggested, the inconstant Proteus transformed. But he is also the other gentleman, the constant Valentine. He is

> Unstaid and skittish in all motions else
> Save in the constant image of the creature
> That is beloved.

So, simultaneously volatile and steadfast, he combines in a single figure those aspects of man's nature which in the earlier comedy had been systematically contrasted and opposed.

In Valentine, of course, we recognize the typical victim of the passion of courtly love. He tells us himself how he suffers

> With bitter fasts, with penitential groans,
> With nightly tears and daily heartsore sighs.

That these groans and sighs survive in Orsino is clear when Olivia asks "How does he love me?" and the messenger replies,

> With adorations, with[7] fertile tears,
> With groans that thunder love, with sighs of fire.

The danger of such a hero is, as Professor Charlton has remarked, that, in fulfilling his conventional role, he may to the quizzical eye seem a fool. Shakespeare guards against this danger by anticipating our ridicule; but his mockery of Valentine and Orsino is quite different in kind. The romantic Valentine is given an unromantic servant who pokes broad fun at his conduct: "to sigh like a schoolboy that has lost his A.B.C.; to weep like a young wench that had buried her grandam; to fast like one that takes diet," and so forth. But Orsino, instead of a servant who laughs at him for loving, has a page who can show him how to do it. "If I did love you in my master's flame," says Cesario, I would

> Make me a willow-cabin at your gate
> And call upon my soul within the house

till all the hills reverberated with the name of the beloved. This famous willow-cabin speech, often praised for its lyricism, is of course no less a parody of romantic love than are Speed's gibes at Valentine. The willow is the emblem of forsaken love and those songs that issue from it in the dead of night apostrophizing the mistress as her lover's "soul"—they are easily recognizable as the traditional love-laments. But the parody, though it has its hint of laughter, is of the kind that does not belittle but transfigures its original. So it comes as no surprise when Olivia, hitherto heedless of sighs and groans, suddenly starts to listen. To the page she says, "*You* might do much," and these words are her first acknowledgement of love's power. Orsino, content to woo by proxy a woman who immures herself in a seven-year mourning for a dead brother, may have the glamor of a knight of romance but he is *not* quite free from the risk of absurdity. He seems, they tell us with some justice, in love not so much with a woman as with his own idea of love. But what they do not so often tell us is how splendid an idea this

[7] Folio omits *with*.

is. His very groans go beyond Valentine's; they were said, it will have been
noticed, to *thunder*, and his sighs were *fire*. If he indulges his own emotions,
this is in no mere dilettantism but with the avidity of hunger.

> If music be the *food* of love, play on,
> Give me *excess* of it, that *surfeiting*,
> The *appetite* may sicken and so die.

This wonderful opening speech suggests no doubt the changeableness of
human emotion. "Play on . . . that strain again! It had a dying fall. . . .
Enough, no more! 'Tis not so sweet now as it was before." But if the spirit
of love is as transitory as music and as unstable as the sea, it is also as living
and capacious. New waves form as often as waves break; the shapes of fancy,
insubstantial as they are, make a splendor in the mind, and renew themselves
as quickly as they fade. So Orsino's repeated rejections by his mistress do
not throw him into despair. Instead he recognizes, in her equally fantastic
devotion, a nature of surpassingly "fine frame" and he reflects on how she
will love when the throne of her heart shall find its "king." How too will
he love, we are entitled to infer, when his inexhaustible but as yet deluded
fancy shall also find the true sovereign it seeks. This of course it does at the
end of the play when he exchanges all his dreams of passion for the love of
someone he has come to know. In the play's last line before the final song
he is able to greet Viola as "Orsino's mistress and his fancy's queen."

Before this consummation Orsino and Viola have only one big scene
together, and in view of all that depends on it it will need to be a powerful
one. Again it finds a model in *The Two Gentlemen of Verona*, where already
there is a scene in which a man declares his love for one woman in the hearing
of another woman who loves *him*. The technique is in each case that of a
scene that centers upon a song, which makes a varying impact upon the
different characters who hear it. In *The Two Gentlemen of Verona* a song of
adoration to a mistress is presented by a faithless lover and is overheard by
the woman he has deserted, while her heartbreak goes undetected by her
escort, who calmly falls asleep. This is admirably dramatic, but its irony
may seem a trifle obvious when set beside the comparable scene in *Twelfth
Night*. The song here is one of forsaken love and it is sung to two constant
lovers. Most artfully introduced, it is called for by Orsino, whose request for
music sustains the role in which he began the play; and the way in which
he calls for the song characterizes both him and it before its opening notes
are heard. It is to be an old and antique song, belonging to some primitive
age, the kind of song chanted by women at their weaving or their knitting
in the sun. It will appeal to Orsino in its simple innocence, or, we may say if
we wish, by its ideal immunity from fact. So the rational mind can disengage
itself from the sentiment in advance, and as soon as the song is ended its
effect is counteracted by the jests of the clown who has sung it and the prac-

tical necessity of paying him. Yet the sentiment of the song remains to float back and forth over the dialogue which surrounds it as Orsino and Viola tell us of their love. The contrast here is not, as in *The Two Gentlemen of Verona*, between the faithful and the faithless, the heartbroken and the heartwhole. It is between one who is eloquent about an imaginary passion and one who suffers a real grief in concealment. Orsino appropriates the song to himself, yet it is Viola who hears in it

> a very echo to the seat
> Where Love is throned.

Orsino is still sending messages to one he calls his "sovereign," but *his* throne, we may say, is still unoccupied. For his splendid fantasies are as yet self-regarding. When Viola objects, "But if she cannot love you, sir?" he dismisses this with "I cannot be so answered." Yet when she simply retorts, "Sooth, but you must," he receives his first instruction in the necessity of accommodating his fantasies to practical realities. And soon he begins, however unwittingly, to learn. As Viola tells the history of her father's daughter, though he does not see that she is speaking of herself, he finds himself for the first time giving attention to a sorrow not his own. "But died thy sister of her love, my boy?" he asks. To this Viola can only reply, "I know not"; for at this stage in the drama the issue is still in the balance, though Orsino's new absorption in another's plight will provide us with a clue to the outcome. In the very act of sending a fresh embassy to his mistress his thoughts are momentarily distracted from his own affair. When it is necessary for Viola to prompt him—"Sir, shall I to this lady?"—though he rapidly collects himself, we know that his development has begun.

    In the emotional pattern of the play Viola represents a genuineness of feeling against which the illusory can be measured. As the go-between she is of course also at the center of the plot. It is her role to draw Orsino and Olivia from their insubstantial passions and win them to reality. But her impact upon each of them is inevitably different. Orsino, whom she loves but cannot tell her love, responds to her womanly constancy and sentiment; Olivia, whom she cannot love but has to woo, is to be fascinated by her page-boy effrontery and wit.

    Now in all the stories of the woman-page who woos for her master and supplants him, the transference of the mistress's affections must be the pivot of the action. In *The Two Gentlemen of Verona*, of course, the lady fails to fall in love with the page at all, which is really a little surprising of her, since she had done so in Shakespeare's source. It is almost as though Shakespeare were reserving this crowning situation, in which the mistress loves the woman-page, for treatment in some later play. At any rate, in *Twelfth Night* he takes care to throw the emphasis upon it from the first. Viola is got into her page-boy clothes before we are halfway through the first act. The plausibility of this, notwithstanding Mrs. Lennox and Dr. Johnson, is not the question. What matters is that the encounter of the lady and the page, upon which the plot is to turn, shall be momentous. And there is no encounter in Shakespeare, not even that of Hamlet with the ghost, which is more elaborately prepared for. Olivia's situation is referred to in each of the first four scenes before she herself appears in the fifth. Out of her love for her dead brother she has abjured the sight of men. This is the plain fact as a plain sea captain tells it to Viola and us. But in the more embroidered description of one of Orsino's gentlemen we may detect perhaps a hint of the preposterous:

> like a cloistress she will veiled walk
> And water once a day her chamber round
> With eye-offending brine.

In the fanciful Orsino this inspires adoration; but how it may appear to a less poetical nature we may gather from the first words of Sir Toby Belch: "What a plague means my niece to take the death of her brother thus?" All these varied views are insinuated naturally into the dialogue, but their cumulative effect is to give Olivia's situation in the round and to make us curious to see her for ourselves. When after all this she appears, curiosity is not satisfied but intensified; she is not, I think, what we expected. Instead of the veiled lady sprinkling her chamber with tears there enters a mistress commanding her household, and her first words are, "Take the fool away." Equally unexpected is the fool's retort, "Do you not hear, fellows? Take away the lady." This great dame is called a fool by one of her own attendants, who then goes on to prove it:

> *Clown.* Good madonna, why mourn'st thou?
> *Olivia.* Good fool, for my brother's death.
> *Clown.* I think his soul is in hell, madonna.
> *Olivia.* I know his soul is in heaven, fool.
> *Clown.* The more fool, madonna, to mourn for your brother's soul being
>   in heaven. Take away the fool, gentlemen.

Now this is excellent fooling, but Shakespeare's incidental gaieties have a way of illuminating important matters and our conception of Olivia is one of them. It is only a fool who calls her a fool, but, as the fool himself has suggested, a fool "may pass for a wise man," while those who think they have wit "do very oft prove fools." The question of Olivia's folly remains open. It is kept alive below the surface of the quipping dialogue which entertains us while Olivia defends the fool and is thanked by the fool in characteristically equivocal terms. "Thou hast spoke for us, madonna, as if thy eldest son should be a fool." One could hardly say more than that. Yet the suggestion that her eldest son might be a fool is at best a left-handed compliment. The fool is quick to right it with a prayer that Jove may cram his skull with brains, but it seems that Jove's intervention may be necessary, for—as Sir Toby enters—"one of thy kin has a most weak pia mater." The chances of brains or folly in the skull of any son of Olivia seem then to be about equal. But what is surely most remarkable is the notion of Olivia's ever having a son at all. We have been made to associate her not with birth but death. The weeping cloistress, as Orsino's gentleman put it, was seasoning a "dead love," and what plagued Sir Toby about this was that care was "an enemy to life." Yet the fool seems to see her as available for motherhood. The remarks of a fool—again—strike as deep as you choose to let them— that is the dramatic use of fools—but Olivia interests us more and more.

By now the page is at the gate. Indeed three different messengers announce him. Sir Toby of the weak pia mater is too drunk to do more than keep us in suspense, but Malvolio precisely catalogues the young man's strange behavior, till we are as curious to see him as is Olivia herself. "Tell him he shall not speak with me," she has insisted; but when this changes to "Let him approach," the first of her defences is down. Our interest in each of them is now at such a height that the moment of their meeting cannot fail to be electric.

How different all this is from what happened in *The Two Gentlemen of Verona*, where only a single soliloquy prepared us before the page and Sylvia just came together pat. But it is interesting to see how the seeds strewn in the earlier play now germinate in Shakespeare's mature inventiveness. When the page came upon Sylvia, he did not know who she was and actually asked her to direct him to herself. This confusion gave a momentary amusement and the dramatic importance of the encounter was faintly underlined. But as Sylvia at once disclosed her identity, this little gambit came to nothing. In *Twelfth Night*, however, Cesario only pretends not to recognize Olivia so as to confound her with his raillery. "Most radiant, exquisite and unmatchable beauty," he begins and then breaks off to enquire whether the lady before him is the radiant unmatchable or not. As he has never seen her, how can he possibly tell? This opens up a brilliant series of exchanges in the course of which the familiar moves of the conventional courtship are all similarly transformed. In *The Two Gentlemen of Verona* Proteus was simply following the usual pattern of suitors when he instructed the page,

> Give her that ring and therewithal
> This letter . . . Tell my lady
> I claim the promise for her heavenly picture.

To be fair, even in this early play the conventional properties, the ring, the letter, and the picture, each made a dramatic point: for Sylvia recognized the ring as that of her rival and so refused to accept it, while she tore the letter up; and if she compliantly handed over her portrait, she was careful

to add the comment that a picture was only a shadow and might appropriately be given for a fickle lover to worship. But in *Twelfth Night* the letter,
the picture, and the ring are changed almost out of recognition. Shakespeare's
superbly original invention allows Orsino to dispense with them; yet they
are all vestigially present. Instead of bearing missives, the page is given the
task of acting out his master's woes, and so instead of the lover's own letter
we are to have the page's speech. This cunningly diverts attention from the
message to the messenger, and the effect is still further enhanced when even
the speech never gets delivered apart from its opening words. Instead there
is talk about the speech—how "excellently well penn'd," how "poetical" it
is—and are you really the right lady so that I may not waste the praise I have
taken such pains to compose? Olivia in turn delights us by matching Cesario's
mockery, but as we watch them finesse about how and even whether the
speech shall be delivered, their mocking dialogue says more than any formal
speech could say. In fact the very circumventing of the speech brings them
to the heart of its forbidden theme. And so we come to the picture. There
is of course no picture, any more than there was a letter; but the convention
whereby the lover asks for a picture of his mistress is made to provide a
metaphor through which the witty duel may proceed. Olivia draws back
the curtain and reveals a picture, they talk of the colors that the artist's
"cunning hand laid on," and Cesario asks for a copy. But the curtain Olivia
draws back is her own veil, the artist is Nature, and the copy of Nature's
handiwork will come as the fruit of marriage. Again the suggestion that
Olivia could have a child. The cloistress who dedicates herself to the dead
is reminded of the claims of life. She waves them aside for the moment by
deftly changing the application of the metaphor. Certainly there shall be a
copy of her beauty; why not an inventory of its items? As she catalogues
them—"two lips, indifferent red . . . two grey eyes, with lids to them"—she
ridicules the wooer's praises; but at the same time, it may not be too much
to suggest, she robs her womanhood of its incipient animation. Yet the
cloistress has removed her veil and presently there is the ring. Orsino again
sent no ring, but that need not prevent Olivia from returning it. And with
this ruse the ring no less than the picture takes on a new significance. By
means of it Olivia rejects Orsino's love but at the same time declares her own.
And as Malvolio flings the ring upon the stage it makes its little dramatic
éclat.

Shakespeare's portrait of Olivia has usually, I think, been underrated.
The critics who used to talk about Shakespeare's heroines fell in love with
Viola, and actresses have naturally preferred the bravura of her essentially
easier role. Besides there is the risk of the ridiculous about a woman who
mistakenly loves one of her own sex. But the delicacy of Shakespeare's handling, once more in contrast with that of his predecessors, steers the situation
right away from farce and contrives to show, through her potentially absurd

and undisguisedly pathetic plight, the gradual awakening of that noble nature which Orsino detected from the first. We have still permission to laugh at her. The fool, reminding us that foolery like the sun shines everywhere, flits between Orsino's house and hers. But when he is called the Lady Olivia's fool he makes one of his astonishing replies. "No indeed, sir. The Lady Olivia has no folly." It is true that his remark is as usual doubleedged. "She will keep no fool, sir, till she be married." Her present exemption, it would seem, lies in her not having yet secured the husband she is seeking. But when the fool now tells us that the Lady Olivia has no folly, we are forcibly reminded that he began by proving her a fool. It seems clear she is making progress. The comic artist only hints this with a lightness which the heavy hand of the critic inevitably destroys; but is there not the suggestion that when Olivia ceases to mourn the dead and gives herself to the pursuit of the living, she has advanced some small way towards wisdom?

There is one character in the play who, unlike Olivia and Orsino, is unable to make this journey. And that brings me to the subplot. For it will already be apparent that I do not agree with a recent paper in the *Shakespeare Quarterly* which makes Malvolio the central figure of the play.[8] The mistake is not a new one. The record of a court performance in the year of the First Folio actually calls the play *Malvolio* and there are other seventeenth-century references, beginning with Manningham in 1602, which go to show that the sublime swagger with which Malvolio walks into the box-hedge trap to emerge in yellow stockings was largely responsible, then as now, for the play's theatrical popularity. The distortion of emphasis this implies is a tribute to Shakespeare's invention of the most novel situation in the play, but if I venture to suggest that it does no great credit to his audience, no doubt some one will rise up like Sir Toby and ask me, "Dost thou think because thou art virtuous there shall be no more cakes and ale?" All I think is that the cake-and-ale jollifications are very jolly indeed so long as they stay, whether in criticism or performance, within the bounds of a subplot, which the whole technique of the dramatic exposition marks them out to be. These more hilarious goings-on make an admirable counterweight to the more fragile wit and sentiment of which the main plot is woven; but attention is firmly directed to the love story of Orsino, Olivia, and Viola before Sir Toby and Malvolio are heard of, and the courtships are well in progress by the time we come to the midnight caterwaulings. So the love-delusions of Malvolio, brilliant as they are, fall into perspective as a parody of the more delicate aberrations of his mistress and her suitor. Like them Malvolio aspires towards an illusory ideal of love, but his mistake is a grosser one than theirs, his posturings more extravagant and grotesque. So *his* illusion enlarges

---

[8] Milton Crane, "*Twelfth Night* and Shakespearean Comedy," *Shakespeare Quarterly*, VI (1955). Cf. also Mark Van Doren, *Shakespeare*, 1939, p. 169: "The center is Malvolio."

the suggestions of the main plot about the mind's capacity for self-deception and if, as Lamb maintained,[9] it gives Malvolio a glory such as no mere reason can attain to, still "lunacy" was one of Lamb's words for it and it is to the madman's dungeon that it leads.

Malvolio's fate, like Falstaff's, has been much resented by the critics. But drama, as Aristotle indicated and Shakespeare evidently perceived, is not quite the same as life, and punishments that in life would seem excessive have their place in the more ideal world of art. In the ethical scheme of comedy, it may be the doom of those who cannot correct themselves to be imprisoned or suppressed. Olivia and Prince Hal, within their vastly different realms, have shown themselves capable of learning, as Malvolio and Falstaff have not.

The comparison between Olivia and Malvolio is one that the play specifically invites. He is the trusted steward of her household, and he suits her, she says, by being "sad and civil." This reminds us that it was with her authority that he descended on the midnight revels to quell that "uncivil rule." Have you no manners, he demands of Sir Toby and his crew; and his rebuke is one that Olivia herself will echo later when she calls Sir Toby a barbarian fit to dwell in "caves Where manners ne'er were preached." But if Olivia and Malvolio are united in seeking to impose an ordered regimen on these unruly elements, that does not mean, though I have found it said, that they share a doctrine of austerity.[10] Indeed the resemblance between them serves to bring out a distinction that is fundamental to the play. It is clearly marked for us on their first appearance. Significantly enough, they are brought on the stage together and placed in the same situation, as if to attract our attention to their contrasting reactions. The first remark of each of them is one of dissatisfaction with the fool, and the fool's retaliation is first to prove Olivia a fool and then to call Malvolio one. But Olivia is amused and Malvolio is not. "I marvel your ladyship takes delight in such a barren rascal." What Olivia delights in, Malvolio finds barren. "Doth he not mend?" she says, suggesting that the fool is getting wittier. But Malvolio rejoins, Yes, he is mending by becoming a more perfect fool—"and shall do till the pangs of death shake him." Olivia too has given her thoughts to death, but whereas she mourns the dead, prettily if absurdly, Malvolio threatens the living in words which betray a cruel relish. This is his first speech in the play and it carries a corresponding emphasis. There are already signs that Olivia may be won from death to life, but the spirit of Malvolio can only be destructive. To say this is again to put it more portentously than it is the nature of comedy to do, but it is Olivia, not

---

[9] In his account of Bensley's Malvolio in the essay "On Some of the Old Actors."

[10] See especially M. P. Tilley, "The Organic Unity of *Twelfth Night*," *PMLA*, XXIX (1914).

Malvolio, whom the comic dialogue invites to have a son, with brains in his skull or otherwise.

The difference in their natures appears in various subtle ways, and I will cite just one example. When Olivia sends after Cesario with the ring, the message that she sends is,

> If that the youth will come this way tomorrow,
> I'll give him reasons for't.

But Malvolio, who bears the message, translates it thus:

> Be never so hardy to come again in his affairs, unless it be
> to report your lord's taking of this.

It is true that Malvolio cannot know, as we do, the secret meaning of the ring, but that hardly leaves him guiltless when he replaces "if" by "unless" and a positive by a negative: "If that the youth will come . . . ," "Be never so hardy to come . . . unless. . . ." An invitation has become a warning off.

As the action proceeds, Olivia opens her heart to the new love that is being born within her, but Malvolio is only confirmed in that sickness of self-love of which she has accused him. At the height of his love-dream, his imaginings are all of his own advancement—"sitting in my state," "in my branched velvet gown," "calling my officers about me" as I "wind up my watch or play with my—some rich jewel."[11] When he showed resentment at the fool, Olivia reproached Malvolio for his lack of generosity and now his very words freeze every generous impulse—"I frown the while," "quenching my familiar smile with an austere regard of control."[12] This is not the language of Olivia. She speaks of the impossibility of quenching those natural feelings which rise up within her, and which we are made to recognize even in the comicality of her predicament:

> Cesario, by the roses of the spring,
> By maidhood, honour, truth and everything,
> I love thee so that maugre all thy pride,
> No wit nor reason can my passion hide.

So Olivia, notwithstanding her mistakes, is allowed to find a husband while Malvolio is shut up in the dark.

The ironic fitness of Malvolio's downfall is dramatically underscored in every detail of his situation. When he dreamed of his own greatness he pictured Sir Toby coming to him with a curtsey and he told Sir Toby to amend his drunkenness: it is now his bitterest complaint that this drunken cousin has been given rule over him. When he rebuked the tipsy revellers,

[11] Cf. John Russell Brown, *Shakespeare and his Comedies*, 1957, p. 167.
[12] On the style of Malvolio's speeches, see Mark Van Doren, *Shakespeare*, 1939, p. 167.

he began, "My masters, are you mad?" and their revenge upon him is to make it seem that he is mad himself. Particularly instructive is the leading part taken in his torment by the fool he began the play by spurning. The fool taunts him in the darkness of the dungeon and he begs the fool to help him to some light. It is to the fool that the man contemptuous of fools is now made to plead his own sanity. But his insistence on his sanity—"I am as well in my wits, fool, as thou art"—leaves the matter in some ambiguity, as the fool very promptly retorts: "Then you are mad indeed, if you be no better in your wits than a fool." And Malvolio ends the play as he began by being called a fool. And if at first it was only the fool who called him so, now it is his mistress herself. Even as she pities him for the trick that has been played on him, "Alas, poor fool" are the words that Shakespeare puts into her mouth.

What then is folly and what wisdom, the comedy seems to ask. The question first appeared in that early cross-talk with the fool which brought Olivia into contrast with Malvolio even while we were awaiting her reception of Cesario. So that the manner in which Malvolio's story is begun clearly puts it into relation with the main plot of the wooing. And of course it is only appropriate that scenes of romantic love should be surrounded by a comic dialogue which gaily tosses off its hints about whether these characters are fools. For the pursuit of the ideal life is not quite compatible with reason. And, as another of Shakespeare's comedies puts it, those who in imagination see more than "reason ever comprehends" are the lover, the poet, and the lunatic. So where does the noble vision end and the madman's dream begin? The greatness and the folly that lie in the mind of man are inextricably entangled and the characters in *Twelfth Night* have each their share of both. Malvolio's moment of lunacy may be, as Lamb suggests, the moment of his glory. Yet Malvolio, so scornful of the follies of others, would persuade us that his own are sane. His sanity is indeed established, but only to leave us wondering whether sanity may not sometimes be the greater folly. What the comedy *may* suggest is that he who in his egotism seeks to fit the world to the procrustean bed of his own reason deserves his own discomfiture. But Olivia, who self-confessedly abandons reason, and Orsino, who avidly gives his mind to all the shapes of fancy, are permitted to pass through whatever folly there may be in this to a greater illumination. Although what they sought has inevitably eluded them, it has nevertheless been vouchsafed to them in another form.

Yet it is the art of Shakespeare's comedy, and perhaps also its wisdom, to make no final judgments. The spirit of the piece, after all, is that of Twelfth Night and it is in the ideal world of Twelfth Night that Malvolio may be justly punished. Perhaps we should also remember, as even the Twelfth Night lovers do, to pause, if only for a moment, to recognize his precisian virtues. Olivia agrees with him that he has been "notoriously abused" and the poet-lover Orsino sends after him to "entreat him to a peace," before they finally enter into the happiness to which "golden time" will summon them. "Golden time"—the epithet is characteristically Orsino's. It is only the wise fool who stays to sing to us about the rain that raineth every day.

Measure for Measure

by R. W. Chambers

In *Measure for Measure* Shakespeare took as his source an old play, *Promos and Cassandra*, written by George Whetstone a quarter of a century before. Now, just as certainly as *Hamlet* was a play of revenge, so was *Promos and Cassandra* a play of forgiveness. In this play Cassandra (like Isabel) pleads for her brother, who (like Claudio) has been condemned to death for unchastity. The judge, Promos (like Angelo) will grant pardon only if Cassandra yield to his passion. Cassandra at last does so. That is the essential difference between the old plot, and Shakespeare's play. Nevertheless, Promos orders Cassandra's brother to be beheaded, and the head to be presented to her. Cassandra complains to the King: the King gives judgment that Promos first marry Cassandra, then lose *his* head. But, this marriage solemnized, Cassandra, now tied in the greatest bonds of affection to her husband, suddenly becomes an earnest suitor for his life. In the end it appears that the kindly jailer has in fact released the brother, and presented Cassandra with a felon's head instead. So, to renown the virtues of Cassandra, the King pardons both brother and judge, and all ends well.

The story shows the violence of much Elizabethan drama. John Addington Symonds says, in *Shakespeare's Predecessors*, that the sympathies of a London audience were like "the chords of a warrior's harp, strung with twisted iron and bull's sinews, vibrating mightily, but needing a stout stroke to make them thrill." The playwrights "glutted their audience with horrors, cudgeled their horny fibers into sensitiveness."

Now mark how Shakespeare treats this barbarous story. According to Professor Dover Wilson, at the time when he wrote *Measure for Measure*, Shakespeare "quite obviously believed in nothing; he was as cynical as Iago, as disillusioned as Macbeth, though he still retained, unlike the first, his sensitiveness, and, unlike the second, his hatred of cruelty, hypocrisy, and ingratitude." [1] According to Sir Edmund Chambers, in *Measure for Measure*

"*Measure for Measure.*" From "The Jacobean Shakespeare and *Measure for Measure*," *Proceedings of the British Academy*, XXIII (1937), pp. 30–58. Reprinted by permission of the author's executor and the British Academy.

[1] *The Essential Shakespeare*, p. 122.

his "remorseless analysis" "probes the inmost being of man, and strips him naked." "It is the temper of the inquisitor": "you can but shudder." [2]

Prepare then to shudder, as you observe William Iago Torquemada Shakespeare at work. Shakespeare, for all the "self-laceration," "disgust," and "general morbidity" [3] which is supposed to have obsessed him and his Jacobean contemporaries, removes from the play the really morbid scene of the heroine kissing the severed head of her supposed brother. Then, he divides the sorrows of the heroine between two characters, Isabel and Mariana. And the object of this duplication is, that, whatever their spiritual anguish, neither of them shall be placed in the "really intolerable situation" [4] of poor Cassandra. Mariana has been contracted to Angelo formally by oath. It is vital to remember that, according to Elizabethan ideas, Angelo and Mariana are therefore man and wife. But Angelo has deserted Mariana. Now I grant that, according to our modern ideas, it is undignified for the deserted Mariana still to desire union with the husband who has scorned her. *We* may resent the elegiac and spaniel-like fidelity of Mariana of the Moated Grange. *But is that the sixteenth-century attitude?* The tale of the deserted bride seeking her husband in disguise is old, approved, beloved. It is a mere anachronism to assume that Shakespeare, a practical dramatist, told this tale with some deep cynical and self-lacerating intention unintelligible to his audience, but now at last revealed to modern criticism. Shakespeare made Mariana gentle and dignified. She, in all shadow and silence, visits her husband in place of Isabel, to save Claudio's life.

And our twentieth-century critics are scandalized over the tale. This surprises me, a Late Victorian, brought up on the Bible and Arthurian story. I did not know that our modern age was so proper. A Professor today cannot deliver a series of lectures on "The Application of Thought to Textual Criticism" without its being reported as "The Application of Thought to Sexual Criticism." Yet this sex-obsessed age of ours is too modest to endure the old story of the substituted bride. I learnt at my Early Victorian mother's knee, how Jacob served seven years for Rachel: "And it came to pass, that in the morning, behold, it was Leah," [5] and Jacob had to serve another seven years for his beloved. I did not exclaim: "Oh my mother, you are lacerating my feelings with this remorseless revelation of patriarchal polygamy." A child could grasp the story of Jacob's service for Rachel, which "seemed unto him but a few days, for the love he had to her."

Sir Edmund Chambers is entitled to say that the story of the substituted bride "does not commend itself to the modern conscience." Jaques was entitled to say that he did not like the name of Rosalind. And Orlando was

[2] *Shakespeare: A Survey*, p. 213.
[3] J. Dover Wilson, *op. cit.*, pp. 117, 118.
[4] *Works of Shakespeare*, ed. G. L. Kittredge, p. 97.
[5] Genesis xxix. 25.

entitled to say, "There was no thought of pleasing you when she was christened." In the sixteenth century the story was a commonplace of romance, and Shakespeare used it in order to make more gentle one of the quite horrible situations of the pre-Shakespearian drama. There was a time when Shakespeare had not shrunk from staging the grossest horrors. It is to avoid them, that he now brings in the substitution which offends "the modern conscience."

It may be objected that Shakespeare is "not for an age, but for all time," and that therefore he ought not to have condescended to use stories which, although current in his day, and although he made them less horrible, nevertheless would not appeal to future ages. But the great poets, Homer, Æschylus, Sophocles, Dante, Shakespeare, speak to all time only through the language, conventions, and beliefs of their own age. How else?

A second fault of the old play is the crudity of the change from Cassandra's thirst for vengeance to her prayer for forgiveness. Shakespeare had permitted himself similar crudities in the past. Now he sets to work to make the plot consistent: he does this by making it turn, from first to last, on the problem of punishment and forgiveness. It is Shakespeare's addition to the story that the Duke is distressed by this problem. Fearing lest his rule has been too lax, he deputes his office to Angelo, whilst remaining, disguised as a friar, to "visit both prince and people." And here many critics, among them Sir Walter Raleigh[6] and Sir Arthur Quiller-Couch,[7] object. It is not seemly for a Duke to "shirk his proper responsibility, and steal back incognito to play busybody and spy on his deputy."

I am reminded of one of the first essays ever shown up to me, by a Japanese student, some thirty-five years ago. He objected to *The Merchant of Venice*. "Bassanio," he said, "did not bring honorable surgeon, to bind up wounds of honorable friend. He did not recognize honorable wife, when disguised as a man."

Why do critics today bring against *Measure for Measure* this kind of objection, which they would be ashamed to bring against Shakespeare's earlier comedies, or later romances?

Disguise and impersonation and misunderstanding are the very life of romantic comedy. The disguised monarch, who can learn the private affairs of his humblest subject, becomes a sort of earthly Providence, combining omniscience and omnipotence. That story has always had its appeal. "Thus hath the wise magistrate done in all ages";[8] although obviously to introduce into our daily life this ancient habit of the benevolent monarch would be to incur deserved satire. There is no doubt how Shakespeare meant us to regard

[6] *Shakespeare*, p. 167.
[7] New Cambridge Shakespeare, *Measure for Measure*, p. xxxiv.
[8] Jonson, *Bartholomew Fair*, 11. i.

the Duke. "One that, above all other strifes, contended especially to know himself: a gentleman of all temperance," says Escalus. Isabel, in her moment of dire distress, remembers him as "the good Duke." Angelo, in his moment of deepest humiliation, addresses him with profound reverence and awe. Lucio (like our moderns) regards the Duke cynically; but he ends by admitting that he deserves a whipping for so doing.

The deputy, Angelo, is not so called for nothing. He *is* "angel on the outward side"—an ascetic saint in the judgment of his fellow citizens, and despite the meanness of his spirit, nay, because of it, a saint in his own esteem. His soliloquies prove this, and Isabel at the end gives him some credit for sincerity.

Now Claudio and Juliet have lived together as man and wife, although their contract has been secret: it has "lacked the denunciation of outward order." (The contract between Angelo and Mariana, on the other hand, had been public, and so had undoubtedly given them the rights of man and wife.) Angelo's puritanical revival of an ancient law, fourteen years out of date, renders Claudio's life forfeit. This Viennese law seems strange, but the Duke says the law is such. If we allow Portia to expound the even stranger law of Venice to the Duke and Magnificoes, we may surely allow the Duke of Vienna to understand the law of his own state. It is a postulate of the story.

Critics speak as if Shakespeare had imagined Claudio a self-indulgent boy, a "poor weak soul." [9] Yet it is only Angelo's retrospective revival which makes Claudio's offence capital. "He hath but as offended in a dream," says the kindly Provost. He "was worth five thousand of you all," says Mistress Overdone to Lucio and his friends. Claudio is first introduced, bearing himself with great dignity and right feeling, under his sudden arrest. He sends his friend Lucio to his sister in her cloister, to beg her to intercede for him, because, he says,

> in her youth
> There is a prone and speechless dialect,
> Such as move men; beside, she hath prosperous art
> When she will play with reason and discourse,
> And well she can persuade.

Such descriptions of characters before they appear—perhaps before Shakespeare had written a word for them to speak—have surely a great weight. They show how Shakespeare wished the audience to see them. Isabel's characteristic when she does appear is exactly this mixture of winning silence with persuasive speech.

But before she can reach Angelo, his colleague Escalus has already inter-

[9] E. K. Chambers, *op. cit.*, p. 209.

ceded for Claudio, urging that, had time cohered with place, and place with wishing, Angelo might himself have fallen. Angelo replies:

> When I, that censure him, do so offend,
> Let mine own judgment pattern out my death,
> And nothing come in partial. Sir, he must die.

Isabel begins her pleading slowly and with characteristic silences: then she grows eloquent, and to Angelo's stern refusal she at last replies:

> I would to Heaven I had your potency,
> And you were Isabel! Should it then be thus?
> No; I would tell what 'twere to be a judge,
> And what a prisoner.

Isabel has no notion as yet of the depth of sin which may have to be pardoned in Angelo. But there is "irony" behind these two speeches, and we can forecast that in the end the places will be reversed: the fate of the convicted Angelo depending upon Isabel.[10]

Will she then be true to the pleas which she now pours forth? "Well she can persuade." Her marvellous and impassioned pleadings, unsurpassed anywhere in Shakespeare, are based on her Christian faith, and upon the Sermon on the Mount: all men are pardoned sinners, and *must* forgive:

> Why, all the souls that were, were forfeit once;
> And he that might the vantage best have took
> Found out the remedy.

"Judge not, that ye be not judged. For with what measure ye mete, it shall be measured to you again." *Measure for Measure*. But how is the Sermon on the Mount to be reconciled with the practical necessities of government? That is the problem which puzzles people—and particularly perhaps young people—so much today. In the Tudor Age men met it by exalting Government. The King is "the image of God's majesty": to him, and to his Government, the divine office of rule and punishment is committed. The private man must submit and forgive. Accordingly, Angelo appeals to his "function": and there is real force in his answers to Isabel—remembering, as we always must, that, for the purposes of the play, Claudio is supposed guilty of a capital offence.

[10] The phrase "dramatic irony" may be misunderstood. Shakespeare, like Sophocles, puts into the mouths of his characters words which they speak in all sincerity, but which, as the play proceeds, will be found to have a deeper meaning than the speaker knew. Dramatic irony does *not* mean that, at every turn, we are justified in suspecting that Shakespeare may have meant the reverse of what he makes his characters say. When he does that ("honest Iago") he leaves us in no doubt. As a great American critic has put it: "However much the *dramatis personae* mystify each other, the audience is never to be perplexed." (G. L. Kittredge, *Shakespeare*, 1916, p. 20.)

Never does Shakespeare seem more passionately to identity himself with any of his characters than he does with Isabel, as she pleads for mercy against strict justice:

> O, it is excellent
> To have a giant's strength; but it is tyrannous
> To use it like a giant. . . .
>   man, proud man,
> Drest in a little brief authority . . .
> Plays such fantastic tricks before high heaven
> As make the angels weep . . . .

Angelo does not fall without a sincere struggle. But more than one of Isabel's pleadings find a mark which she never meant:

> Go to your bosom;
> Knock there, and ask your heart what it doth know
> That's like my brother's fault . . .
> Hark how I'll bribe you . . . .

Angelo has thought himself superior to human weakness, because he is free from the vulgar vices of a Lucio. And the "beauty of mind" of a distressed, noble woman throws him off his balance.[11] If we fail to see the nobility of Isabel, we cannot see the story as we should. The plot is rather like that of Calderon's *Magician*, where the scholarly, austere Cipriano is overthrown by speaking with the saintly Justina. Cipriano sells himself literally to the Devil to gain his end by magic. Angelo tempts Isabel in a second dialogue, as wonderful as the first. In her innocence Isabel is slow to see Angelo's drift, and it is only her confession of her own frailty that gives him a chance of making himself clear. "Nay," Isabel says,

> call us ten times frail;
> For we are soft as our complexions are,
> And credulous to false prints.

If Shakespeare is depicting in Isabel the self-righteous prude which some critics would make of her, he goes strangely to work.

But when she perceives Angelo's drift, Isabel decides without hesitation. Now whatever we think of that instant decision, it is certainly not un-Christian. Christianity could never have lived through its first three hundred years of persecution, if its ranks had not been stiffened by men and women who never hesitated in the choice between righteousness and the ties to their kinsfolk. We may call this fanaticism: but it was well understood in Shake-speare's day. Foxe's *Martyrs* was read by all; old people could still remember

[11] Cf. Masefield, *William Shakespeare*, p. 179.

seeing the Smithfield fires; year after year saw the martyrdoms of Catholic men (and sometimes of Catholic women like the Ven. Margaret Clitherow). It was a stern age—an age such as the founder of Christianity had foreseen when he uttered his stern warning: "He that loveth father or mother more than me . . . ." "If any man come to me, and hate not his father, and mother, and brethren and sisters, he cannot be my disciple." [12]

It is recorded of Linacre, the father of English medicine, that, albeit a priest, he opened his Greek New Testament for the first time late in life, and came on some of these hard sayings: "Either this is not the Gospel," he said, "or we are not Christians," and refusing to contemplate the second alternative, he flung the Book from him and returned to the study of medicine. Now it is open to us to say that we are not Christians: it is not open to us to say that Isabel's instant decision is un-Christian. So she goes to her brother, not because she hesitates, but that he may share with her the burden of her irrevocable decision. Claudio's first reply is, "O heavens! it cannot be"; "Thou shalt not do't." But the very bravest of men have quailed, within the four walls of a prison cell, waiting for the axe next day. I am amazed at the way critics condemn Claudio, when he breaks down, and utters his second thoughts, "Sweet sister, let me live." Isabel overwhelms him in the furious speech which we all know. And I am even more amazed at the dislike which the critics feel for the tortured Isabel. But when they assure us that their feeling towards both his creatures was shared by the gentle Shakespeare, I am then most amazed of all.

It is admitted that no greater or more moving scenes had appeared on any stage, since the masterpieces of Attic drama ceased to be acted. Yet our critics tell us that Shakespeare wrote them in a mood of "disillusionment and cynicism," "self-laceration," and, strangest of all, "weariness." [13] "A corroding atmosphere of moral suspicion" [14] hangs about this debate between "the sainted Isabella, wrapt in her selfish chastity," and "the wretched boy who in terror of death is ready to sacrifice his sister's honor." [15] Isabel's chastity, they say, is "rancid," and she is "not by any means such a saint as she looks";[16] her inhumanity is pitiless, her virtue is self-indulgent, unimaginative, and self-absorbed.[17]

And yet, think of Rose Macaulay's war poem, "Many sisters to many brothers," and let us believe that a sister may suffer more in agony of mind than the brother can suffer in physical wounds or death. Shakespeare has made Isabel say to Claudio

[12] Matthew x. 37; Luke xiv. 26.
[13] J. Dover Wilson, *op. cit.*, pp. 116, 117.
[14] E. K. Chambers, *op. cit.*, p. 214.
[15] J. Dover Wilson, *op. cit.*, p. 116.
[16] New Cambridge Shakespeare, *Measure for Measure*, p. xxx.
[17] U. M. Ellis-Fermor, *The Jacobean Drama*, pp. 261, 262.

> O, were it but my life,
> I'ld throw it down for your deliverance
> As frankly as a pin.

It is standing the play on its head,[18] to say that Shakespeare wrote those words in irony and cynicism. How did he convey that to his audience? If such assumptions are allowed, we can prove anything we like, "eight years together, dinners and suppers and sleeping-hours excepted."

Isabel then, as Shakespeare sees her and asks us to see her, would frankly, joyously, give her life to save Claudio—and, let there be no mistake about it, *"greater love hath no man than this."* And now Claudio is asking for what she cannot give, and she bursts out in agony. Have the critics never seen a human soul or a human body in the extremity of torment? Physical torture Isabel thinks she could have stood without flinching. She has said so to Angelo:

> The impression of keen whips I'ld wear as rubies,
> And strip myself to death, as to a bed
> That longing have been sick for, ere I'ld yield
> My body up to shame.

To suppose that Shakespeare gave these burning words to Isabel so that we should perceive her to be selfish and cold, is to suppose that he did not know his job. The honor of her family and her religion are more to her than mere life, her own or Claudio's.

Sir George Greenwood prefers Cassandra's character. The New Cambridge Shakespeare quotes this dictum of Sir George with more approval than it would give to his other dicta.[19] Still, though Cassandra may yield, Isabel can't. And most of those who have criticized her, from Hazlitt downwards, agree that she can't. And she has got to make that clear to Claudio. It is just here that her critics quarrel with her. Sir Arthur Quiller-Couch digs out Mrs. Charlotte Lennox from the obscurity of the mid-eighteenth century to tell us how the scene should have been written. Isabel, Charlotte says,

> should have made use of her superior understanding to reason down Claudio's fears, recall nobler ideas to his mind, teach him what was due to her honour and his own, and reconcile him to his approaching death by arguments drawn from that religion and virtue of which she made so high a profession.

---

[18] I borrow this very excellent phrase from W. W. Lawrence (p. 70). The brevity of a lecture compels me to pass over many points that a critic may think should have been more fully argued, but I do this the more cheerfully, because they have been already so fully discussed by Lawrence in his *Shakespeare's Problem Comedies*, 1931, and their moral emphasized in an excellent leading article in *The Times Literary Supplement* of July 16, 1931.

[19] p. xxxi.

"To reason down Claudio's fears!" "By arguments drawn from religion and virtue!" Why, the Duke had just preached to Claudio the most eloquent Sermon Against the Fear of Death that has ever been written since Lucretius completed his Third Book. Claudio had expressed himself convinced; and then the Duke's discourse had shrivelled like a thread in the flame of Claudio's longing for life.

How will pi-jaw help Claudio? Shakespeare imagined Claudio as a good lad, but not, like his sister, devout; he doesn't keep devout company, exactly. Isabel "well can persuade." She is one of a few women in Shakespeare who can persuade. (Not Portia: "The quality of mercy is not strain'd" produces no persuasion in the soul of Shylock.) Volumnia is a special case. The other great persuaders are Isabel, Beatrice and Lady Macbeth. And they all use the same arguments—the arguments which, I expect, the first cave-woman, when in dire straits, used to her cave-man: You are a coward; You have no love or respect for me; I have no longer any love for you.

Isabel is the most vehement of the three. Sisterly technique has its own rules; there is a peculiar freedom about the talk of those who have known each other from babyhood. And Isabel can use arguments outside the range of Beatrice or Lady Macbeth. Don't forget that Escalus, when he first pleaded for Claudio, remembered his "most noble father." Isabel had exclaimed, when she first found Claudio firm,

> there my father's grave
> Did utter forth a voice.

And now she cries,

> Heaven shield my mother play'd my father fair.

Isabel appeals to the passion which, in an Elizabethan gentleman, may be presumed to be stronger than the fear of death—pride in his gentle birth and in the courage which should mark it. Don't people see that there are things about which we cannot argue calmly? The fierceness of Isabel's words is the measure of the agony of her soul. "The fortress which parleys, the woman who parleys, is lost." I grant that, at the end of a lifetime's training, a saint like Thomas More could smile on his daughter when she tempted him, "What, Mistress Eve?" But the young martyrs are apt to be more stern, whether it be Cordelia or Antigone, the spitfire St. Eulalia, or St. Juliana putting the fear of death upon the Devil. And it is our fault if we don't see that Isabel is suffering martyrdom none the less because her torment is mental, not physical.

One of the most significant of Shakespeare's alterations of his original is to make the heroine a "votarist of St. Clare." At the root of the movement of St. Francis and St. Clare was the intense remembrance of the sufferings of Christ, in atonement for the sins of the whole world—the "remedy" of which

Isabel in vain reminds Angelo. Isabel, as a novice, is testing herself to see whether she is called to that utter renunciation which is the life of the "poor Clare." Whether she remains in the Convent or no, one who is contemplating such a life can no more be expected to sell herself into mortal sin, than a good soldier can be expected to sell a stronghold entrusted to him.

Imagine an officer and his subaltern commanded to hold to the uttermost a fortified post against rebels. In a sortie the rebels capture the subaltern, and threaten to shoot him unless the fort surrenders. The subaltern breaks down, and implores his commandant to save his life. I can imagine that the commandant would reply, firmly but gently, that surrender is impossible. But suppose the subaltern were his beloved younger brother, or his only son. I can imagine that then the commandant would reply to his son's appeal by passionate denunciation, telling him that he is a disgrace to his family. To discuss the matter calmly would lead to the surrender which he knows he must not make: his instinct would tell him that. So, at least, it seems to me in my ignorance. And when I find Shakespeare in his wisdom depicting the matter so, I don't see anything cynical about it.

Those who dislike the vehemence of Isabel would do well, in Ben Jonson's phrase, to "call forth Sophocles to us," and to ponder on the *Philoctetes*. In that play Neoptolemus is asked to sell his honor and betray his father's friend by a base lie, for the good of his country, and for the ultimate good of the friend who is to be deceived. Neoptolemus refuses indignantly, but he lets himself be drawn into discussion, and so sells his honor and his friend. But the anticipated good does not follow, and Neoptolemus has to make amends to his friend, though this means treason to the Greek army. The play is ending, with Neoptolemus deserting the army, and even contemplating war with his own countrymen, when the god appears from the machine to solve the knot. All this follows because Neoptolemus listens and debates when he hears the voice of the tempter: "Now give thyself to me for one short, shameless day, and then, for the rest of thy time, be called of all mortals the most righteous." We cannot argue with the tempter, when our own desires are already so much enlisted on his side. We can only refuse, instinctively, vehemently.

It is precisely the alternation of vehemence with silence which gives Isabel her individuality. Remember that when she first understands the real drift of Angelo's temptation, the poor child flies at him with a pathetic attempt at blackmail: "Sign me a present pardon for my brother, or . . . I'll tell the world . . . ." Remember also that when she is told that Angelo has slain Claudio, she exclaims:

> O, I will to him and pluck out his eyes!

Shakespeare sometimes puts his heroines in pairs, coupling the fierce, vehement girl, with the gentle, swooning girl: Hermia with Helena, Beatrice with

Hero, Isabel with Mariana. For all her silence and modesty, Isabel has the
ferocity of the martyr. Yet I don't think Shakespeare disliked his vixens.
Hermia has nails which can reach her enemy's eyes. Benedick foresaw a
predestinate scratched face for the husband of Beatrice. Yet would you, Mr.
Chairman, take Hero in to dinner, if you could get Beatrice? Would you,
Mr. Secretary, go hiking through the Athenian forest with Helena, if you
could get Hermia?

Critics ask, as does Sir Edmund Chambers, whether Isabel too "has not
had her ordeal, and in her turn failed," whether she was "wholly justified in
the eyes of her creator." They are entitled to ask the question. But they ought
to wait for the answer. The Duke enters, takes Claudio aside, and tells him
there is no hope for him. And we find that Claudio, who before Isabel's outburst had been gripped by the mortal fear of death, is now again master of
his soul:

> Let me ask my sister pardon. I am so out of love with life, that I will sue to
> be rid of it.

"Hold you there," says the Duke. Claudio does. Later, we see him quiet and
self-possessed when the Provost shows him his death warrant. To the Provost
he is "the most gentle Claudio": and to Shakespeare, the word "gentle" is a
word of very high praise, not consistent with any want of spirit.[20] "Gentle"
and "most gentle" is how his worthy friends and fellows—Ben Jonson,
Heminge, Condell—described Shakespeare. Claudio, "most gentle" in his
cell, has passed his ordeal well, showing quiet courage equally removed from
the hilarity of a Posthumus and the insensibility of a Barnardine.

Mrs. Lennox says that Isabel ought to have taught Claudio what is due
to her honor and his own. She has.

Now, if Isabel's speech had been intended to depict a "cold," and "remorseless" woman, "all for saving her own soul," acting cruelly to her
brother in the "fiery ordeal" which (we are told) "his frail soul proves ill-
fitted to endure," why does Shakespeare show Claudio, far from resenting
his sister's reproaches, only wishing to ask her pardon, and henceforth courageous and resolute? Why, above all, does Shakespeare make the Duke, when
he overhears Isabel's whole speech, comment on the beauty of her goodness?
This is intelligible only if Shakespeare means Isabel's speech as an agonized
outcry, working on her brother as no calm reasoning could have done. If
Shakespeare's critics think they could have written the scene better, they are
welcome to try; but it does not follow that Shakespeare was a disillusioned
cynic because he did not write Isabel's speech as Charlotte Lennox would
have done.

---

[20] "He's gentle, and not fearful," says Miranda to Prospero, warning him not to presume
too much on Ferdinand's patience.

When the Duke suggests that Isabel may yet be able to save her brother, she replies, "I have spirit to do any thing that appears not foul in the truth of my spirit." And now Isabel's critics disapprove of her because of the "businesslike" way in which she sets about saving her brother and assisting the Duke's plot. If Shakespeare's Jacobean audiences were as perverse as his modern critics, I can well understand how "gloom and dejection" may have driven the poor man "to the verge of madness," as critics assert that it did. That Shakespeare imagined Isabel as businesslike, should be clear to any one who studies with care her words in the earlier scenes. She is a sensible Elizabethan girl, with no nonsense about her, and she knows that it is no sin to bring husband and wife together.

So Mariana takes Isabel's place, to save Claudio's life.

Again, if Shakespeare meant us to regard Isabel cynically, why did he picture her not only as touching by her goodness both Angleo and the Duke, though to different issues, but even as aweing the frivolous Lucio into sobriety and sympathy? To Lucio she is "a thing ensky'd and sainted,"

> an immortal spirit;
> And to be talk'd with in sincerity,
> As with a saint.

Sir Arthur disqualifies Lucio's evidence because Lucio is a sensualist, and sensualists, he says, habitually divide women into angels and those who are "their animal prey." [21] Even if that be true, could Shakespeare seriously expect his audience to grasp such a subtlety? Critics see Isabel "hard as an icicle." [22] If Shakespeare meant that, why did he make Lucio see her differently: "O pretty Isabella, I am pale at mine heart to see thine eyes so red" IV. iii. 158. Even a sensualist can tell when people's eyes are red.

Angelo's own words make it clear that it is his conviction of the innocence and goodness of Isabel which overthrows him.

As for Claudio—the critics may despise him, but Angelo knows better. He knows that Claudio is a plucky lad who, "receiving a dishonour'd life with ransom of such shame," might take his revenge in time to come. So he commands Claudio's execution. The Duke, of course, prevents it, and continues to weave his toils round Angelo, till the moment when he will fall on him, and grind him to powder.

And, immediately, Angelo's remorse begins. He realizes what he really is: "This deed unshapes me quite." Yet his state is more gracious now, when he believes himself to be a perjured adulterer, than it was a few days before, when he believed himself to be a saint.

I pass over the agonies of Angelo's repentance. "Dull to all proceedings,"

[21] New Cambridge Shakespeare, p. xxvii.
[22] U. M. Ellis-Fermor, *op. cit.*, p. 262.

he fights to maintain all that is left him, the "credent bulk" of a public esteem which has become a mockery to him. When Lucio brings the struggle to an end, by tearing the Friar's hood off the Duke, Angelo realizes that his master is one from whom no secrets are hid:

> *Duke.*   Hast thou or word, or wit, or impudence,
> That yet can do thee office? . . .
> *Angelo.*   O my dread lord,
> I should be guiltier than my guiltiness,
> To think I can be undiscernible,
> When I perceive your Grace, like power divine,
> Hath looked upon my passes.

A cold-hearted, self-righteous prig is brought to a sense of what he is, in the sight of his Master. A few hours before, Angelo had turned a deaf ear to the plea "Why, all the souls that were, were forfeit once." But now he can conceive no depth of guilt so deep as his own, "Guiltier than my guiltiness." It is like the repentance of Enobarbus, "I am alone the villain of the earth," or of Posthumus,

> it is I
> That all the abhorred things o' the earth amend
> By being worse than they.

For Angelo, as for Enobarbus and for Posthumus, nothing remains save a passionate prayer to be put out of his misery:

> Then, good prince,
> No longer session hold upon my shame,
> But let my trial be mine own confession:
> Immediate sentence then, and sequent death,
> Is all the grace I beg.

Surely it is concerning repentance like this that it is written, "There is joy in the presence of the angels of God."

The ninety-and-nine just persons which need no repentance naturally think otherwise. Coleridge began the outcry against *Measure for Measure*, which he found most painful because, he said, cruelty, lust, and damnable baseness cannot be conceived as repented of or forgiven.[23] Swinburne endorsed this judgment at great length. Justice, he said, "is buffeted, outraged, insulted, struck in the face." "We are tricked out of our dole, defeated of our due, lured and led on to look for some equitable and satisfying upshot,

[23] *Notes on Shakespeare.*

defrauded and derided and sent empty away." [24] Hazlitt could not allow
Mariana to love Angelo "whom we hate." [25] To enumerate the ninety-six
other just persons would be to write a bibliography of *Measure for Measure*,
which is no part of my intention. Rather I turn to Mariana as she implores
pardon for her husband—a scene which Coleridge thought degrading to the
character of woman. Yet repentance, intercession, and forgiveness are the
stuff of Christianity and of the old stories of Christendom. In the story which
Calderon used, Cipriano, after selling himself to the Devil in order to win
Justina to his will, repents and dies a martyr at her side, comforted by her
words: "So many stars has not the Heaven, so many grains of sand the sea,
not so many sparks the fire, not so many motes the sunlight, as the sins which
He forgives."

But the Duke again and again rejects Mariana's plea for mercy. She turns
at last to Isabel:

> Sweet Isabel, take my part;
> Lend me your knees and all my life to come
> I'll lend you all my life to do you service.

Isabel stands silent.

A second time Mariana appeals:

> Isabel,
> Sweet Isabel, do yet but kneel by me;
> Hold up your hands, say nothing, I'll speak all.

Still Isabel stands silent, whilst Mariana pleads on pitifully:

> They say, best men are moulded out of faults;
> And, for the most, become much more the better
> For being a little bad: so may my husband.

At her third appeal,

> O Isabel, will you not lend a knee?

Isabel kneels at the feet of the Duke.

While Isabel is pleading for his life, Angelo is longing for death. Escalus
turns to him, regretting his fall. Angelo only says:

> I am sorry that such sorrow I procure:
> And so deep sticks it in my penitent heart,
> That I crave death more willingly than mercy;
> 'Tis my deserving, and I do entreat it.

[24] *Study of Shakespeare.*
[25] *Characters of Shakespeare's Plays.*

The wheel is come full circle.

Only two days before, Angelo had rejected the plea of mercy for Claudio with the words

> When I, that censure him, do so offend,
> Let mine own judgement pattern out my death.

And Isabel had longed for the potency of Angelo that she might "tell what 'twere to be a judge, and what a prisoner." Later we have seen Angelo "unshaped" by his remorse, though still confident that he will escape undetected, whilst Isabel longs to "pluck out his eyes," and is promised revenges to her heart on "this wretch" who has murdered her brother. And now Angelo, publicly shamed, longing for death, faces an Isabel who can bring herself to say, after an agony of silent struggle, "let him not die." It was not in a spirit of "weariness, cynicism, and disgust" that the Master Craftsman made the whirligig of time bring in revenges like these.

Isabel's sufferings are over. The muffled Claudio is brought in. Sister meets brother with that "prone and speechless dialect" which moves, or should move, men.

Sir Edmund Chambers asks, Why does the Duke conceal from Isabel in her grief the knowledge that her brother yet lives? Sir Walter Raleigh asked the same question thirty years ago. His answer was that the reason is dramatic; the crisis must be kept for the end. And, as a piece of stagecraft, the ending justifies itself; it is magnificent. But Sir Edmund Chambers is surely right when he says that a play dealing seriously with the problems of life must be taken seriously; the Duke, he thinks, symbolizes the workings of Providence. Is not such treatment of Providence, then, he asks, ironical?

The Duke certainly reminds us of the ways of Providence. And we feel so in the great final scene, where Mariana is imploring the silent Isabel to intercede for Angelo. Why, then, does the Duke gather up all his authority, as former Friar and present Monarch, and crash it, with a lie, in the path Isabel must tread?

> Should she kneel down in mercy of this fact,
> Her brother's ghost his paved bed would break,
> And take her hence in horror.

Yet all this time the Duke is keeping her brother in reserve, to produce him when Isabel shall have fulfilled her destiny, by making intercession for the man she most hates.

I can only reply that life undoubtedly *is* sometimes like that. There are some souls (Isabel is one) for whom it is decreed that no trial, however agonizing, no pain, however atrocious, is to be spared them. Nevertheless, it is also true that there is no trial so agonizing, no pain so atrocious, but that some souls can rise above it, as Isabel does when, despite the Duke's stern warning, she kneels at his feet to intercede for Angelo.

Is it then true, as Sir Arthur Quiller-Couch says, that Isabel writes no lesson on the dark walls, and that they teach none to her soul? Or is it true when Sir Edmund Chambers echoes the complaint of Coleridge, and says that *Measure for Measure* "just perplexes and offends," because there is no poetic justice? Is it true that "to no profit of righteousness has Isabella's white soul been dragged through the mire"?

I know that many readers find a stumbling block in this culminating scene, in Isabel's pleading for Angelo. Why should she plead, they ask, for her brother's murderer?

We must be prepared to accept the postulates of Shakespeare's plays, as we do, for example, of Sophocles' *Œdipus Tyrannus*. And, generally, we are so prepared: we accept the caskets and the pound of flesh, King Lear's love-test and Prospero's art. It is a postulate of our story that Claudio has committed a capital offence. Angelo has not committed a crime in letting the law take its course upon Claudio; he has not committed a crime in his union with Mariana, to whom he has been publicly betrothed; those are assumptions on which the play is based. Angelo would be despicable if he put forward any such plea for himself, and he does not. But the fact remains that Angelo's sin has been, not in act, but in thought, and human law cannot take cognizance of thought: "thoughts are no subjects." Besides, Isabel is conscious that, however innocently, she herself has been the cause of Angelo's fall:

> I partly think
> A due sincerity govern'd his deeds,
> Till he did look on me; since it is so,
> Let him not die.

And Angelo is penitent. There can be no doubt what the words of the Sermon on the Mount demand: "Judge not, and ye shall not be judged." That had been Isabel's plea for Claudio. It is a test of her sincerity, if she can put forward a plea for mercy for her dearest foe, as well as for him whom she dearly loves.

Criticism of *Measure for Measure*, from Coleridge downwards, has amounted to this: "There is a limit to human charity." "There is," says Chesterton's Father Brown, "and that is the real difference between human charity and Christian charity." Isabel had said the same:

> O, think on that;
> And mercy then will breathe within your lips
> Like man new made.

Shakespeare has so manipulated the story as to make it end in Isabel showing more than human charity to Angelo, whilst at the same time he was avoided, by the introduction of Mariana, the error, which he found in his crude original, of wedding Isabel to Angelo.

Is it then true that in *Measure for Measure* "the evidence of Shakespeare's profound disillusionment and discouragement of spirit is plain enough," that "the searchlight of irony is thrown upon the paths of Providence itself"?[26]

The way in which the Duke, an earthly Providence, tortures Isabel till he wrings her agonized forgiveness out of her, reminds us of the way in which, in Shakespeare's contemporary tragedies, Providence seems to ordain that no suffering is spared to Lear or Cordelia, to Othello or Desdemona. It is very terrible. But it cannot be called, as it often is called, un-Christian, when we observe how Lear and Othello, Cordelia and Desdemona rise "superior to the world in which they appear." [27] The last word on this has been said by that wise critic, A. C. Bradley:

> The extremity of the disproportion between prosperity and goodness first shocks us, and then flashes on us the conviction that our whole attitude in asking or expecting that goodness should be prosperous is wrong; that, if only we could see things as they are, we should see that the outward is nothing and the inward is all.[28]

This rather grim thought was, perhaps, better understood by the Englishmen of Shakespeare's day than it is now. Mr. Bettenham, Reader of Gray's Inn, was wont to say "that virtuous men were like some herbs and spices, that give not their sweet smell, till they be broken and crushed." And Francis Bacon, of the same Inn, put this doctrine into his essay *Of Adversity*, to show that "Prosperity is the blessing of the Old Testament; adversity is the blessing of the New, which carrieth the greater benediction, and the clearer revelation of God's favor."

And I heard A. E. Housman, who, of all men I have known, was sternest in refusing to break his proud reserve, say in his first lecture:

> Fortitude and continence and honesty are not commended to us on the ground that they conduce, as on the whole they do conduce, to material success, nor yet on the ground that they will be rewarded hereafter: those whose office it is to exhort mankind to virtue are ashamed to degrade the cause they plead by proffering such lures as these.

Forty-one years later, in his last great public utterance, in which he bade us "Farewell for ever," he quoted: "Whosoever will save his life shall lose it, and whosoever will lose his life shall find it." "That," he said, "is the most

---

[26] E. K. Chambers in the *Encyclopaedia Britannica* (1911), xxiv, p. 785.

[27] A. C. Bradley, *Shakespearean Tragedy*, p. 324.

[28] *Ibid.*, p. 326.

important truth which has ever been uttered, and the greatest discovery ever made in the moral world; but I do not find in it anything which I should call poetical."

Now it would take me altogether out of my depth, to discuss whether there is anything poetical in those words. But it can surely be contended that Shakespearian tragedy is an expression *in poetry* of that "most important truth which has ever been uttered." And so, equally, is *Measure for Measure* an expression of "the greatest discovery ever made in the moral world": the highly unpleasant discovery that there are things more important, for oneself and for others, than avoiding death and pain.

That, of course, is not a Christian discovery. One of the founders of modern Japan uttered it in two lines of Chinese verse, as he was led to execution, speaking with a loud voice, so that he might take farewell of his friend without implicating him by turning his head:

> It is better to be a crystal and be broken
> Than to remain perfect like a tile upon the housetop.

It is not Christian, but it is a foundation upon which Christianity, in common with every other religion worth the name, is built.

Measure for Measure is a play of forgiveness, more distinctly even than *The Tempest*. Isabel forgives in her moment of direst loss; Prospero only when he has recovered his Dukedom. Isabel urges forgiveness because a Christian must forgive; Prospero forgives because he does not condescend to torment his enemies further. And the contrast applies also to those forgiven. Angelo longs for death, because the Duke, *"like power divine,"* has seen his sinfulness. Sebastian and Antonio learn from Prospero, when he forgives them, that besides their crimes against him, he knows also how they have plotted to kill their king; to the pardoned Sebastian, just as to Angelo, there naturally seems to be something superhuman in such knowledge; but Sebastian expresses his conviction differently from Angelo:

> The devil speaks in him.

'No!' says Prospero; and then he turns to his brother Antonio:

> For you, most wicked Sir, whom to call brother
> Would even infect my mouth, I do forgive
> Thy rankest fault . . . .

Antonio makes no answer to this forgiveness. But he and Sebastian, unabashed, continue their joyless jests to the end.

Now, when we mark how evil, and its forgiveness, is depicted in *Measure for Measure* in 1604, can we agree that Shakespeare's philosophy about 1604 was "obviously not a Christian philosophy"? On the contrary, it seems to me

more definitely Christian than that of *The Tempest*, though I don't deny that
the philosophy of the Romances can also be called Christian. I would not
deny that, on the whole, Shakespeare's last plays *are* "happy dreams,"
"symbols of an optimistic faith in the beneficent dispositions of an ordering
Providence." [29] But I see no ground to believe that there is any "complete
breach" between the mood of 1604 and that of 1611, or that we must assume
a "conversion," caused by "a serious illness which may have been a nervous
breakdown, and on the other hand may have been merely the plague." [30]

We are told that the low-comedy characters of *Measure for Measure*
are "unwholesome company": that whereas Shakespeare, in Falstaff and
his associates, had represented sin as "human," he now represents it as
"devilish." [31] But is this really so? Surely the answer was given by Sir Walter
Raleigh years ago. These characters "are live men, pleasant to Shakespeare."
Pompey is "one of those humble, cheerful beings, willing to help in anything
that is going forward, who are the mainstay of human affairs. . . . Froth is an
amiable, feather-headed young gentleman—to dislike him would argue an
ill-nature, and a small one. . . . This world of Vienna, as Shakespeare paints
it, is not a black world; it is a weak world, full of little vanities and stupidities,
regardful of custom, fond of pleasure, idle, and abundantly human." [32]

As to Barnardine, his creator came to love him so much that he had not the
heart to decapitate him, although Barnardine was only created to be
decapitated.

In *Measure for Measure* sin is not represented as "devilish", it is represented
as sinful, and that is necessitated by the serious and earnest character of the
whole play. Yet there are few things funnier in all Shakespeare than Lucio
pouring his scandal about the Duke into the hooded ears of the Duke himself;
the poor Duke trying to keep his end up by giving himself a handsome testi-
monial as "a scholar, a statesman, and a soldier"; asking the name of his
libeler, and being told, "Lucio; well known to the Duke"; and at last frus-
trated when he tries to escape from his tormentor by Lucio's, "Nay, friar, I
am a kind of burr; I shall stick." And when the unmasked Duke finally taxes
Lucio with his slanders, he is not unequal to the occasion:

> Faith, my lord, I spoke it but according to the trick. If you will hang me for it,
> you may; but I had rather it would please you I might be whipt.

One of my women students once told me that her greatest regret over not
being born a man was that she could not act Lucio. I admit that the lady was
a greater ornament of the College Dramatic Society than of my lecture room,

---

[29] E. K. Chambers, in the *Encyclopaedia Britannica* (1911), xxiv, p. 785.
[30] E. K. Chambers, *William Shakespeare*, 1930, i, pp. 86, 274.
[31] E. K. Chambers, *Shakespeare: A Survey*, 1935, p. 211.
[32] *Shakespeare*, p. 166.

and that she ultimately left the University without taking a degree. When I last heard of her, she had entered the nursing profession, where I hope she will find scope for her generous and truly Shakespearian sympathy.

This, then, is how Shakespeare treats the barbarous old story of *Promos and Cassandra*, removing its morbid details, harmonizing its crudities, giving humanity and humor to its low characters, turning it into a consistent tale of intercession for sin, repentance from and forgiveness of crime. Yet *Measure for Measure* is adduced as the supreme proof that, about 1603, Shakespeare was in a mood of "self-laceration, weariness, discord, cynicism, and disgust." [33] He has been in that mood for the two years since the execution of Essex, and will remain in it for another four or five. This dominant mood of gloom and dejection will bring him on one occasion to the verge of madness, and lead him to write dramas greater than any other man ever wrote save Æschylus and Sophocles alone. Then in 1608 Sir Edmund Chambers will cure him of his seven years of "profound disillusionment and discouragement of spirit" by giving him either the plague, or (alternatively) a nervous breakdown.

I hear a gentle voice from Stratford murmur

Good frend, for Jesus sake forbeare.

Yet the critics have one final kick at *Measure for Measure*. More Papistical than the Pope, they feel outraged that Isabel should "throw her novitiate headdress over the mill" [34] and marry the Duke. Even the sober A. C. Bradley thought that here Shakespeare lent himself to "a scandalous proceeding." [35] Yet Isabel is a novice, and her business as a novice is to learn her Creator's intentions for her future. Whether she ought to return to the cloister from which she has been so urgently summoned rests with her creator— William Shakespeare. And he leaves her silent, and us guessing. For myself, I am satisfied that Isabel will do her duty in that state of life unto which it shall please William Shakespeare to call her, whether as abbess or duchess.

Yet in Shakespeare's greatest plays, his greatest characters, for all their individuality, have also an imaginative, a symbolic suggestion. It is so in *The Tempest*, it is so in *Hamlet*. Thus also in the person of Lear, not only a helpless old man, but Paternity and Royalty are outraged; and "Glamis hath murder'd Sleep." No woman in Shakespeare is more individual than Isabel: silent yet eloquent, sternly righteous yet capable of infinite forgiveness, a very saint and a very vixen. But, first and last, she "stands for"

[33] J. Dover Wilson, *op. cit.*, p. 117.
[34] New Cambridge Shakespeare, p. xxxi.
[35] *Shakespearean Tragedy*, p. 78.

mercy.[36] The Duke is shown to us as a governor perplexed about justice, puzzled in his search for righteousness, seeking above all things to know himself. Is it altogether fanciful to remember once again that *Measure for Measure* was acted before the court at Christmas, 1604, that when Isabel at the beginning urges her plea for mercy (which she also makes good at the end) it is on the ground that

> He that might the vantage best have took
> Found out the remedy.

The day before *Measure for Measure* was acted, the finding out of that remedy was being commemorated. All sober criticism must remember the part which the accepted theology played in the thought of Shakespeare's day; that the Feast of the Nativity was—is—the union of Divine Mercy and of Divine Righteousness, and was—is—celebrated in the Christmas psalm:

> Mercy and truth are met together: righteousness and peace have kissed each other.

Shakespeare's audience expected a marriage at the end; and, though it may be an accident, the marriage of Isabel and the Duke makes a good ending to a Christmas play.

[36] This does not make her allegorical, any more than Beowulf is an allegory because, as W. P. Ker says, he "stands for" valor.

The "Meaning" of *Measure for Measure*

by *Clifford Leech*

The nineteen-twenties, distrustful of "enthusiasm," strove to see Shakespeare as above all the practical dramatist, led to the choice and the manipulation of his stories, to his manner of theatrical speech and character-presentation, by the stage-conditions of his time and the passing fashion of dramatic taste. This approach strengthened our understanding of Elizabethan stage technique, and it was a useful corrective to the heavily romanticized Shakespeare of earlier years. But when the student of stage-conditions set up as the complete interpreter, the limitations of the approach were obvious enough. The poetic and the dramatic power were only foster children of the industrious apprenticeship to the stage: the heart of the matter was not to be weighed in a Shakespeare laboratory.

The realization that the greatness of the poet lies, partly at least, in the scope of his mind has led in recent years to a close study of the ideas communicated through the plays. We now tend to see the histories as dramatic essays on a political theme, the final romances as embodiments of religious truth. Even the tragedies are dredged for underlying "meanings." But in one characteristic these searchers for theses do not differ from the stage-conditions men of a generation ago. They, too, emphasize the Elizabethanism of Shakespeare, and relate the significance of his plays to the general current of Elizabethan thought on political and religious themes. In the two tetralogies, we are told, Shakespeare speaks after the fashion of Halle and the Homilies; in the romances he is at one with the Christian attitude, adding—as G. Wilson Knight has it[1]—his *Paradiso* to complete the structure of his collected works. And Miss Elizabeth M. Pope, in her article on "The Renaissance Background of *Measure for Measure*," [2] has set out to demonstrate that Shakespeare's handling of this dark comedy gives a thoughtful examination of the Christian views of justice and pardon. If we accept these interpretations

"The Meaning of *Measure for Measure*." From *Shakespeare Survey 3* (Cambridge University Press, 1950), pp. 66-73. Reprinted by permission of the author, the editor, and the publishers.

[1] *The Crown of Life* (1947), p. 30.
[2] *Shakespeare Survey*, II (1949), 66-82.

unreservedly, we may see Shakespeare as the superb expositor of his age's thought, but perhaps we shall be giving both to the Shakespeare plays and to the Elizabethan age a consistency of texture that they can hardly claim. Historically it was a time of important social transition, and the birth pangs of the new order often induced doubt of old premise and new practice: the Homilies are of necessity orthodox, but we would do violence to *Tamburlaine* to interpret it exclusively in their light; Chapman's tragedies and Jonson's comedies are the products of independent minds, ever ready to scrutinize an accepted code; in *Troilus and Cressida* the traditional values of Hector and Ulysses are seen as unavailing in a world given over to disorder. If, then, we are to think of Shakespeare as the dramatic champion of the Tudor supremacy and the Anglican Church, we must recognize that this makes him, not the complete Elizabethan, but the sturdy partisan.

Yet it would appear particularly strange for Shakespeare's plays to be the embodiments of theses. In all matters of detail we find contradictions between one part of a play and another: the time-schemes are hardly ever consistently worked out; the manner of the dialogue may be rhetorical, intimate, sententious, euphuistic, compact, staccato, orotund, facetious, according to the particular demands of the individual scene; the statement of one passage may be at odds with others in the play, as with the differing accounts of Ophelia's death, the riddle of Macbeth's children, and Prospero's claim that he has raised men from the dead on his enchanted isle. Of course we can argue that contradictory time-schemes will fuse in the theatre, that the style in the best plays brings diversity into unity, and that incidental contradictions of statement will go unnoticed by an audience under a poet's spell. It remains significant that there are these discrepancies, for they may lead us to expect to find contradictory "meanings" juxtaposed in the plays, to see the ending of *Macbeth* as simultaneously the destruction of a brave spirit and the reassertion of a political and moral order. In fact, when Shakespeare wrote *Macbeth*, he was thinking with part of his mind in the fashion of the Homilies, and at the same time he conveyed something of Seneca's concern with the individual's destiny, something of Euripides' cosmic challenge. For this reason, perhaps, *Macbeth* and the other tragedies leave us uneasy, in suspense. If we can, we shall escape from our uneasiness by disregarding certain parts of the dramatic statement, we shall claim *Macbeth* as first cousin either to *Gorboduc* or to *Jude the Obscure*, according as the fashion of the moment and our personal inclinations may lead us. But to escape in either direction is to do violence to the play.

In Miss Pope's account of *Measure for Measure* we have, I think, a corresponding simplification. Her relation of certain utterances in the play to Elizabethan statements of Christian doctrine does indubitably throw light on those utterances, and on the strands in the play's thought and feeling that they represent. But the total impression she leaves with us hardly coheres

with the effect produced by the play in the theatre or when read as a whole.
We are disturbed by it, not because its Christian doctrine is strict and uncompromising—as we may be disturbed by François Mauriac or Graham
Greene—but because the very spokesmen for orthodoxy in the play repel us
by their actions and the manner of their speech: they are not too hard for us,
but rather too shifty, too complacant, too ignorant of their own selves, and
for these failings they are nowhere explicitly reproved. That there is a
Christian coloring in the play Miss Pope has securely demonstrated, particularly in the prayer of Isabella for Angelo's life and in the ultimate transcendence of justice by mercy. But this Christian coloring is, I hope to show,
not more than intermittent in the play: it wells up, as it were, from Shakespeare's unconscious inheritance, and it does not determine the play's
characteristic effect.

   We should note first of all that *Measure for Measure* is not free from those
incidental contradictions of statement that are to be found in almost all of
Shakespeare's plays. Dover Wilson has observed gross inconsistency in the
time-references and has drawn attention to the way in which Mistress
Overdone in I, ii first tells Lucio and the others of Claudio's imprisonment
and immediately afterwards, in her talk with Pompey, displays ignorance of
it.[3] A much more serious puzzle is provided by the Duke's statements about
Angelo in different parts of the play. In I. i. the Duke is presumably serious
in his profession of trust in Angelo. If he were not, the appointment of
Angelo would be inexcusable. Moreover, he professes that Angelo's high
character is fully manifest:

>   There is a kind of character in thy life,
>   That to th' observer doth thy history
>   Fully unfold;

and he adds that such merit should not go unused. Yet, in his conversation
with Friar Thomas, the Duke is by no means so sure: part of his object in
deserting his post and turning spy is to find out whether Angelo is all that he
appears:

>   Lord Angelo is precise;
>   Stands at a guard with envy; scarce confesses
>   That his blood flows, or that his appetite
>   Is more to bread than stone: hence shall we see,
>   If power change purpose, what our seemers be.   (I. iii. 50-4)

We will not stay to consider whether, in view of these suspicions, the appointment of Angelo should have been made. In III. i. however, the Duke professes
himself amazed at Angelo's fall from grace:

---

[3] New Cambridge edition (1922), pp. 99-100.

but that frailty hath examples for his falling, I should wonder at Angelo;

and then, some forty lines later, tells Isabella of Angelo's former relations with Mariana. We should in particular note the Duke's assertion that Angelo, wishing to escape from his dowerless bride, pretended "in her discoveries of dishonor." His past conduct is, in fact, here presented as so infamous that Isabella is moved to cry:

> What corruption in this life, that it will let this man live!

Yet the Duke knew all this long before, we must assume. Not only, therefore, does Angelo's appointment reflect on the Duke, but we must find Shakespeare curiously engaged in deceiving his spectators: we have been led to believe that Angelo was honest in his puritanism, was convinced of his own strength against temptation, was horrified when Isabella was used to bait vice's hook. It is difficult to see how even a revision-theory could explain these inconsistencies. Rather it seems likely that, as so often, it was the immediate situation that primarily engaged Shakespeare's attention.

If that is the case, however, should we expect to find consistency of thought and feeling through the play? Are we to try to reconcile the deeply Christian cry of Isabella:

> Why, all the souls that were were forfeit once;
> And He that might the vantage best have took,
> Found out the remedy;   (II. ii. 73-5)

with the Duke's speech on death in III.i? In this connexion we should remember that, though Miss Pope will not accept Roy Battenhouse's view of the Duke as representing "the Incarnate Lord," she does see him as the good ruler, doing God's work and moving through the play as "an embodied Providence." [4] Yet, despite his Friar's gown, the Duke offers no hint of Christian consolation: Claudio must welcome death because there is no real joy to be found in life: he denies even personality itself:

> Thou art not thyself;
> For thou exist'st on many a thousand grains
> That issue out of dust.

Man, he says, is not master of his own mind:

> Thou art not certain;
> For thy complexion shifts to strange effects,
> After the moon.

And there could hardly be a more dreadful or more sober denunciation of human lovelessness than we are offered here:

[4] *Op. cit.* p. 71.

> Friend hast thou none;
> For thine own bowels, which do call thee sire,
> The mere effusion of thy proper loins,
> Do curse the gout, serpigo, and the rheum,
> For ending thee no sooner.

We can, of course, see the dramatic reason for this speech. It provides the thesis to which Claudio's shrinking from death is the antithesis. But it cleaves too near the bone to be regarded as a mere dramatic convenience. We have to recognize that the ideas in the speech reverberated in Shakespeare's own mind, that they could coexist with echoes of redemption and of a human as well as divine forgiveness.

The Duke, ultimately the dispenser of pardon, has something of Prospero's magisterial place and nature, is indeed at certain moments a morality-figure, a god out of the playwright's pigeonhole. G. Wilson Knight assures us that "Like Prospero, the Duke tends to assume proportions evidently divine," [5] while W. W. Lawrence argues that the Duke is but "a stage Duke," a mere instrument in the play's economy.[6] Both these judgments, however, overlook the strong antipathy which the Duke has aroused in many readers during the past hundred years. The contrast between Wilson Knight's view and that, for example, of H. C. Hart[7] suggests an ambivalence in the character, a contradiction between its dramatic function and the human qualities implied by its words and actions. As F. P. Wilson has briefly shown, the character's morality-outline cannot be preserved in a play where other characters are as fully realized as Isabella, Angelo, Claudio, and Lucio.[8]

Raleigh pointed out how the Duke plays at cat-and-mouse with Angelo in the last act,[9] and indeed his supreme indifference to human feelings is as persistent a note as any in the play. In II. iii. he catechizes Juliet, and in bidding her farewell casually breaks the news of Claudio's imminent execution:

> Your partner, as I hear, must die to-morrow,
> And I am going with instruction to him.
> Grace go with you! *Benedicite!*

We should note perhaps that as yet there is no hint that the Duke will interfere with the sentence: he has no criticism of Angelo's severity to make here, and in IV. ii. he insists that the sentence would be unjust only if Angelo fell short of the standards he is imposing on others. If, however, we are to assume that the Duke undergoes a "conversion" which brings him to the exercise of

---

[5] *The Wheel of Fire* (1930), p. 87.
[6] *Shakespeare's Problem Comedies* (1931), pp. 104-5.
[7] Arden edition (1905), pp. xxii-xxiii.
[8] *Elizabethan and Jacobean* (1945), p. 118.
[9] *Shakespeare* (English Men of Letters), ed. 1939, p. 158.

mercy, we should be given some clear token of this in the play: as things stand, it appears as if the Duke pardons because he has not the strength to be severe and because he enjoys the contriving of a last-minute rescue. He is indeed like Prospero in this, who pretends sorrow for Alonso's loss of his son, and then extracts a stage manager's thrill from the sudden discovery that Ferdinand is safe. When Lucio refers to "the old fantastical duke of dark corners," he gives us a phrase that our memories will not let go: it comes, too, most appropriately in IV. iii, just after the Duke has told us that he will proceed against Angelo "By cold gradation and well-balanc'd form" and has informed Isabella that Claudio is dead. Of course, he gives us a reason for this behavior: Isabella shall have "heavenly comforts of despair, When it is least expected," but this implies an odd principle of conduct, which we should challenge even in "an embodied Providence." Indeed, it appears that there is nothing the Duke can do directly. After he has spied on the interview between Isabella and her brother in III. i. he tells Claudio that Angelo has merely been testing Isabella's virtue: one can see no reason for this beyond the Duke's love of misleading his subjects. Having, moreover, hit upon the Mariana-plan, he still urges Claudio to expect immediate death. We should note, too, that he claims to know Angelo's mind by virtue of being Angelo's confessor. One does not have to be deeply religious to be affronted by this piece of impertinence, but later we find that the Duke takes a special delight in the confessor's power which his disguise gives him: in Angelo's case he doubtless lied, but in IV. ii. he is prepared to shrive Barnardine immediately before execution and in the last speech in the play he recommends Mariana to Angelo as one who has confessed to him. We have reason to believe that the home of Shakespeare's childhood was one in which the old religion was adhered to:[10] be that as it may, however, it is difficult to believe that he could look with favor on a man who deceived a condemned criminal with a pretence of priestly power and who tricked Mariana into giving him her confidence.[11]

But mystification is his ruling passion. He sends "letters of strange tenour" to Angelo, hinting at his own death or retreat into a monastery (IV. ii); he gives Angelo a sense of false security at the beginning of v. i, announcing:

> We have made inquiry of you; and we hear
> Such goodness of your justice, that our soul
> Cannot but yield you forth to public thanks,
> Forerunning more requital.

[10] Cf. J. H. de Groot, *The Shakespeares and 'The Old Faith'* (1946).
[11] W. W. Lawrence, *op. cit.* p. 105, is at pains to convince us that the Duke did not confess Angelo, but he does not consider the implications of his exercise of priestly function with Mariana and (in intention) with Barnardine.

Then he orders Isabella to prison, calls Mariana "thou pernicious woman," and then, in his Friar's disguise, tells them both that their cause is lost. Later he laments with Isabella that he was not able to hinder Claudio's death:

> O most kind maid!
> It was the swift celerity of his death,
> Which I did think with slower foot came on,
> That brain'd my purpose.

Apart from considerations of common decency and kindness, we must assume at this point that Isabella is a woman he loves. Later he pretends to discharge the Provost for beheading Claudio, though here presumably only the standers-by were deceived.

It may be argued that we are taking the last act too seriously, that here, as Raleigh put it, we have "mere plot, devised as a retreat, to save the name of Comedy." [12] Indeed, there is evidence that Shakespeare's mind was not working at full pressure in this part of the play: Isabella tells Mariana in iv. vi. that the Friar may "speak against me on the adverse side": this he does not do and we may assume that then writing iv. vi. Shakespeare had not fully worked out the conduct of the final scene. Nevertheless, the stage-managing Duke of v. i. is of a piece with the man we have seen eavesdropping and contriving throughout the play. But now he forsakes his "dark corners," focuses the light on himself as Richard did at Conventry, gives pardon to all, even to Escalus for being shocked at the Friar's seeming impudence, and promises himself an added delight in further discourse of his adventures.

We should not forget in this last scene that the Duke is still outraged by the manner of Viennese life. Speaking as the Friar, he puts forward the same view as at the beginning of the play:

> My business in this state
> Made me a looker-on here in Vienna,
> Where I have seen corruption boil and bubble
> Till it o'er-run the stew: laws for all faults,
> But faults so countenanc'd, that the strong statutes
> Stand like the forfeits in a barber's shop,
> As much in mock as mark.   (v. i. 318-24)

Apart from his desire to spy on Angelo, his whole object in abandoning his ducal function was that the law should be exercised with greater rigor; yet at the end all are forgiven—except Lucio, whose punishment is grotesque rather than stern—and it would seem inequitable to discriminate between Barnardine and Mistress Overdone. But perhaps at the end, like the Duke

[12] *Op. cit.* p. 169.

himself, we forget Vienna and the governmental function: it may be that a *coup de théâtre* should not supply a legal precedent.

There is, moreover, something odd in the relations between the Duke and Lucio. Miss Pope, in exalting the Duke's ultimate dispensation of mercy, says that Lucio has to make amends "to the girl he has wronged." [13] This is a sententious way of putting it, for Shakespeare seems to take it much less seriously: in III. ii. Mistress Overdone gives us the lady's name, and "wronging" seems too romantic a term for Lucio's association with her. Our reaction to the Duke's punishment of the one man he could not forgive is compounded of amusement at Lucio's discomfiture and astonishment at the intensity of the Duke's spite. When Lucio protests against the sentence, the Duke's reply is "Slandering a prince deserves it": this is a different matter from righting a wrong done to Mistress Kate Keepdown. Before that, I think, most readers and spectators have frankly enjoyed Lucio's baiting of the Friar. Not only do his words "old fantastical duke of dark corners" bite shrewdly, but it is amusing to see how the Friar tries in vain to shake Lucio off when he is garrulous concerning the Duke's misdemeanors. Critics, searching for ethical formulations, are apt to forget that in the theatre the low life of Vienna and Lucio's persevering wit can arouse our sympathetic laughter.[14] And because we have earlier tended to side with Lucio against the Duke, we are amused when the Duke is petulant at Lucio's interruptions in the final scene. As for the judgment, we may remind ourselves as we hear it that, about this time, Shakespeare wrote in *Lear* of a judge and a condemned thief who might exchange places.

But much in this play seems to provide a comment on the administration of justice. The law's instruments include Abhorson, Elbow, and, as a recruit from the stews, Pompey: their combined efforts take something away from the law's majesty. During Shakespeare's middle years he made much use of trial scenes and other ceremonial unravellings. There is the Venetian court in *The Merchant of Venice*, the dismissal of Falstaff by the newly crowned Prince in 2 *Henry IV*, the King's putting of things to rights in *All's Well*, and the Duke's similar exercise of his function in this play. In each instance the sentence given can be justified; some clemency is allowed to mitigate the letter of the law; the way is cleared for the return of common conditions. And yet in every case our feeling is hardly of complete satisfaction. Shylock, Falstaff, Lucio arouse some resentment on their behalf, and we have little pleasure in the assertion of the law. It is frequently argued that we are too sensitive in our attitude to these victims of justice, and Miss Pope[15] suggests that Shakespeare's first audience would have been at least as well contented

[13] *Op. cit.* p. 80.
[14] Raleigh, *op. cit.* p. 166, is here as so often an exception.
[15] *Op. cit.* p. 79.

if Angelo, Lucio and Barnardine had been, like Shylock, punished severely. But perhaps the attitude of the audience is not so necessary to an understanding of Shakespeare's purpose as his own attitude must be, and it is in *Measure for Measure* that we are given one of the clearest statements of his wide-reaching sympathy: Isabella herself reminds us that

> the poor beetle, that we tread upon,
> In corporal sufferance finds a pang as great
> As when a giant dies.   (III. i. 79-81)

We may remember too that Barnardine, a convicted malefactor, seems to be introduced into the play for the sake of providing a substitute for Claudio's head: that he is not executed and that Ragozine dies so conveniently would suggest that Shakespeare could feel the horror of execution in the case of the common ruffian as well as in that of the gentlemanly, merely imprudent Claudio. It would be dangerous to base a judgment of Shakespeare's purpose on the assumption that his feelings were less fine than ours.[16]

No more than the other plays incorporating "trial scenes" is *Measure for Measure* to be interpreted as a dramatic satire. It is indeed the overt purpose of the play to demonstrate, as Miss Pope has suggested, a governor's duty to practice mercy, to requite evil with forgiveness or with the gentler forms of punishment. Even the Duke's cat-and-mouse tricks with Claudio and Angelo may be justified as the mitigated punishment for their wrongdoing. Miss Pope has judiciously drawn attention to the Duke's soliloquy at the end of Act III, where in gnomic octosyllabics he speaks with chorus-like authority:[17] here, indeed, the morality-element in the play is uppermost, and Wilson Knight has noted the resemblance of these lines to the theophanic utterances of the last plays.[18] But, as so often with Shakespeare, the play's "meaning" is not to be stated in the terms of a simple thesis: there are secondary as well as primary meanings to be taken into account, and the secondary meanings may largely determine the play's impact. We can see 2 *Henry IV* as a play with a morality-outline, with the Prince tempted by disorder and finally won over to the side of Royalty. At the same time, that play seems a dramatic essay on the theme of mutability, with sick fancies, the body's diseases, senile memories, and lamentations for a lost youth constitut-

---

[16] Even with the trick of the substituted bed-fellow, we should not too readily argue that its frequency in earlier literature would make it acceptable to Shakespeare. It is noticeable that the Duke broaches the subject with some hesitation and seems to anticipate opposition from Isabella. He has, indeed, to suggest that the end justifies a doubtful means: "If you think well to carry this, as you may, the doubleness of the benefit defends the deceit from reproof. What think you of it?" Isabella's quick assent is in sharp contrast to the Duke's laborious persuasions.

[17] *Op. cit.* p. 73.

[18] *The Wheel of Fire*, p. 87.

ing its lines of structure. And we can see it, too, as part of the great historical design, of the chain of actions that led from Gloucester's murder to Bosworth Field. There is a satiric element as well, which appears uppermost when Prince John teaches us not to trust the word of a noble, and which is perhaps latent in Falstaff's rejection scene.

It is this complexity of meaning that makes it possible for us to see and read these plays so often, that enables the theatrical producer to aim at a new "interpretation." We are tempted always to extract a meaning, and the undertaking may be profitable if it leads us to inquire into the bases of Elizabethan thought and does not limit our perception to those things in the play that are easy to fit in place. In *Measure for Measure* in particular we should be careful of imposing a pattern on Shakespeare's thought, for the silence of Isabella in the last hundred lines suggests either a corrupt text or a strange heedlessness of the author. But we should always be ready for the by-paths which Shakespeare's thoughts and feelings may take at any moment of a play. If we would penetrate into his state of mind during the composition of *Measure for Measure,* we should not, I think, overlook the name he gave to Claudio's young mistress[19] and the light thrown on Isabella's childhood when she cries that she would rather think her mother a strumpet than her father Claudio's begetter. Shakespeare cannot have forgotten an earlier Juliet when he used her name again, and the words of Isabella illuminate her cult of chastity. In our search for the play's "meaning," we should not neglect these hints of a suppressed but deep sympathy with Juliet and of an almost clinically analytic approach to Isabella. In *Measure for Measure* we have a morality-framework, much incidental satire, a deep probing into the springs of action, a passionate sympathy with the unfortunate and the hard-pressed. Only if we concentrate our attention on one of these aspects will the play leave us content.

[19] In Whetstone her name is Polina.

Virtue Is the True Nobility:

A Study of the Structure of *All's Well that Ends Well*

by M. C. Bradbrook

All's Well that Ends Well might have as its subtitle "Two Plays in One." In this article I shall be concerned with one of the plays only—the play that is revealed by the structure and the plot. Such a partial and one-sided approach is justified because, I believe, it reveals the governing idea[1] of the whole composition. This is perhaps a dangerous assumption, for

> in attempting to isolate the idea that governs a play we run the risk of fixing it and deadening it, especially when the idea discerned is expressed as a philosophical proposition and stated in a sentence or two.[2]

The governing idea of this particular play is one which I believe belongs rather to Shakespeare's age than to all time. To display it therefore requires what may seem a humorless and over-detailed study of the background of ideas. The method by which the idea is presented is not quite Shakespeare's usual one, though not unlike that discerned by modern critics elsewhere in his work.[3] No one could dare to suggest that Shakespeare took a moral idea and dressed it up in human terms; yet the allegorical mode of thought and the conception that literature should promote good actions were still very much alive in his day. They were not secure.[4] Shakespeare himself, in that period of the mid-nineties when he more or less has the stage to himself —the period between the death of Marlowe and the arrival of Jonson— transformed the conception of dramatic art and produced those ripe and humane works which for ever made impossible such plays as Robert Wilson's.

The modern reader of *All's Well*—"the new Cambridge production is the first for many years"—may feel that the play contains one superb character

"Virtue Is the True Nobility." From *The Review of English Studies*, XXVI (1950), pp. 298-301. Reprinted by permission of the author and the Clarendon Press.
[1] See Nevill Coghill, "The Governing Idea, Essays in the Interpretation of Shakespeare—I," *Shakespeare's Quarterly*, i (1948), pp. 9-16.

[2] Coghill, *loc. cit.*

[3] E.g. Tillyard, Rossiter, Bethell, Danby.

[4] Cf. Rosemary Freeman, *English Emblem Books* (London, 1948), pp. 19-22.

study, that of Bertram; and at least one speech of great poetic power, Helena's confession to the Countess. Seen through Helena's eyes Bertram is handsome, brave, "the glass of fashion and the mould of form": seen through the eyes of the older characters he is a degenerate son, an undutiful subject, a silly boy. The two images blend in the action, as we see him sinking from irresponsibility to deceit, but making a name for himself in the wars. He ends in an abject position, yet Helena's devotion continues undiminished. Her medieval counterpart, patient Griselda, whose virtues are passive, is not called on for more than obedience,[5] and the audience need not stop to wonder what kind of a person the Marquis could be, whether such barbarity could be justified as an assay of virtue, and how the final revelation could leave his wife with any palate for his company. As a character, he exists only to demonstrate Griselda's patience. But Bertram is not "blacked out" in this way. The connection of his character and Helena's feelings with the general theme can be explained, but they are not identified with it.

In *All's Well* the juxtaposition of the social problem of high birth versus native merit and the human problem of unrequited love recalls the story of the Sonnets; the speeches of Helena contain echoes from the Sonnets,[6] but the story to which her great speeches are loosely tied does not suit their dramatic expression. It illustrates the nature of social distinctions, of which the personal situation serves only as example. It might be hazarded that this first tempted Shakespeare, who then found himself saying more, or saying other, than his purely structural purpose could justify. Helena's speech to the Countess is the poetic center of the play, but the structural center is the King's judgment on virtue and nobility. For once, the dramatist and the poet in Shakespeare were pulling different ways. *All's Well that Ends Well* expresses in its title a hope that is not fulfilled; all did not end well, and it is not a successful play.

My contention is that *All's Well* fails because Shakespeare was trying to write a moral play, a play which he proposed to treat with the gravity proper, for example, to "a moral history." [7] He was not writing allegorically but his characters have a symbolic and extra-personal significance. To write such a play the writer must be detached and in complete control of his material; and Shakespeare was not happy when he was theorizing. Here he is not driven to bitter or cynical or despairing comment on the

[5] Helena shows herself similarly passive in her two scenes as wife (II. iv, v). Unlike Parolles, she calls Bertram her "master," both before and after marriage (I. iii. 166, III. iv. 9).

[6] Helena's three great speeches (I. i. 91-110, I. iv. 199-225, III. ii. 102-32) have a number of parallels with the sonnets, especially the second of the three. Cf. Sonnets xxvi, lvii, lviii, lxxxvii. The way in which Bertram is condemned recalls also the plain speaking which is so unusual a feature of the Sonnets (e.g. xxxv, lxvii, lxxxii, lxxxiv, xcv, xcvi).

[7] A term defined by A. P. Rossiter in his edition of *Woodstock* (London, 1948): roughly, a chronicle history built on a moral theme.

filth that lies below the surface of life. Instead of the stews of Vienna, the activities of Pandarus and Thersites, we have the highly moral comments of the young Lords on Bertram. Yet compared with *Measure for Measure*—to which it is most closely linked by similarities of plot[8]—the play appears more confused in purpose, more drab and depressing, if less squalid. Both are concerned with what Bacon called Great Place; the one with the nature and use of power, the other with the nature and grounds of true nobility. The characters are occasionally stiffened into types: the King becomes *Vox Dei*, which means that he is merely a voice. Yet at other times, but chiefly in soliloquy, deep personal feeling breaks through. Angelo's temptations and Helena's love are not completely adjusted to the stories which contain them. These feelings burst out irrepressibly, and in a sense irrelevantly, though they are the best things in the plays.

To compare *Measure for Measure* with its source play, *Promos and Cassandra*, is to see the shaping process of imagination at work: to compare *All's Well* with Painter's translation of Boccaccio is at least revealing.[9] The alterations are perfectly consistent, tending to greater dependence, humility, and enslavement on Helena's part and greater weakness and falsehood on Bertram's. New characters are added to voice Helena's claims to virtue and dignity— this is the chief purpose of the Countess, Lafeu, and the additions to the King's part—while others are created to stigmatize Bertram. An outline of Painter will make this clear.

Giletta of Narbonne is brought up with Beltramo and several other children; though not noble she is rich, and refuses many suitors for love of him. After his departure she waits some time—years are implied—before following him, and she sees him before she seeks the King. The conditions of her bargain are that she cures the King in eight days or she offers to be burnt, the King spontaneously adding that he will give her a husband if she succeeds. She asks the right to choose and, somewhat to the royal chagrin, names Beltramo. The King almost apologizes to the firmly protesting Count, but pleads that he has given his royal word. After the wedding Giletta goes to Rossiglione, puts the estate in order, tells the people the whole story and goes away openly with a kinsman and a good deal of treasure. She reaches Florence, ferrets out Beltramo's mistress, plans the substitution and eventually gives birth to twin sons. At her leisure she returns, and entering on a day

---

[8] E.g. the rejection of a devoted bride for insufficiency, and a compelled marriage ordered by the ruler: the substitution of one woman for another: the false self-accusation of the chaste woman, followed by prolonged lying from the culprit, culminating in his exposure through the arrival of an absent person: the slanderer who speaks ill of his lord and is unmasked in public.

[9] William Painter, *The Palace of Pleasure* (1566), contains as the xxxviii novel the story of "Giletta a phisition's doughter of Narbon," the orignal being Boccaccio, *Il Decamerone*, III. ix. The subject of the relations of *All's Well* to its sources is, I understand, being considered in detail by Professor H. G. Wright.

of feast, presents her two sons; Beltramo, to honor his word, and to please his subjects and the ladies, his guests who make suit to him, receives her as his wife.

These shrewd, unsentimental, vigorous Italians, who come to terms after a brisk skirmish, resemble Benedick and Beatrice rather than their own Shakespearian descendants. Two principal characters, the Countess and Parolles, have been added by Shakespeare, and two lesser ones, Lafeu and the Fool. The climaxes are heightened, and in the last scene Bertram is in danger of the law.[10] Shakespeare's hero is a very young man, highly conscious of his birth. He is handsome, courageous in battle, winning in manners: he is also an inveterate liar.

The Elizabethan code of honor supposed a gentleman to be absolutely incapable of a lie. In law his word without an oath was in some places held to be sufficient.[11] To give the lie was the deadliest of all insults and could not be wiped out except in blood. Honor was irretrievably lost only by lies or cowardice. These were more disgraceful than any crimes of violence. Alone among Shakespeare's heroes Bertram is guilty of the lie. Claudio, in *Much Ado*, is clear, and Bassanio, though he thinks of a lie to get himself out of an awkward situation at the end of the play, does not utter it. By such conduct Bertram forfeits his claims to gentility: a gentleman, as Touchstone remembered, swore by his troth, as a knight by his honor.[12] For this he is shamed and rebuked openly, not only by his elders but by his contemporaries and even by his inferiors.[13] The feelings of a modern audience towards Claudio or Bassanio may be due to a change in social standards, but Bertram is roundly condemned.

The fault, however, is not entirely his, for like Richard II, Prince Hal, and all other great ones in search of an excuse, he can shelter behind ill company. Parolles, or Wordy, a character of Shakespeare's own invention, is perceived in the end by Bertram himself to be the Lie incarnate. From the beginning the Countess had known him as

> a verie tainted fellow, and full of wickednesse,
> My sonne corrupts a well-derived nature
> With his inducement   (III. ii. 90-2)

[10] Bertram's own lies cause this, and the exposure of his treatment of Diana. Her use in this scene is entirely Shakespeare's own invention, and much increases the melodrama. Helena in Act II also increases the tension by offering to have her name traduced as a strumpet if she fails to cure the King, and by cutting down the period required from eight days to two.

[11] R. Kelso, *The Doctrine of the English Gentleman* (Urbana, 1929), p. 78.

[12] *As You Like It*, I. ii. Cf. Mulcaster, *Positions* (reprinted London, 1898), p. 198.

[13] E.g. IV. ii. 11-30 where Diana, who is perhaps his social equal, being descended from the ancient Capilet, rebukes him; IV. iii. 1-30, where the young Lords criticize him. Parolles's sonnet contains some nasty home truths: in the last scene the King and Lafeu are quite uncompromising. Bertram's word is not to be trusted (v. iii. 184-6).

whilst Helena describes him before he appears as "a notorious Liar," "a great way foole, solie a coward." It is not till the final scene that Bertram too acknowledges him　　　·

> a most perfidious slave . . .
> Whose nature sickens: but to speake a truth.　　　(v. iii. 207-9)

In the earlier part of the play he is completely gulled by Parolles, who gains his ends by flattery. To the Elizabethan, the flatterer was the chief danger of noble youth, and his ways were exposed in most of the manuals of conduct. In Stefano Guazzo's *Civile Conversation*, a book of manners designed for the lesser nobility, much of Book II is taken up with the subject. Shakespeare in his comedy makes little use of the figure of the flatterer, and this differentiates him from Chapman, Jonson, and Middleton, who took the parasite of ancient comedy and furnished him with the latest tricks of the coney-catcher. Falstaff is in some sense a flatterer, but he is never more deceived than when he thinks to govern his sweet Hal.[14]

Flattery thrives on detraction, and Parolles's evil speaking, which finally exposes him, has been anticipated by his double-dealing with Helena and Lafeu. His cowardice is of no power to infect Bertram, but his lying is contagious, and in the last scene the count shows how deeply he is tainted. The unmasking of Bertram re-echoes the unmasking of Parolles.

Shakespeare is unlikely to have felt deeply about the minutiae of social procedure, the punctilio of a modern and Frenchified fashion like the duel, or the niceties of address. Saviolo's discourse on the lie is put into the mouth of Touchstone, Segar's observations on Adam *armigero* are given to the First Gravedigger, and Falstaff has the longest if not the last word on Honor. But the question "Wherein lies true honor and nobility?" was older than the new and fantastic codes of honor, or the new ideas of what constituted a gentleman. It is the theme of the first English secular drama, *Fulgens and Lucres* (*c.* 1490), where Medwall gave the lady's verdict for the worthy commoner against the unworthy nobleman, thereby proving his independence of his original, Buonaccorso, who in *De Vere Nobilitate* had left the matter open. In 1525, Rastell, *Of Gentylnes & Nobylyte*, treated the same subject, and it was an obvious theme for secular moralities. The question of blood and descent had been touched on by Shakespeare in *King John* in the triple contrast of Arthur, the legal successor, John the King *de facto*, and Richard the Bastard, whose royalty of nature makes him the natural leader. Civil nobility seen in relation to courtly life was a different aspect of the same problem and it is with this that Shakespeare is concerned in *All's Well*.

When at the turn of the fifteenth century, the ruling caste had ceased also to be a fighting caste, there remained for the elder and wiser the role of

---

[14] Hamlet's discrimination between Polonius, his two schoolfellows, and Osric is a mark of the wise prince: Timon's failure to discriminate is his downfall.

statesman or politician and for the younger sort that of courtier. The feudal
tenant-in-chief had derived his standing from his military prowess and his
local territorial responsibilities of delegated rule. Although the military
profession was no longer paramount, the young noble was trained in war.
The perfect courtier was required to be witty, full of counsel and of jests,
skilled in music and poetry, a horseman, a patron of all noble science. Such
arts of living could be learned only at the court. He should be ambitious of
honor—like Hotspur and Prince Hal—truthful and loyal, kindly and modest.
His life was devoted to glory, and his reward was good fame. Such employ-
ments as the professions afforded—of which that of physician was held least
worthy, as too close to the barber and the apothecary—were the refuge of
impoverished families and of younger sons. As the king was the fount of
honor, the young noble's place was at court; but the vanity and corruption
of court life were especially dangerous for the young. In actuality, the
scramble for preferment was a dangerous game in which the player might
lose his all.[15] Warnings against the court had been set forth in literature for
more than a century. Spenser's *Colin Clout's Come Home Again* depicts both
the glories and miseries of the court. A sick or aging ruler left the courtiers
exposed to all the natural dangers of the place without restraint. Such a
situation is depicted at the beginning of *All's Well*. The metaphor of the
sick king was always something more than a metaphor for Shakespeare.
The Countess bids farewell to her "unseason'd courtier" with open misgivings, and Helena, too, is openly afraid of the influence of the court on
Bertram: Parolles's description is not inviting, and even the clown is not
improved by it.[16] When the court is reached, all the virtuous characters turn
out to be elderly. The King describes the perfect courtier in the person of
Bertram's father, recalled to his mind by the young man's likeness (a resemblance already twice commented on):[17]

> Youth, thou bear'st thy Father's face,
> Franke Nature rather curious then in hast
> Hath well compos'd thee: Thy Father's morall parts
> Maist thou inherit too.   (I. ii. 18-21)

The elder Rousillon is but lately dead when the play opens. In an extensive
picture or mirror of his father, the King sets up to Bertram that model which

---

[15] See Lawrence Stone, "The Anatomy of the Elizabethan Aristocracy," *Economic History Review*, xviii (1948).

[16] I. i. 71, 80-2; 182-93, 224: III. ii. 13-29. See Kelso, *op. cit.*, pp. 50-2, for a comparison between the English and Italian courtly traditions, which suggests that English courtiers were more frequently employed in administration and that mere attendance at court was in England not considered an occupation in itself. Yet in spite of this, Sidney, like Bertram, stole away to the wars, though "with a copy of Castiglione in his pocket."

[17] I. i. 1, 71-2.

had already been recommended to him by his mother. It constitutes one of the main statements of the play, embodying the idea of true nobility.

> He did look farre
> Into the service of the time, and was
> Discipled of the bravest . . . in his youth
> He had the wit, which I can well observe
> To day in our yong Lords: but they may iest
> Till their owne scorne returne to them unnoted
> Ere they can hide their levitie in honour:
> So like a Courtier, contempt nor bitternesse
> Were in his pride, or sharpnesse; if they were,
> His equall had awak'd them, and his honour
> Clocke to it selfe, knew the true minute when
> Exception bid him speake: and at this time
> His tongue obeyd his hand. Who were below him,
> He us'd as creatures of another place,
> And bow'd his eminent top to their low rankes,
> Making them proud of his humilitie,
> In their poor praise he humbled. . . .   (I. ii. 26 ff.)

The model which Bertram actually takes is the very antithesis of this. Parolles claims to be both courtier and soldier, but his courtliness is entirely speech, as his soldiership is entirely dress. Even the clown calls Parolles knave and fool to his face (II. iv). He is ready to play the pander and to tempt Bertram ("a filthy Officer he is in those suggestions for the young Earle," III. v. 17-18), yet at the end he crawls to the protection of old Lafeu, who had been the first to meet with provocative insults the challenge of the "counterfeit."

Affability to inferiors was indeed not always recommended: Elyot held that courtesy consisted in giving every man his due, whilst Guazzo thought "to be too popular and plausible, were to make largesse of the treasures of his courtesie, to abase himself, and to shew a sign of folly or flatterie." [18] Yet on the other hand, Theseus's gracious kindness to the tradesmen, or Hamlet's sharp answer to Polonius's "I will use them according to their desert"—

> Gods bodykins, man better. Use everie man after his desert, and who should scape whipping: use them after your own Honor and Dignity. The lesse they deserve, the more merit is in your bountie

illustrate the same virtue which the King praised in the elder Rousillon. The arts of speech were indeed in themselves the very stuff of which a

---

[18] S. Guazzo, translated by Pettie, *Civile Conversation* (reprinted London, 1925), i. 158.

courtier was made. Guazzo describes first of all the speech and bearing to be cultivated, and then the truthfulness, fair speaking, and modesty which should characterize the matter of discourse. Hence the ungraciousness of Bertram's petulance. "A poore Physitian's daughter my wife?" did not perhaps sound quite so outrageous as it does now, for marriage out of one's degree was a debasing of the blood which blemished successive heirs. But Helena is of gentle, though not of noble blood, and all the other young nobles who have been offered to her have been ready to accept her.

The question that is raised by Bertram's pride and the King's act is one central to all discussion on the nature of nobility.

> One standard commonplace on nobility took shape: that lineage alone was not enough, but that the son of a noble family should increase and not degrade the glory of his ancestors.[19]

Aristotle had said that Nobility consisted in virtue and ancient riches.[20] Lord Burghley, a potent authority in his day, lopped the phrase down: "Nobility is nothing but ancient riches." Whilst it was admitted that the King could confer nobility upon anyone, gentility was sometimes held to be conferred only by descent; hence the saying, "The King cannot make a gentleman." At the court of Elizabeth, herself the granddaughter of a London citizen and surrounded by new nobility, the more rigid views were not likely to prevail. Nevertheless "nobility native" was inevitably preferable to "nobility dative." [21] Through inheritance it conferred a disposition to virtue, and even the degenerate were shielded in some manner by their descent, "the fame and wealth of their ancestors serves to cover them as long as it can, as a thing once gilded, though it be copper within, till the gilt be worn away." [22] Education and the example of his ancestors would also help the nobleman, though a bad education might corrupt him entirely.[23] The debate on old and new titles in Osorio's *Discourse of Civil and Christian Nobility* went in favour of blood, while Nenna's *Il Nennio* supported the lowly born. But all would agree with Mulcaster: 'The well-born and virtuous doth well deserve double honor among men . . . where desert for virtue is coupled with descent in blood.'[24]

Desert for virtue is Helena's claim, and the two words echo significantly throughout the play. The causes for ennobling the simple were headed by

[19] John E. Mason, *Gentlefolk in the Making* (Philadelphia, 1935), p. 8.
[20] *Politics*, iv. viii. 9.
[21] Kelso, *op. cit.*, p. 22.
[22] Sir Thomas Smith, *De Repub. Anglorum* (reprinted London, 1906), p. 38.
[23] Kelso, *op. cit.*, p. 24, quotes La Perrière, *Mirour of Policie* (translated 1598): "If he be evilly instructed in his young years, he will as long as he liveth have such manners as are barbarous, strange, and full of villainy." The education of a prince or noble was the subject of constant discussion.
[24] Mulcaster, *Positions, op. cit.*, p. 199; quoted by Kelso, *op. cit.*, p. 30.

"virtue public," i.e. some great public service, and this it is which ennobles her. Learning and riches were other causes. Elyot declared that nobility is "only the prayse and surname of virtue" and set forth the eleven moral virtues of Aristotle as the model for his Governor.[25] The essentially competitive nature of honour, while it was recognized, was not stressed.

In Helena and Bertram, the true and the false nobility are in contest. Helena seeks recognition: Bertram denies it. The King, with the Countess and Lafeu, whom Shakespeare created to act as arbiters, are all doubly ennobled by birth and virtue and therefore judge dispassionately. By these three judges the young people are compared at intervals throughout the play, to the increasing disadvantage of Bertram. In the first scene, the Countess introduces Helena as inheriting virtue and yet improving on it. The technical terms of honor emphasize her point:

> I have those hopes of her good, that her education promises: her dispositions shee inherits, which makes faire gifts fairer . . . she derives her honestie, and atcheeves her goodnesse (I. i. 47 ff.).

Of Bertram she cherishes hopes less assured, but wishes that his blood and virtue may contend for precedence, and his goodness share with his birthright.

By making his social climber a woman, Shakespeare took a good deal of the sting out of the situation. Helena's virtues were derived from her father and from heaven, to whose intervention she ascribes all her power to cure the King. She protests she is richest in being simply a maid, and the King offers her to Bertram with the words

> Vertue and shee
> Is her owne dower: Honour and wealth, from mee.

The promotion of a modest but dignified young woman is far from arousing jealousy.[26] Helena had been conscious of her lowliness and in her first soliloquy she almost despairs:

> Twere all one,
> That I should love a bright particuler starre,
> And think to wed it, he is so above me. (I. i. 97-9)

To the Countess, before making her confession, she says:

> I am from humble, he from honored name:
> No note upon my Parents, his all noble,
> My Master, my deere Lorde he is, and I
> His servant live, and will his vassall die. (I. iii. 164-7)

[25] *The Governor*, ed. Croft, ii, 38. Quoted by Mason, *op. cit.*, p. 26.

[26] Her many hesitations, her disclaimer of any aspiration to a royal match, show Helena's decorum. No Elizabethan could, like a modern writer, have called it "canny."

These words are not retracted by her confession for she protests that she does not follow him by any token of presumptuous suit: "Nor would I have him till I doe deserve him" (I. iii. 199). At her first encounter with the King, Helena is almost driven off by her first rebuff. In stately couplets which mark out the solemnity of the moment she suddenly returns and offers herself as "the weakest minister" of heaven. She frankly claims "inspired Merit" and warns the King that it is presumption to think Heaven cannot work through the humble. "Of heaven, not me, make an experiment." The King recognizes the power of something greater than herself in Helena's voice and he submits. She is "undoubted blest."

Such claims shift the ground of Helena's nobility. To fail to recognize her as already ennobled in a superior way by the choice of heaven is an aggravation of Bertram's offence in refusing the consummation of the marriage —itself a religious duty as Diana reminds him (IV. ii. 12-13). The countess feels nothing but indignation with the "rash and unbridled boy," for

> the misprising of a Maide too vertuous
> For the contempt of Empire.   (III. ii. 27-8)

Even before the journey to court she had loved Helena as her own child (I. iii. 98, 143-4) and now she prefers her, disclaiming her proper son (III. ii. 68-9), who in rejecting such a wife has lost more honor than he can ever win with his sword. Helena's penitential pilgrimage raises her yet higher in the Countess's estimation, and finally, with the report of her death, she becomes "the most vertuous gentlewoman, that ever Nature had praise for creating" (IV. v. 9-10).

In bestowing a wife on one of the royal wards, the King was certainly doing no more than Elizabeth and James had done. Much lesser persons regarded their wards as legitimate matrimonial prizes. The customary formula (which the King uses): "Can you like of this man?" "Can you like of this maid?" did not imply love but only the ability to live harmoniously together. Bertram, who is succinctly described by Lafeu as an "asse," has, it is clear from the first scene, no dislike to Helena, but he knows her as his mother's servant and "I cannot *love* her, nor will strive to doo't." Only later does the brilliant idea occur to him that he was really in love with Lafeu's daughter.[27] His seduction of Diana "contrives against his owne Nobilitie," and his responsibility for the death of Helena means that "the great dignitie that his valour hath here acquir'd for him (i.e. in Florence), shal at home be encountred with a shame as ample" (IV. iii. 25-30, 79-82).

Bertram's "folly," though excused as the fault of Parolles's ill counsel (IV. ii. 1), and as "Naturall rebellion, done i' th blaze of youth" (V. iii. 6),

---

[27] The King had long ago arranged the match, in the young people's childhood, and Bertram's affection may be assumed to be politic; but his readiness to accept the plan undermines his claim to freedom of choice in his first marriage.

remains in the eyes of Lafeu a blot upon his honor. However much Bertram wronged his King, his mother, and his wife, he wronged himself much more (v. iii. 12-19). Lafeu champions Helena's memory rather in the way in which Paulina champions Hermione's, and the rapidity with which the King jumps to thoughts of murder when he sees the royal gem offered as "an amorous token for fair *Maudlin*" is a proof of his feeling for Helena no less than of his well-merited distrust of Bertram. Like the rings of Bassanio and Portia, the jewels which are bandied about in the last scene are symbolic of a contract and an estate of life. The King's gem derived from him to Helena, and Bertram neither knows nor cares what it is. His own monumental ring symbolizes all that he has thrown away:[28]

> an honour longing to our house,
> Bequeathed downe from manie Ancestors,
> Which were the greatest obloquie i' th world,
> In me to loose.   (IV. ii. 42-5)

This jewel, with which he had taunted Helena, is found at the end in her keeping.

Nevertheless, though Helena is wise and Bertram foolish, though she is humble and he is proud, his final acknowledgment of her would constitute a strong ending. When Brachiano marries Vittoria, or when in *A Woman Killed with Kindness*, Sir Francis marries Susan, the condescension of the noble partner is matter for astonishment. Even in realistic comedy, such as *Eastward Ho!*, the marriage of court and city provides grounds for satire and for farce. Helena's success would lose all point if it were not a great exception. If this suggests that social theory enabled the judicious spectator both to eat his cake and have it, the answer is that the same dilemma lies at the center of the play, and is expounded by the king in a full account of the nature of title and dignity—a speech which had tradition behind it, but which is sharply at variance with the nigglers who measured whether honor came with the first or third generation of a new title.

> Tis onely title thou disdainst in her, the which
> I can build up: strange is it that our bloods
> Of colour, waight and heat, pour'd all together,
> Would quite confound distinction: yet stands off
> In differences so mightie. If she bee
> All that is vertuous (save what thou dislikst),
> A poore Phisitian's daughter, thou dislikst

---

[28] In Painter's story the ring is not an heirloom, but prized by Beltramo "for a certain virtue that he knew it had." Bertram's use of Diana's ring as a love-token should not be pressed as a point against him, though it is hardly suitable: but his lying repudiation and slander of Diana is ignoble.

> Of vertue for the name: but doe not so:,
> From lowest place, whence vertuous things proceed,
> The place is dignified by th' doers' deede.
> When great additions swells, and vertue none,
> It is a dropsied honour. Good alone,
> Is good without a name. Vilenesse is so:
> The propertie by what it is, should go,
> Not by the title. She is young, wise, faire,
> In these, to Nature shee's immediate heire:
> And these breed honour: that is honour's scorne,
> Which challenges it selfe as honour's borne,
> And is not like the sire: Honour's thrive
> When rather from our acts we them derive
> Then our fore-goers: the meere words a slave
> Deboshed on everie tombe, on everie grave:
> A lying Trophee, and as ofte is dumbe,
> Where dust, and damn'd oblivion is the Tombe
> Of honour'd bones indeed. . . .   (II. iii. 124 ff.)

Helena already possesses the essential attributes and therefore the potentiality of honor, which the King by his recognition of her claims will bestow. "The name and not the thing" is vanity.[29]

Medieval tradition recognized three classes of nobility.[30] Christian, natural, and civil. Pre-eminence must be given to sanctity, but the saints included poor fishers, even slaves. Natural nobility or perfection of kind might be ascribed to animals, and a noble falcon justly so termed. The writers of books of honor often mentioned these two classes but pointed out that they could not discuss them. One of the fullest treatments of the subject is by Dante in his *Convivio*. He denies civil nobility any real value.[31] Nobility, he says, cannot be defined by riches, which in themselves are vile,[32] or by time, because all men ultimately derive from a common stock, but only by its effects. The necessary outcome or effect of Nobility is Virtue: where Virtue exists, Nobility must therefore exist as its cause. Nobility descends upon an individual by the grace of God (*Convivio*, IV. xv) and is "the seed of blessedness dropped by God into a rightly placed soul." Dante goes on to expound the eleven moral virtues (much like Elyot). The claim to nobility by descent is then refuted, natural and Christian nobility identified, and civil nobility

[29] So, when she has fulfilled Bertram's conditions, Helena turns to seek, not her lord, but the King (IV. iv), because public recognition of her right is essential.

[30] Kelso, *op. cit.*, p. 21, where it is mentioned that later writers tended to ignore these divisions, or to pay them lip-service only.

[31] *Convivio*, Fourth Treatise.

[32] *Nobile* is derived by Dante from *not vile* (IV. xvi).

wiped out. Dante's Third Ode, upon which this section of the *Convivio* provides a commentary, is addressed to Beatrice, who, like Helena, is an example of active virtue, received by a direct infusion of grace. The language of religion is used with particular frequency by Shakespeare in this play,[33] and the gravest words of all are spoken by the Clown (IV. v. 50-9) when he describes how "the Prince of this world" entices nobility "into his court."

> I am for the house with the narrow gate, which I take to be too little for pompe to enter: some that humble themselves may, but the manie will be too chill and tender, and theyll bee for the flowrie way that leads to the broad gate, and the great fire.

Helena is "a Jewell" (v. iii. 1) which Bertram throws away. His rejection of her must be seen not in isolation but as linked with his choice of Parolles.[34] The first dialogue of Helena and Parolles, the Liar and Vertue as she herself has labelled them, must be seen as the encounter of Bertram's good and evil angels, who, if this were a morality, would contend for his soul in open debate.[35] In the final scene Parolles turns the tables on Bertram, and though the King dismisses the informer with contempt, an elaborate and inexorable shaming of the now utterly silenced young man proceeds. This last scene, in which Shakespeare completely forsakes his original, has the closest affinities with *Measure for Measure*. It is a judgment scene with charge and countercharge piled up in bewildering contradiction till they are resolved as if by miracle in the sudden appearance of the central figure. In this scene the King appears as the fount of justice: he deprives Bertram of all honor (v. iii. 184-6), though the revenges with which he threatens the young man should not be taken in any personal sense. Such a finale, with a royal judgment, and a distribution of rewards and punishments, was a well-established comic convention,[36] though it is difficult to resist the thought that in offering Diana a husband, the King shows some inability to profit by experience. The riddles with which Diana led up to the *dénouement* recall those in which Portia swore she lay with Doctor Balthazar to obtain the ring, and they are not to modern taste.

Bertram's conversion must be reckoned among Helena's miracles. What is well ended is her struggle for recognition, which he concedes her. Her devotion, tinged for the first time with bitterness, requires another mode of

---

[33] E.g. I. i. 109-10, 239-40; I. ii. 57-8, 65-7; I. iii. 20-1, 212-13, 253; II. i. 139-44, 151-7, 163, 178-9; II. iii. 1-7, 28-9, 69; III. iv. 28-9; IV. ii. 21-9, 66-8; IV. iii. 55-63.

[34] The pride of Parolles and the humility of Helena have been contrasted in their use of the term "master": they are shown at the beginning as more or less social equals.

[35] Bertram's ultimate rejection of Parolles, though well deserved, is expressed with a wilful petulance, not with shame: "I could endure anything but a Cat, and now he's a Cat to me" (IV. iii. 242-3).

[36] E.g. *Friar Bacon and Friar Bungay, The Shoemaker's Holiday, An Humorous Day's Mirth.*

expression than the last dozen lines allow. She has been acknowledged by her lord: that her personal happiness is simply irrelevant, and the ending therefore neither hypocritical nor cynical, can be granted only if the play is seen as a study of the question of "Wherein lies true honor and nobility?"

Helena

by G. Wilson Knight

Helena possesses those old-world qualities of simplicity, sincerity, and integrity which Bertram lacks. She is loving, humble, and good, and in her there is no lack of piety to her forbears: instead, her father's art descends to, and is used by, her.

Her first words sound a note of wistful suffering. The Countess thinks that she is grieving for the loss of her father:

> *Countess.* No more of this, Helena, go to, no more; lest it be rather thought you affect a sorrow than have it.
> *Helena.* I do affect a sorrow, indeed, but I have it too. (I. i. 60)

The note is that of Julia's "Tne musician likes"—i.e. "pleases"—"me not" in *The Two Gentlemen of Verona* (IV. ii. 58); and of Imogen in *Cymbeline*. Helena, like those, might seem to be going to play the part of a wronged woman, suffering for love. But there is a difference: her feminine humility becomes an active and challenging, almost a *male*, force.

She is generally praised. From her father she inherits fine qualities, and shows honesty and goodness (I. i. 45-53); the Countess regards her as, in effect, her daughter (I. iii. 150-61; IV. v. 11-13); she possesses "wisdom and constancy" amazing in one of her age (II. i. 86-8). But she is always "humble" (II. iii. 89), and will only have Bertram on terms just to him: "Nor would I have him till I do deserve him" (I. iii. 207). Even when her healing of the King has proved her desert, her way of choosing Bertram is to offer her "service" to his "guiding power" in uttermost feminine humility (II. iii. 109): that is her conception of marriage, recalling Portia's in *The Merchant of Venice* (III. ii. 149-75). The Countess clearly asserts that she "deserves a lord that twenty such rude boys" as her own son should "tend upon" whilst calling her "mistress," and regards her supposed death as "the death of the most virtuous gentlewoman that ever nature had praise for creating" (III. ii. 83; IV. v. 9). Our social valuations are reversed: nature's aristocracy,

"Helena" [Editor's Title]. From "The Third Eye" in *The Sovereign Flower* (London: Methuen & Co., Ltd., 1958), pp. 131-57. Reprinted by permission of the author and publishers.

as in the poetry of *The Winter's Tale*, replaces man's. "We lost a jewel of"—
i.e. "in"—"her," says the King (v. iii. 1), the image recalling Thaisa in
Pericles. Again

> He lost a wife
> Whose beauty did astonish the survey
> Of richest eyes, whose words all ears took captive,
> Whose dear perfection hearts that scorn'd to serve
> Humbly called mistress.   (v. iii. 15)

She is almost beyond the human, with the kind of idealization accorded
Thaisa, Marina, and Hermione. She is one whose "prayers" Heaven itself
"delights to hear and loves to grant" (III. iv. 27). But she is not showy:
"all her deserving is a reserved honesty" (III. v. 61). Nor is there anything
priggish in her: she can engage in broad sex-talk with Parolles. She alone
of our people has the sympathy to recognize in this strange creature, whom
she loves for Bertram's "sake," both the vicious falsity of his play-acting and
yet a certain fitness in his scandalous behavior which somehow wins our
approbation whilst "virtue's steely bones" are left "bleak i' the cold wind."
To this point the contrast is in Parolles' favor: the imagery of cold contrasted
with the rich humor of his shameless absurdity constitutes a kind of approbation, aesthetic rather than moral; and though in her next lines, calling it an
example of the way "cold wisdom" often has to take second place to "super-
fluous folly" ("luxurious folly"), she registers a disapproval, the point has,
poetically, been made (I. i. 111-17). However that may be, Helena herself
certainly stands for more than an ethical ideal; she is feminine "honour"
incarnate, her excellence a way of life, to be interpreted in the realm of being
rather than of precept.

Helena can best be discussed under two main headings, and we shall next
consider her as (i) the supreme development of Shakespeare's conception of
feminine love, and (ii) as miracle worker.

She is utterly humble. Her love is characterized less by desire and possessiveness than by service and adoration, reminiscent of the Sonnets. Her
father is forgotten:

> What was he like?
> I have forgot him: my imagination
> Carries no favour in't but Bertram's.
> I am undone: there is no living, none,
> If Bertram be away. 'Twere all one
> That I should love a bright particular star
> And think to wed it, he is so above me:
> In his bright radiance and collateral light
> Must I be comforted, not in his sphere.
> The ambition in my love thus plagues itself:

> The hind that would be mated with the lion
> Must die for love. 'Twas pretty, though a plague,
> To see him every hour; to sit and draw
> His arched brows, his hawking eye, his curls,
> In our heart's table; heart too capable
> Of every line and trick of his sweet favour:
> But now he's gone, and my idolatrous fancy
> Must sanctify his reliques. (I. i. 93)

Here is a Bertram very different from the man we have been discussing; it is Bertram known by love; the potential, perhaps the real, man. Observe that Helena herself subscribes whole-heartedly to those social and aristocratic valuations which her own personality, as a dramatic force, serves to attack. Notice, too, he peculiar tone of it, like Paulina's words over Leontes' child (*The Winter's Tale*, II. iii. 97-102), exquisitely handling physical detail with a consummate purity of perception. "Our heart's table" recalls the difficult Sonnet 24 on perfect love-sight (G. Wilson Knight, *The Mutual Flame* [1955], pp. 40-1).

Here is another revealing passage, spoken to the Countess:

> Then I confess,
> Here on my knee, before high Heaven and you,
> That before you, and next unto high Heaven,
> I love your son.
> My friends were poor, but honest; so's my love.
> Be not offended; for it hurts him not
> That he is loved of me. I follow him not
> By any token of presumptuous suit;
> Nor would I have him till I do deserve him;
> Yet never know how that desert should be.
> I know I love in vain, strive against hope;
> Yet in that captious and intenible sieve,
> I still pour in the waters of my love,
> And lack not to lose still: thus, Indian-like,
> Religious in mine error, I adore
> The sun, that looks upon his worshipper,
> But knows of him no more. My dearest madam,
> Let not your hate encounter with my love
> For loving where you do: but if yourself
> Whose aged honour cites a virtuous youth,
> Did ever in so true a flame of liking
> Wish chastely and love dearly, that your Dian
> Was both herself and love; O, then give pity
> To her, whose state is such, that cannot choose

> But lend and give where she is sure to lose;
> That seeks not to find that her search implies,
> But riddle-like lives sweetly where she dies.   (I. iii. 199)

Here I point less to any especial accents in the poetry than to the statement.
"Next high Heaven" recalls "next my Heaven the best" in Sonnet 110.
Especially important is the reference to Dian, our central deity. Helena's
love exists at the meeting-place of Dian and desire: "was both herself and
love." We are continually forced towards a paradoxical identification of
virginity and *sexual love*, pointing to the "married chastity" of *The Phoenix and
the Turtle*. That, if it means "married virginity," cannot be, and is not,
dramatically maintained; but the equivalent of purity may have been
maintained in Shakespeare's personal love for the Fair Youth adored in the
Sonnets; and he may be working from that.

The powers of virgin love are exquisitely described in one of Helena's
early speeches. Parolles has been arguing against virginity, and she breaks
in with:

> Not my virginity yet:[1]
> There shall your master have a thousand loves,
> A mother and a mistress and a friend,
> A phoenix, captain and an enemy,
> A guide, a goddess, and a sovereign,
> A counsellor, a traitress, and a dear;
> His humble ambition, proud humility,
> His jarring concord, and his discord dulcet,
> His faith, his sweet disaster; with a world
> Of pretty, fond, adoptious christendoms
> That blinking Cupid gossips. Now shall he—
> I know not what he shall. God send him well!
> The court's a learning place, and he is one—   (I. i. 181)

The lines, with their broken conclusion, insistently remind us of Viola's
semi-confession of her love to Orsino in *Twelfth Night*, breaking off on "Sir,
shall I to this lady?" (II. iv. 105-24); and of Cleopatra's

> Sir, you and I must part, but that's not it;
> Sir, you and I have loved, but there's not it;
> That you know well. Something it is I would—
> O, my oblivion is a very Antony,
> And I am all forgotten.   (*Antony and Cleopatra*, I. iii. 87)

The thoughts are different, but the hesitant phrasing, the sense of unutterable
worlds behind, is the same in each.

---

[1] I follow the Folio pointing in printing a colon here.

Helena's speech is difficult, but there is no reason to suppose a missing line. "There" cannot surely, as has sometimes been argued, mean "at the Court." Helena's words show an enjoyed *fondling* of love-thoughts, and must accordingly refer to her own love of Bertram rather than that of any rival, or rivals. The opening I take, in direct succession to her preceding remarks to Parolles, to mean: "I shall not part with my virginity to anyone yet, because therein your master has an infinite love." I do not think that, at this early stage in her story, it can mean "In giving your master my virginity I shall give him a thousand loves," since she has no good reason at this stage to expect such an event. Not that the total meaning would be so very different, either way, since virginity, given or withheld, remains the key thought. As in the Christian scheme virginity is here less the denial of love than an expression of it: it is conceived as a positive power. In *The Christian Renaissance* (revised ed. [1962], p. 29) I have, in emphasizing the importance of virginity in Christian dogma, suggested that "to hold up virginity as an ideal is merely to raise sex to an infinite value." That is what happens here: the love is infinite, "a thousand loves"; it is the window to a great insight. It may be related to the state of perfect integration from which poetry is born, a state which is, as Shelley in his *Defence of Poetry* tells us, "at war with every base desire." Such a state is a state of inclusion, wisdom, and forgiveness: this Helena claims, and her ability later on to work the miracle is evidence of her right.

This love, like Shakespeare's own ranging poetic vision, is universal and so a number of human categories are contained. It is not sexually limited: it is simultaneously maternal, sexual, and a friendship in the Elizabethan sense, whereby "friend" was as strong a term as "lover," partly perhaps because of the many ardent man-to-man friendships and idealizations, such as Shakespeare's in the Sonnets. The "Phoenix" must be understood in terms of its use throughout *Love's Martyr*, the collection in which Shakespeare's *The Phoenix and the Turtle* appeared. The symbol appears at key moments in Shakespeare's esoteric thought from *Timon of Athens* onwards, and is fully discussed in *The Mutual Flame*. The Phoenix is bisexual, an idealized creature, and chaste. In precise terms of "Phoenix" and "Turtle" Bertram, from Helena's view, would more exactly be "Phoenix," with her adoring self as "Turtle"; but she is imagining herself as she might be from his view, and her own bisexuality, her blend of female love and male vigor, her virgin chastity combined with beauty and wisdom, all entitle her to the term as that to which he might, and should, aspire. War categories are also involved: she will be both his "captain" and his "enemy." All Bertram's interests and ambitions as warrior are somehow contained, and the male values safeguarded, Helena boldly entering this domain as his "captain," so asserting the priority of her love, and even as his "enemy." Why? The next lines clarify the word. This love is as a "guide"; being in touch with his greater self and speaking thence, it naturally becomes a "goddess" and, in human terms, his "sovereign." Every value, sacred or secular, is included, and from this height Bertram is to be counselled, advised, warned, even opposed, for his failings are admitted; and so her love is, in its way, a "traitress," aligning itself with opposing forces, and yet simultaneously, and accordingly, a "dear," or thing of highest worth.

Paradox is involved, and becomes now explicit. Love such as Helena's is, at its best, a great aspiration, and yet one born of humility; in her pride and humility are unified; and this is one with *his* reasons for both pride and humility. She has become almost a divine or poetic principle, overruling, watching, containing him; or rather it is not she, but the Love overarching, overruling, both, as we find it in the Sonnets (*The Mutual Flame*, pp. 41, 61, 94). "His jarring concord and his discord dulcet" suggests the whole Shakespearian universe in its blend of tempests and music; but here in particular it denotes both Helena's effect on him and also his own lack of integration as surveyed by the now almost impersonal Love for which it exists as harmony; as when Helena accepts Parolles's faults since "they sit so fit in him" that "virtue" appears "bleak," "cold," and metallic in comparison (i. i. 113). This is the poetic, Shakespearian, view of man. Helena's love sees Bertram as he potentially is, that core and inmost music of his personality which no faults can disturb—Parolles's "simply the thing I am"—and this outspaces the moral judgment, which, though present, is surpassed, as when Mariana says of Angelo that she craves "no other nor no better man," since "best men are moulded out of faults" (*Measure for Measure*, v. i. 440). So here Helena is "his faith," that which believes in, recognizes, and works for, his own highest good and potential excellence; but, since that may, as in the greater scheme of God's dealings with man— and these are never far from Helena's thinking—bring suffering, she, or the great Love, is, too, his "sweet disaster," recalling Saint Paul's sense of happy bondage in servitude to Christ. But the thought is getting too weighty, and returns to all the little ways and sentimentalities of love, though even here remembering religion in the word "christendoms," Christian names or nicknames, sponsored by ("gossips") blind ("blinking") Cupid.

The speech offers a definition of perfect love, which labors for its object's good; which, seeing the "heart" (*A Midsummer-Night's Dream*, ii. ii. 155), the Hindu *atman*, or divine spark, knows, includes, and forgives all; and which, in Shakespeare's own experience, made him see all humanity, including all that was evil and ugly, as aspects, like Helena's understanding of Parolles, of the wondrous being whom he loved (Sonnets 113 and 114): this is the exact opposite of Bertram's distorted, scornful vision of man. What Helena is describing is an authentic part of the great poetic panorama, of the same stuff and significance as the lucid patterns of Pope's *Essay on Man* and Shelley's *Defence of Poetry*.

This careful definition serves as a prologue to Helena's story. Directly after it we find her love beginning to *act* in her as a source of magical power:

> Our remedies oft in ourselves do lie
> Which we ascribe to Heaven: the fated sky
> Gives us free scope; only doth backward pull
> Our slow designs when we ourselves are dull.
> What power is it which mounts my love so high,
> That makes me see, and cannot feed mine eye?
> The mightiest space in fortune nature brings
> To join like likes, and kiss like native things.
> Impossible be strange attempts to those
> That weigh their pains in sense, and do suppose
> What hath been cannot be: who ever strove
> To show her merit that did miss her love?
> The King's disease—my project may deceive me,
> But my intents are fixed, and will not leave me.   (I. i. 235)

This is the moment of conception. Emphasis is laid on man's, or woman's, "free" abilities, given by the "sky," to use what is "in" himself, the more cosmic suggestion of "sky" marking a distinction from reliance on a transcendental, or theological, "Heaven." The psychic potentialities in question are hampered by the "dull" elements of material inertia (as at Sonnet 44). The "power" is either directly born of Helena's love, or at least intimately associated with it, infusing it with confidence, even pride ("mounts . . . high"): we may recall the powers of love described by Biron in *Love's Labour's Lost* (IV. iii. 289-365). It is recognized as a reality beyond sense-perception ("That . . . eye"), which can break through even the strongest ("mightiest space") social barriers in the cause of *natural* affinity ("nature . . . things"). We must not stifle enterprise by assessing difficulties in terms of common sense ("weigh . . . sense"), nor forget that such things have happened before.

The emphasis falls on natural, yet spiritual, power, though the contrast of "Heaven" and "sky" is not elsewhere maintained, the more orthodox concepts being generally used. The distinction, though often valuable and sometimes inevitable, cannot be more than provisional. So Helena goes ahead with her plan to heal the King, and succeeds. The actual healing we shall discuss later.

Helena claims always to serve Bertram; he remains her master. When, after the healing, she chooses him for her husband, she first takes the great step from Dian to Love, from virginity to marriage:

> Now Dian, from thy altar do I fly;
> And to imperial Love, that god most high,
> Do my sighs stream.   (II. iii. 80)

Then, coming to Bertram, she proposes as follows:

> I dare not say I take you; but I give
> Me and my service ever whilst I live,
> Into your guiding power.   (II. iii. 109)

She speaks like other Shakespearian heroines, recognizing the man as her lord and master; and yet here that very recognition has taken the initiative, assuming the male prerogative.

After Bertram has gone to the war, she recognizes that she has driven him away, and speaks poignantly of his danger. It is, as a Shakespearian woman, her part both to fear and to respect, like Katharina (*The Taming of the Shrew*, v. ii. 148-52), the hardships and dangers which fall to man. She, whose art is healing, fears the very thought of the dangers which Bertram must incur.

He has written: "Till I have no wife, I have nothing in France" (III. ii. 77). So in remorse she will leave France. Here is her soliloquy, remarkable for its maternal, protective, tone, for its fine depicting, unusual in Shakespeare, of contemporary warfare, and above all for the sudden dignity, witnessing to the ability of Shakespeare's poetry to live its own lines of thought, with which she, who has long recognized his nobler self, now, as it were, crowns the scornful young man before our eyes by the simple use of his title. The name "Rousillon" (spelt in the Folio "Rossillion") sounds twice, like an awakening, and perhaps nowhere else in Shakespeare is a name used with so resounding an effect:

> Nothing in France until he has no wife!
> Thou shalt have none, Rousillon, none in France;
> Then hast thou all again. Poor lord! is't I
> That chase thee from thy country and expose
> Those tender limbs of thine to the event
> Of the non-sparing war? And is it I
> That drive thee from the sportive court, where thou
> Wast shot at with fair eyes, to be the mark
> Of smoky muskets? O you leaden messengers,
> That ride upon the violent speed of fire,
> Fly with false aim; move the still-piecing air
> That stings with piercing; do not touch my lord.
> Whoever shoots at him, I set him there;
> Whoever charges on his forward breast,
> I am the caitiff that do hold him to't;
> And, though I kill him not, I am the cause
> His death was so effected; better 'twere
> I met the ravin lion when he roar'd
> With sharp constraint of hunger; better 'twere

> That all the miseries which nature owes
> Were mine at once. No, come thou home, Rousillon,
> Whence honour but of danger wins a scar,
> As oft it loses all: I will be gone;
> My being here it is that holds thee hence.
> Shall I stay here to do 't? No, no, although
> The air of paradise did fan the house
> And angels officed all. I will be gone,
> That pitiful rumour may report my flight,
> To consolate thine ear.   (III. ii. 103)

Here there is full recognition both of her own fault, if for once we may so call it, and also of the true greatness of her husband; for a warrior's is a great calling. From a woman's, maternal, view, she surveys its terror, the danger it is to be a man. So Bertram is twice given his title, "Rousillon." In direct contrast to her earlier soliloquy she here resigns her rights to the intimacy of a Christian name, while freely allowing him *his* rights to all that aristocratic honor which made him reject her, but which she herself never repudiates; and on her lips the splendid name makes him seem noble, creating for us his true self, known by love, the word's music sounding as the music of his young warrior soul.

So she composes a letter in sonnet form for the Countess, admitting the fault of her "ambitious love" and saying how she will do penance as a pilgrim, and labor to "sanctify" her husband's "name" with a "zealous fervour" (III. iv. 4-17). It is a religious and penitential act; she is still laboring to serve his interests.

Whether we can respond as we are meant to to her later actions is less certain. Though she certainly knew that Bertram had gone to serve the Duke (III. i. 54), we must not suppose that her finding him in Florence was part of a deliberate plan, since her letter to the Countess had already urged his immediate return to France (III. iv. 8); and as for her substituting of herself for Diana as the object of Bertram's passion, we can at least note that in doing this she is in effect saving him from a sin which she regards as serious: again she is, in fact, serving his best interests. As for the symbolic ring which she wins from him, we can endow this with whatever ancestral powers we like: possessing that, she may be supposed to know that, according to the terms of his own semi-oracular letter (III. ii. 60), she will eventually possess his love. All this we must accept as best we may: we have to forgive as much, as Tolstoy saw, in most of Shakespeare's plays. No doubt such dramatists could do better were we willing to sit in the theatre for treble the time they normally demand, but we are not. What we can say is this, that her later actions all tend, finally, to serve and rebuild Bertram's better self; and whatever we think of these scenes, they do certainly serve to show that, except when on the field of battle, Bertram needs guiding, since his judgment is immature and his values in chaos. It may seem presumptuous in Helena to cast herself for such a role, but she is no ordinary woman; or rather she has the best qualities of an ordinary woman developed to so high a pitch that she becomes almost a saint.

Religious categories are involved: they cluster round her as the values of war surround Bertram; and she actually performs a miracle. We pass now to consider Helena as miracle-worker.

The miracle grows from a world well saturated with religious thought and language. Religious phrases are continual, such as: "Heaven aiding," "Doubt not but Heaven," "O dear Heaven, bless" (iv. iv. 12, 18; v. iii. 71); and so on. A "quarrel" may be called "holy"; so may love, even by a seducer (iii. i. 4; iv. ii. 32). Theological terms occur: "With the divine forfeit of his soul," "He will sell the fee-simple of his salvation"; "Dost thou put upon me at once the office of God and the Devil?" (iii. vi. 33; iv. iii. 314; v. ii. 52). The Countess's prayers hope to "pluck down" blessings on her son's head (i. i. 79); Helena has influence with a religious dignitary said to be "one of the greatest in the Christian world" (iv. iv. 2). Parolles tells how Bertram in love "talked of Satan, and of Limbo, and of Furies" (v. iii. 264). People moralize naturally on human life as "a mingled yarn" of "good and ill," of virtues and vices (iv. iii. 83). The Clown knows himself a "wicked creature," and marries in order to "repent" (i. iii. 38), going on to talk of "young Charbon the puritan and old Poysam the papist" (i. iii. 58). The Countess, he says, is well but for two things:

> One, that she's not in Heaven, whither God send her quickly! the other, that
> she's in earth, from whence God send her quickly!   (ii. iv. 12)

He takes, indeed, a bitter view, talking of "the black prince," "the prince of darkness," "the devil," and continuing:

> I am a woodland fellow, sir, that always loved a great fire; and the master I
> speak of ever keeps a good fire. But, sure, he is the prince of the world; let his
> nobility remain in's court. I am for the house with the narrow gate, which I take
> to be too little for pomp to enter. Some that humble themselves may; but the
> many will be too chill and tender, and they'll be for the flowery way that leads
> to the broad gate and the great fire.   (iv. v. 50)

"Pomp" is satirized, and humility, the humility of a Helena, honored. The speech marks a complete surrender to the religious, ascetic, point of view. Naturally it displeases Lafeu, the Lord. It is not so much that the Clown is wrong as that this recognition of human evil is just where the real problem of living, as Lafeu would see it, begins. Parolles has no morals; the Clown has little else. Neither face the complexities of life.

Helena functions as a *bridge* between religion and the court, between humility and honor. In a world of divided, sin-struck humanity she is a redeeming power, a perfect unit; that is her function. Even the Clown admits "that she was the sweet marjoram of the salad, or rather the herb of grace" (IV. v. 17). She it is who can speak words which Imogen might have spoken, like:

> No, no, although
> The air of paradise did fan the house
> And angels officed all. (III. ii. 127)

Her very prayers, according to the Countess, are peculiarly valid:

> What angel shall
> Bless this unworthy husband? He cannot thrive
> Unless her prayers, whom Heaven delights to hear
> And loves to grant, reprieve him from the wrath
> Of greatest justice. (III. iv. 25)

She functions, within the play, almost as Christ within the Christian Scheme. The play is a microcosm of that scheme. Naturally, her love is "religious":

> Thus, Indian-like,
> Religious in mine error, I adore
> The sun, that looks upon his worshippers
> But knows of him no more. (I. iii. 212)

That is spoken from her humility: we are not to regard her love as idolatry. Her love possesses, as we have seen, both poetic integrity and religious purity, and it is right that in its pursuit she should become a pilgrim in holy dress, going to the sanctuary of Saint Jaques le Grand and lodging "at the Saint Francis" (III. v. 34-7), the whole venture being called "a holy undertaking" accomplished "with most austere sanctimony" (IV. iii. 59). Like the Duke's disguise as a Friar in *Measure for Measure*, all this has a more than plot-meaning; associatively and visually it marks an addition to the protagonist's stature. And yet there is nothing prudish or ascetic about her. Nor does she in any sense oppose the courtly, aristocratic, valuations. She both accepts and admires them; they are part of her.

The idealization is so uncompromising, and yet so inclusive and so firmly based, since, as we have seen, her consciousness functions on the plane of Shakespearian poetry itself, that we are all but forced to believe that her very being is beyond criticism, and see Bertram's behavior accordingly. This is, pretty nearly, equivalent to calling the play a religious morality, with Helena as a semi-divine person, or some new type of saint. And it is true that our central scenes are formal and ritualistic, rather like the formality of the tournament in *Pericles* (II. ii). Her choosing of a husband is formal;

she passes from lord to lord as in a sort of trance, her rhymed speeches driving
home the ritual meaning.

The earlier and crucial scene of the healing is also ritualistically felt, with
formal rhymes and chant. And here indeed we approach the play's heart.
For, whatever the poetry says it is hard to believe it alone; we want dramatic
action. Here we have it. Helena from the start insisted that she did not want
Bertram until she deserved him. She wins her right by the miracle, and by
that alone; and yet the miracle is itself, as we shall see, a derivative from her
love.

We shall now inspect this crucial event. It is, as happens in other late
plays, a development on a more metaphysical level of dramatic patterns in
the Comedies. Here we can point to Rosalind functioning as miracle-worker
in *As You Like It*. Our nearest analogy from the latest plays is the art of
Cerimon, together with the "sacred physic" and "skill" of Marina, in
Pericles (iii. ii; v. i. 74, 76). But our present miracle is not quite like anything
else in Shakespeare; it is closer to us, more realistically conceived in point
of detail, it speaks less to a "mystical" than to what might be called a
psychical or "spiritualistic" understanding. Since Helena's function is so
clearly stated to be that of a medium only for the greater powers, we have
the less excuse for questioning it on grounds of probability.

Helena comes to the King with a power which descends from her father.
She is thus credited with preserving and using her parental heritage in
contrast to Bertram whose qualities are precisely those which did not characterize his father, and who parts with his ancestral ring.

Her father, Gerard de Narbon, was more than an ordinary physician,
and nearer to Cerimon in *Pericles*, who says:

> I hold it ever
> Virtue and cunning were endowments greater
> Than nobleness and riches. Careless heirs
> May the two latter darken and expend,
> But immortality attends the former,
> Making a man a god.   (*Pericles*, iii. ii. 26)

So, too, de Narbon's skill is closely associated with "honesty," or integrity.
He was one, according to the Countess,

> whose skill was almost as great as his honesty; had it stretched so far, would have
> made nature immortal, and death should have play for lack of work.
>
> (i. i. 22)

Indeed, adds Lafeu, "he was skilful enough to have lived still, if knowledge
could be set up against mortality" (i. i. 35). The skill concerned appears to
exist in close relation to its owner's personal virtues ("honesty"), and to be
nearer to some variety of occult wisdom, or spirit-power, than to anything

which we can call medical science. As in *The Winter's Tale*, only with more
of a close-pinned realism, such esoteric secrets are, so far as may be, hinted,
and indeed emphasized, without breaking the bounds of dramatic propriety,
as normally understood. Helena possessed her father's notes:

> You know my father left me some prescriptions
> Of rare and proved effects, such as his reading
> And manifest experience had collected
> For general sovereignty; and that he will'd me
> In heedfull'st reservation to bestow them
> As notes, whose faculties inclusive were,
> More than they were in note; amongst the rest,
> There is a remedy, approved, set down,
> To cure the desperate languishings whereof
> The king is render'd lost. (I. iii. 229)

This is the basis of our miracle. It sounds at first ordinary enough; but we
may observe that the notes are considered of more general ("inclusive")
application than a superficial reading would suggest.

The Countess fears that the King and his physicians would scorn a "poor
unlearned virgin" after the "doctrine" of their "schools" has already pro-
nounced its verdict (I. iii. 243-50). This may appear strange in view of her
earlier remark that, had de Narbon been alive, the King might have been
cured (I. i. 25), but the discrepancy is, as we shall see, part of the dramatic
plan. Helena replies:

> There's something in't,
> More than my father's skill, which was the great'st
> Of his profession, that his good receipt
> Shall for my legacy be sanctified
> By the luckiest stars in Heaven. (I. iii. 250)

The lines are obscure. I take "receipt" to refer to the prescription (as at
II. i. 108), rather than to the King's "acceptance." If so, it means: "There is
more to it than my father's skill, for I feel that his valuable prescription will
in my hands ('for my legacy') somehow be blessed by God." She herself,
whose prayers, as we are elsewhere told, are peculiarly valid, is claiming to
have divine assistance and support. And here we may recall that her plan's
original conception (i) grew directly from out of her own love of Bertram and
(ii) entered her consciousness as a power independent of sense-perception:

> What power is it which mounts my love so high,
> That makes me see, and cannot feed mine eye? (I. i. 239)

Her determination to visit the King flowered directly from a state of strong
spiritual impregnation, born of love. So now, asked if she really believes in

divine support, she answers briefly: "Ay, madam, knowingly" (i. iii. 258). We are beyond science; transcendental, or occult, categories have entered our field. She goes to Paris.

We are, as happens in *The Winter's Tale*, gradually attuned to the possibility of miracle by Lafeu's introductory speech to the King, wherein he reports, in a light semi-humorous style, that he has seen a medicine "able to breathe life into a stone," and raise the dead. Next, claiming to have left his "light deliverance" for serious talk, he tells how he has spoken

> With one that, in her sex, her years, profession,
> Wisdom and constancy, hath amazed me more
> Than I dare blame my weakness.   (II. i. 86)

Will the King see her, and after that "laugh" (II. i. 90) at him, if he wishes to? Again, we see that it is not all "science"; Helena's own qualities are involved. Lafeu is amazed at her blend of female with male "wisdom" and "constancy." It is all very strange. Observe that there is some risk of *mockery*.

Helena is brought before the King, and tells him of her father's art:

> On's bed of death
> Many receipts he gave me; chiefly one
> Which as the dearest issue of his practice,
> And of his old experience the only darling,
> He bade me store up as a triple eye,
> Safer than mine own two, more dear. I have so;
> And, hearing your high majesty is touch'd
> With that malignant cause, wherein the honor
> Of my dear father's gift stands chief in power,
> I come to tender it and my appliance,
> With all bound humbleness.   (II. i. 107)

The legacy appears now to be rather more than a written prescription. It is a choice secret, to be "stored up," and actually compared to a "triple eye." This is the "third eye" of occult doctrine and practice, located on the forehead and used in spirit-healing as a source of powerful rays. It is here regarded as a sense more valuable ("dear") than the physical senses, and we shall naturally relate it to that experience of a love-born power offering a *sight* other than *sense-perception* which was the motivating impulse of Helena's whole scheme. Helena accordingly offers not merely a "prescription," but rather this secret together with her own "appliance." Her own mediumistic gifts, developing from love, will be engaged; but it is all offered with humility.

The King is at first incredulous. But why? We know that he has been speaking "mourningly" of de Narbon (i. i. 35), and we have heard him remark to Bertram, "If he were living, I would try him yet," since the other

doctors have only worn him out "with several applications" (I. ii. 73). Now
he gets a wonderful posthumous opportunity, and refuses:

> We thank you, maiden;
> But may not be so credulous of cure
> When our most learned doctors leave us, and
> The congregated college have concluded
> That labouring art can never ransom nature
> From her inaidable estate. I say we must not
> So stain our judgement, or corrupt our hope,
> To prostitute our past-cure malady
> To empirics, or to dissever so
> Our great self and our credit, to esteem
> A senseless help, when help past sense we deem.   (II. i. 117)

This constitutes a contradiction, both of the King's own former speech—
though perhaps even there "try him" underlined a doubt—and of the
general recognition, by the Countess and Lafeu, of de Narbon's superlative
abilities. And yet it is easy to see what is happening. The Countess has
already warned us that the King will refuse, and we can say that Shakespeare
has been very subtly at work attuning us by degrees to regard Helena's cure
as within the realm of spirit-healing in strong contrast to the official services
of the medical profession. We could only make complete sense of the King's
attitude by supposing that the term "triple eye" has made him realize that
more was involved in de Narbon's art than he had supposed. Either way,
the main issue is clear, and from now on there is no doubt. The King, to
put it bluntly, is afraid of making a fool of himself.

Helena's argument in reply is important. She does not waste time urging
her father's famous skill, but rather insists that divine powers can work
through so humble an instrument as herself. Hitherto, except for two con-
cluding and *abrupt* couplets from the King, both have spoken in blank verse,
but now Helena speaks wholly in rhyme:

> What I can do can do no hurt to try,
> Since you set up your rest 'gainst remedy.
> He that of greatest works is finisher
> Oft does them by the weakest minister:
> So holy writ in babes hath judgement shown,
> When judges have been babes; great floods have flown
> From simple sources; and great seas have dried
> When miracles have by the greatest been denied.
> Oft expectation fails, and most oft there
> Where most it promises; and oft it hits
> Where hope is coldest, and despair most fits.   (II. i. 137)

Observe the gnomic, formal, incantatory quality of the rhymes, functioning, as in Helena's first recognition of her own magical powers, as the language of inspiration. She seems to be mesmerizing the King. He is, however, still reluctant, though from now on the two speakers interweave with each other in rhyme. Helena continues, in directly religious, and here orthodox, terms:

> Inspired merit so by breath is barr'd:
> It is not so with Him that all things knows,
> As 'tis with us that square our guess by shows;
> But most it is presumption in us when
> The help of Heaven we count the act of men.
> Dear sir, to my endeavors give consent;
> Of Heaven, not me, make an experiment.   (II. i. 151)

The King asks how long the cure will take? She answers in powerful incantatory style:

> The great'st grace lending grace,
> Ere twice the horses of the sun shall bring
> Their fiery torcher his diurnal ring;
> Ere twice in murk and occidental damp
> Moist Hesperus hath quench'd his sleepy lamp;
> Or four and twenty times the pilot's glass
> Hath told the thievish minutes how they pass;
> What is infirm from your sound parts shall fly
> Health shall live free, and sickness freely die.   (II. i. 163)

Uttermost humility is maintained. Helena claims no power of her own. Even on the plane of nature, it is clear that no health is given; it is there already; only the obstruction is removed, so that nature, the full cosmic powers, may function unimpeded.

The King asks Helena what she is prepared to stake on her own belief. She has already told the Countess that she is prepared to risk her life (I. iii. 255-7) and now proposes the alternative of death with torture. It is precisely this willingness on her part, this embracing of the male values of mortal hazard, the Fortinbras values, which turns the scale. Now the King enters Helena's world, his surrender being marked by his first full-length speech in the full flood of rhyme, beginning:

> Methinks in thee some blessed spirit doth speak
> His powerful sound within an organ weak . . .   (II. i. 178)

Helena's weakness is throughout emphasized, by herself and others; but she is a channel for greater powers, and in that trust risks her life. The King recognizes that "impossibility" may, after all, make sense; for such a girl so to hazard her "youth," "beauty," "wisdom," and "courage," he says, argues either "skill infinite," or some form of desperation (II. i. 184-7). He accepts her contract of healing or death; but, if successful, she asks in return for the hand of any lord it is in the King's "power" to give (II. i. 197). The King, now wholly under her influence, speaks a rhymed speech, in high excitement, almost triumph; and so this extraordinary scene, offering probably the most skilful dramatic use of rhyme in Shakespeare, closes.

That the healing is, as near as may be, or at least to science appears, a miracle, is re-emphasized by the subsequent dialogue of Lafeu and Parolles, with Bertram significantly both present and tongue-tied:

Lafeu. They say miracles are past; and we have our philosophical persons to make modern and familiar things supernatural and causeless. Hence it is that we make trifles of terrors, ensconcing ourselves into seeming knowledge, when we should submit ourselves to an unknown fear.

Parolles. Why, 'tis the rarest argument of wonder that hath shot out in our latter times.

Bertram. And so 'tis.   (II. iii. 1)

We have recently found blank verse catching fire, as it were, and blossoming into rhyme; now we circle back to prose, used to mark the appallingly realistic, near-distance, non-visionary, impact of the miracle. Perhaps nowhere else in Shakespeare are such stylistic variations so effective. Observe that Parolles is genuinely interested, while Bertram remains perfunctory and unimpressed. Knowing Helena so well as a humble retainer in his mother's house, he probably finds it impossible to see her as a person of importance. He may be jealous, or just uninterested; but the fact remains that throughout the subsequent dialogue he says no more. This is most important, and should be underlined in production: his silent presence on the stage should speak volumes.

The more Lafeu expatiates on the miracle, the more keenly Parolles tries to draw level, finding phrases or pretending that he would have found them. Comedy is used, as Bernard Shaw uses it in *Saint Joan*, as a bridge towards reception of an event so utterly beyond the normal, beyond the ken "of all the learned and authentic fellows" who gave out the King as "incurable" (II. iii. 14-16). But Lafeu's phrases are themselves weighty enough, and deeply significant: a "novelty to the world," "a showing of a heavenly effect in an earthly actor," "the very hand of Heaven" (II. iii. 24-38). The personal weakness of Helena as merely the medium, the purified channel, of the transcendent, or cosmic, powers, is rightly stressed:

In a most weak and debile minister, great power, great transcendence: which should, indeed, give us a further use to be made than alone the recovery of the King, as to be generally thankful.   (II. iii. 40)

That is, Lafeu thinks that such powers should be more widely developed. Helena functions as a medium only; but this function is one with her poetic,

Shakespearian, insight, born of love; and both may be related to her virginity. We may seem to have moved far from social considerations, and yet they, too, are contained. This speech marks a fine extension of our former thoughts regarding the relative merits of virtue and rank. It is found that Heaven works directly through a simple girl, of humble origin.

This is the girl whom Bertram, who shows no interest in the miracle, rejects on grounds of birth; and Parolles, who does at least try to show interest, has told us that "he's of a most facinorous spirit that will not acknowledge it to be the ——": he breaks off, and perhaps gestures to Bertram to complete his sentence; but it is Lafeu who continues with "very hand of Heaven" (ii. iii. 35). Any able producer would make full use of Bertram's silent, sulking, presence.

Such an invasion of the story by an event beyond normality is nothing strange among Shakespeare's greater plays. We have only to think of the ghosts and other supernatural phenomena of *Julius Caesar, Hamlet,* and *Macbeth,* the inflated naturalism of *King Lear,* the symbolic and semi-transcendental tempests in work after work, the magical powers of Cerimon, the resurrections of Thaisa and Hermione, the visionary appearances of Diana and Jupiter, Queen Katharine's vision in *Henry VIII.* Some of these events, such as the *unusual* storms in *King Lear* and elsewhere, are poetic fabrications, for a purpose; nor need we ourselves believe in Jupiter as our god. But much of what happens in *Macbeth* can be paralleled among the phenomena of spiritualism; and the resurrection of Hermione may be allowed to shadow a truth regarding death which no Christian should find strange. What, however, is so remarkable in *All's Well that Ends Well* is the more near-distance, immediate and detailed, treatment of transcendence, the dramatist laboring hard to convince us of its reality; a quality driven home by Lafeu's exquisite prose comments, the more effective in that they follow our earlier poetic excitement like a douche of cold water, which nevertheless merely awakes us to the amazing fact. We are faced with an example of spirit-healing of a kind which anyone who chooses can witness in the public demonstrations of our own day. This is not the same as faith-healing, but rather the release, through a medium, of cosmic powers which so reinforce the organism that the obstructing element is dissolved. Such is the "miracle," if so we choose to call it, of *All's Well that Ends Well.* No one who has read, and taken to heart, the New Testament, need be surprised, either at Helena's, or for that matter Cerimon's, powers. Certainly if we do not respond properly to Helena's achievement—if we regard it merely as an impossible fiction—we shall receive little of importance. We shall merely rank ourselves beside Bertram as one who fails to recognize the transcendent when he meets it; and there is probably no more dangerous error than that.

True, we need not wish to be married to it, and a difficulty remains. But then Helena is herself no more than a medium. She is a very ordinary, if exceptional, girl—that is her paradox. However we look at it, Bertram's rejection is to be regarded as a great sin, given weighty theological expression. When, after her supposed death, he claims to have come to love her, the King comments:

> That thou did'st love her, strikes some scores away
> From the great compt, but love that comes too late
> Like a remorseful pardon slowly carried
> To the great sender turns a sour offence,
> Crying, "That's good that's gone." (v. iii. 55)

Who is the "great sender"? King or God? Perhaps the lover is being imagined as carrying God's royal and redemptive pardon to the loved one; and failure incurs wrath. As in the Final Plays, the human drama is regarded as sacramental.

Much depends on our understanding of Helena as a channel, or medium, for the divine, or cosmic, powers. She is drawn directly as a medium, in contrast to Paulina whose function as miracle-worker is less realistically strutted. Like that of Cerimon, another such medium though a thumbnail study only, Helena's miraculous powers grow from, or through, her own, personal, qualities. They are one with her virgin "honor," her calling as Diana's "knight" (i. iii. 122), her beyond-good-and-evil, Shakespearian and Nietzschean, insight, her purified and all-embracing love. Such are Shakespeare's steps towards his conception of what might be termed a "Renaissance sainthood." Sainthood cannot be fully explained; but each of us can, in his own way, use his own best gifts as an approach to an understanding, and Shakespeare seems to have done so here, using his own inward experience of love, the creative bisexuality, and the ranging poetry born from it, to conceive his Helena; using that wholeness of his own poetic experience for which Helena is, as we have seen, a voice. For poetry may be allowed to have functioned as his "third eye," the expression of a unity beyond, and yet including, the male and female principles, a faculty of purity, perception, and power.

The Winter's Tale

by Derek Traversi

[*The author has been discussing the earlier scenes of* The Winter's Tale—Ed.]
The next decisive extension of the play's conception, which takes place
in the great pastoral scene (IV. iv), is preceded by the successive taking up
of a number of threads which contribute in different measure to the complete
effect and indeed add something to its scope and inclusiveness. The first
of these is the intervention of the Chorus (IV. i) which, from its suitable
position at this, the point of balance of the plot, stresses the importance of
the action of time. This, in so far as the temporal process contributes to the
main plan, is worth noting; so too is the reference, made as it were in passing,
to Perdita's growth in "grace." The following exchange between Polixenes
and Camillo is mainly concerned with keeping the plot in motion, though it
also contributes, in the form of passing phrases, to laying the principal
themes before us. The dialogue, indeed, is couched in terms of age, sickness,
and penitence, terms which suit the state of the speakers and correspond to
their position, at this moment, in the general scheme. For Polixenes, it is a
"sickness" to deny anything to Camillo, and "death" to part from him;
whilst Camillo, in his reply, expresses himself as anxious to return to his
country, not only to die ("to lay my bones there"), but also to "allay"
the sorrows of his "penitent master." In both of them, the state of winter,
expressed through a combination of age and exile, predominates, although
the connection with Leontes's penitence already looks forward to the future.

The last-mentioned idea, indeed, is also in the mind of Polixenes, and
already associated with the idea of reconciliation; though his thoughts at
this stage still turn mainly on the "loss" of his former friend's "most precious
queen and children" rather than on the mutual estrangement of the kings
themselves. He does, however, refer in a spirit akin to remorse ("Sicilia . . .
whose very naming *punishes* me") to his own share in the events which
brought that estrangement about. In the latter part of the scene, Polixenes'
concern over the behavior of his own son is itself seen in relation to the

"*The Winter's Tale.*" From *Shakespeare: The Last Phase* (London: Hollis and Carter, 1954;
Stanford: Stanford University Press, 1965), pp. 136-52. Reprinted by permission of the
author and publishers.

conception held by him of the royal dignity: "Kings are no less unhappy, their issue not being gracious, than they are in losing them when they have approved their virtues." The idea of "grace" is here connected with the reference, a little below, to the "princely exercises" which Florizel appears to be neglecting; it is part of the play's intention to stress that the reconciling love of the two royal children is a *princely* love, and that the virtues which they are called upon to embody in their situation are an essential part, properly understood, of the life of "grace." This will be further developed in the handling of the courtly theme, in its relation to pastoral convention, in the scene towards which all this part of the play is deliberately leading.

It is similarly as an anticipation of the pastoral episode that we are, in the main, to understand the introduction into the action of Autolycus, which immediately follows (IV. iii). Autolycus, indeed, has a part of his own to play in the complete conception. His comic function is that of one who is regarded as a little apart from the main structure, whose behavior is in some sense irreducible to the social values of the play, calculated to throw upon the symbolic symmetry itself a touch of relativity, a sense of the incalculable individuality of the processes of life. Yet, although he is not identified, or indeed identifiable, with any neatly rounded scheme, there exists a relation between Autolycus and the complete conception; his vivacious spontaneity has something to contribute to the lifeblood of the action, to the vitality without which it would be no more than an abstract play of empty symbols. This is indicated clearly in the song with which he makes his entry. If *The Winter's Tale* is built upon a pattern which reflects the movement of the seasons, from winter through the rebirth of spring to the full consummation of summer, it is clearly fitting at this point, as an introduction to the following Whitsun pastoral, that this song should indicate the restoration to life of the processes of nature after the prolonged recess of winter. Autolycus's song represents "the sweet," the tender, reborn heart of the year; its concern is with the daffodil newflowering and the impulse of the "blood" that sets the "pugging tooth" on edge, that finds its human counterpart, intensely alive and impatient of all social restraint, in the meeting with "the doxy over the dale" and in "tumbling in the hay." In Autolycus the sense of freedom takes the form of an abandonment of all normal social forms and restraints, the positively valuable and the merely conventional alike. He tells us that he once served Prince Florizel but is now "out of service"; his relation to the social world is in one sense that of an outcast, threatened with the terrors of "beating and hanging," but in another that of a free man exercising a vitality which rests on the action of "blood" and needs itself to be considered in relation to the complete experience offered by the play.

The key to Autolycus, and to his peculiar position in the action, can, indeed, be defined in the phrase from his own song that "the red blood reigns in the winter's pale." The reference to winter implies at once a contrast and a point of reference. It connects the episode now before us with the play's title, and establishes a relationship between the birth of spring in the heart of winter and the affirmation of the warm, living "blood" of youth against the jealousy and care-laden envy of age, an affirmation shortly to be confirmed in the contrast between the young lovers and their elders. In Autolycus himself, of course, this outpouring of spontaneous life moves on the margin of social forms. It has indeed a predatory aspect comically expressed in his first action, the picking of the Clown's pocket; but this itself is, to some degree, a devaluation of his victim's newfound riches and the social pretensions which these have aroused in him. It represents, in any case, an element which will have in due course to be related, as far as may be, to the growing harmony. For the new and natural life expressed in the resurrection of spring is to be, once assumed into fully "gracious" forms of living, a prelude to the final reconciliation; and the main significance of the pastoral which follows, thus stated in the form of an introductory theme, lies in its relation to the birth of spring out of winter, and life—even in the form of wayward, anarchic impulse—on the margin of social forms and conventions.

Thus introduced by this varied and tentative enunciation of its main themes, it is not difficult to see that the great pastoral scene (IV. iv) which constitutes the third "movement" of *The Winter's Tale*, far from being simply, almost naïvely contrasted to the preceding bitterness, is an artistically logical development of the situation. The opening exchange between Florizel and Perdita, indeed, balances the sense of delicate, poetic beauty against a richer, more complex content. The theme of spring, of life reborn but not yet come to full maturity, is stressed from the first; it is explicit in Florizel's apostrophe to Perdita as:

> no shepherdess, but Flora
> Peering in April's front.

If this stood alone, the pastoral, decorative element might still be held to prevail, producing an effect of delicate make-believe which could then be regarded as implicit in the following comparison of the sheep-shearing to "a meeting of the petty gods" of which Perdita, dressed out in the naïve finery her father has produced for her, would be no more than the "queen." Perdita's replies, however, both here and in the following dialogue, indicate that the true situation is more intricate. Behind the pastoral idyll lies the real world, with differences of social station of which she is throughout entirely conscious. Florizel's poetic expressions she sees as "extremes," beneath which lie the fact that he has obscured his "high self" as "the gracious mark o' the land" at the same time as she, in her lowliness, has been "prank'd up," raised to the imitation indeed of a goddess but in no sense endowed with any corresponding reality.

The introduction by Perdita of the vital conception of "grace," now clearly associated with rank and courtliness, reminds us that it is no part of the purpose of the play to set up pastoral simplicity as a final, self-sufficient ideal. It is at best a condition associated with spring, an intermediate state which has much to offer to the courtly order, but which will need before the play is completed to be assimilated into that order if the effect to be achieved is to be something more than a pathetic illusion. Neither of the lovers, indeed, is destined to find fulfilment within the pastoral order. Meanwhile, the sense of happiness which Florizel finds in his love is from the first precarious, its validity doubtful in a way which anticipates the future development. When he blesses the accident which has brought him into contact with Perdita she, far from responding directly with emotions of the same kind, can only pray "Now Jove afford you cause!" and add, in explanation of her misgivings:

> To me the difference forges dread; your greatness
> Hath not been used to fear.

In this exchange, as elsewhere, it is the stranger to pastoral life, the courtier and son of Polixenes, who expresses a naïve, romantic idealism, who is prepared to read into his passion a permanence which, although finally justified, is at least premature; whereas Perdita, supposedly a shepherd girl whose experience of the world is apparently limited by her status, is consistently realistic in her attitude. From Polixenes's point of view, as she knows, her external dignities as queen of the feast are no more than "borrow'd flaunts," her attraction for Florizel no more than a sign that "his work, so noble" has been in her "vilely bound up." The judgment so stated is not to be ignored; if, by the end of the action, it will have become irrelevant, it will yet be strong enough, during the course of this scene, to prevent the consummation of a union which would, in this context, still be premature.

A further indication of the presence of complexities that surpass mere idyllic feeling emerges from a careful reading of Florizel's effort to allay Perdita's misgivings.

> Apprehend
> Nothing but jollity,

he says, and goes on to argue that

> The gods themselves,
> Humbling their deities to love, have taken
> The shapes of beasts upon them: Jupiter
> Became a bull, and bellow'd; the green Neptune
> A ram, and bleated; and the fire-robed god,
> Golden Apollo, a poor humble swain,
> As I seem now.

This cataloguing of divine misdeeds, based on Ovidian commonplaces familiar to the Elizabethan mind, reads oddly indeed in contrast to the effect of
pastoral simplicity also indicated in the speech. The conception of love to
which the gods humbled themselves, losing their divine nature to assume
that of beasts, is neither simple nor idyllic; the passage stands for the introduction of "blood" as an element in the poetic structure, associated indeed
with the reborn greenness of spring—"*green* Neptune"—and even, by indirect
implication, with the fire of Whitsun in the reference to Apollo, "the *fire-robed*
god," but also with the "shapes of beasts" through which they achieved their
purposes. At the end of the speech the rarity of Perdita's beauty is linked,
in the speaker's mind, with the chastity of her love in a way that is far from
simple or merely decorative; so much so, indeed, that the gods, originally
quoted to justify Florizel's own behavior, are implicitly rebuked for the
inferior purity of their motives:

> Their transformations
> Were never for a piece of beauty rarer,
> Nor in a way so chaste, since my desires
> Run not before mine honor, nor my lusts
> Burn hotter than my faith.   (IV. iv.)

It is natural to read this as an effort towards clarification, in which "desires"
are balanced against "honor," and "lusts"—strangely chosen word, one
would have said, to use in a context of purely decorative pastoral—"burn,"
indeed, in accordance with their natural condition, but less hotly than the
"faith" which will eventually lead to their transformation.

In the light of this new indication of conflicting readings of the implications
of "blood," Perdita's characteristically realistic comment—"Your resolution
cannot hold"—and her sense of the irresistible "power of the king" lead her
logically to conclude that the kind of relationship imagined by Florizel is
not, and cannot in the nature of things be, final; either he will have to bow
to the will of Polixenes, thus breaking their union in order to return to the
social world, or she will have to change her own state, thus raising their
relationship to a level not definable in strictly pastoral terms:

> One of these two must be necessities,
> Which then will speak, that you must change this purpose,
> Or I my life.

To Florizel, still unaware of the true complexities into which he is entering,
these forebodings are no more than "forced thoughts," and he begs her
accordingly to

> Strangle such thoughts as these with anything
> That you behold the while.

In support of this advice, he asserts his own constancy in the face of destiny, announces—

> I'll be thine, my fair,
> Or not my father's,

and affirms, more profoundly,

> I cannot be
> Mine own, nor anything to any, if
> I am not thine.

The last statement is emphatically true, and upon this truth their union will in due course be built and exercise its healing function; but before this can take place, it will have to be related to depths of experience of which the speaker, at least, is still unaware. When this has been achieved, and the pressure of external events already foreseen by Perdita has taken its course, the time will be ripe for a "nuptial" of which this pastoral scene is no more than an anticipation.

The following episode, after Perdita has taken upon herself "the hostess-ship o' the day" is, in turn, a great deal more than the beautiful piece of decoration which we might be inclined to see in it. The distribution of the flowers to the assembled guests has, indeed, an essential place in the development of the symbolic motives of the play; the fact that these motives are superbly realized in poetry adds to the force of their impact, but in no way changes their true nature. To her two elderly guests, Polixenes and Camillo, Perdita gives "rosemary and rue," both flowers, as Polixenes himself points out, "of winter," and therefore at once recalling the tragedy through which this pair has already passed and anticipating the part they (or at least the king) are shortly to play in breaking up the spring-like mood of consecrated love; but, as she is careful to point out, these are also flowers associated with "remembrance," and therefore ultimately with the penitence—the choice of "rue" is, in this respect, significant—which will in due course be a prelude to the restoration of "grace." It is this suggestion of a possible redeeming quality that gives force to Perdita's observation that these are flowers which keep

> Seeming and savour all the winter long,

implying thus the presence of the sap of life beneath the apparent death of the season.

This, however, is no more than a prelude to the main part of the flower episode, which takes up and develops themes already foreshadowed in Polixenes's earlier account of his youthful friendship with Leontes. Its purpose, in fact, is to give the particular situation there outlined a setting in

the universal processes of nature, and the pastoral convention is never used
to more subtle effect than in Perdita's reply to Polixenes:

> Sir, the year growing ancient,
> Not yet on summer's death, nor on the birth
> Of trembling winter, the fairest flowers o' the season
> Are our carnations and streak'd gillyvors,
> Which some call nature's bastards: of that kind
> Our rustic garden's barren; and I care not
> To get slips of them.   (IV. iv.)

A reader aware of the possibilities of Shakespearean language will not pass
by as mere poetic decoration the beautiful linking of summer and winter,
birth and death, into continuity. "Death" is joined to summer, and "birth"
and "trembling" are given to winter, so as to suggest that the passage of
the seasons is only part of one inseparable process; and, since we know
already that the relations of birth and death are central to the play, we now
realize that the various developments of *The Winter's Tale* are, like the cycle
of the year, a necessary and connected whole. The contrast of the two
seasons has, moreover, a further meaning. Summer is coupled with the
flowering of youth into the love of Florizel and Perdita, whilst "winter"
reminds us that the age of their parents, just recalled by Perdita through her
gift of flowers, will before the end of this same scene once more affect their
children's relationship. It is, indeed, a winter of lust and egotism, a winter
which implies the vanity and barrenness of jealous, impotent age, in contrast
to the summer of youth in which it fails to see its own natural, normal fulfilment by succession. The coming brutality of Polixenes in separating the
lovers is an exact complement to Leontes' earlier sin; it proceeds from the
same impotence of aged blood, as we are shown by the continual emphasis
upon age and bitterness. By the time Camillo has brought his two masters
together, both will have had cause to regret the importunities of passion. At
present, however, the play has only reached a stage midway between the
winter of disordered passion and the full summer of "grace." Perdita, in the
second part of her speech, goes on to make this clear. Between the terminal
seasons, so to call them, of winter and summer, unregenerate "nature" and
the fullness of "grace," there are flowers which have a certain beauty of
their own, but a beauty imperfect and, as it were, alloyed, like that of human
passion unconsummated by "grace." These flowers are "*car*nations" (the
root has a clear connection with the flesh) and "streak'd gillyvors," "bas-
tards" between crude nature and the realm of "grace."

It is important to catch these associations; but more striking still is the
discussion with Polixenes which arises from Perdita's attitude to the flowers
she herself has mentioned. To her refusal to "get slips of them," Polixenes
replies by asking her to explain the motive which has led her to reject them,

and receives an answer which is in effect a statement of Perdita's position in the play as Hermione's daughter, and so as a manifestation of the pure, undiluted essence of "grace":

> I have heard it said
> There is an art which in their piedness shares
> With great creating nature.

For Perdita, in her simple integrity, "piedness," the creation of "art," or artifice, is contrary to the creative simplicity of 'nature'; the ambiguous and the artificial are rejected by her, in flowers as in human beings, and her conception of life is one which admits of no possible addition to, or "sharing" with, natural perfection. This is, however, one conception of "nature," and Polixenes greatly extends the scope of the discussion when he points out that the "streak'd" process is after all engrained in nature herself; in the same way, the action of "blood," though capable of producing—as it has produced in the earlier scenes—the disruption of harmony and natural relationship, is essential to a full growth into maturity:

> Say there be;
> Yet nature is made better by no mean,
> But nature makes that mean: so, over that art
> Which you say adds to nature, is an art
> That nature makes. You see, sweet maid, we marry
> A gentler scion to the wildest stock,
> And make conceive a bark of baser kind
> By bud of nobler race: this is an art
> Which doth mend nature, change it rather, but
> The art itself is nature.   (IV. iv.)

The expression of this argument is worth the most careful attention, because it brings us very close to the central meanings of the play. To Perdita's conception of "art" as an addition to "nature," and therefore, from the standpoint of her absolute simplicity, as a deformation of it, Polixenes opposes another of "art" as completing "nature," based on it, indeed, but as its crown and perfection. The conception is clearly one which is capable of expression in human and social terms, and Polixenes, in what follows, proceeds to make this relation explicit. After describing Perdita as "sweet maid"—the reference to virginity is capable, for all its beauty, of indicating an incompleteness which will shortly be taken up more openly—he goes on to discuss the process of grafting in terms of marriage, the union, in this case, of "the wildest stock" (in other words, "nature," or, in human terms, "blood," unregenerate humanity) to "a gentler scion," the product of civilized urbanity, of "nature" in its complete, fulfilled sense, which is "grace." In this sense, the process of grafting, far from being, as Perdita

fears, a perversion of natural virtue, is itself natural, merely the unfolding
in man of the full possibilities of "nature," which require a civilized soil
and a spiritual end for their complete flowering. The "bark of *baser* kind"—
the adjective is now clearly indicative of the lack of the civilized graces—
is made to "conceive" by "a bud of *nobler* race": the idea of birth following
on marriage thus acquires a new and wider meaning, becomes a completion,
itself natural, of "nature," an assumption by normal humanity of the crown-
ing qualities, social and spiritual, of "grace."

Perdita's reply, however, shows that the achievement of this union is still
premature. To Polixenes's attempt, on the strength of this argument, to
dissuade her from excluding these flowers, she turns away with an extreme
repulsion which is most significant:

> I'll not put
> The dibble in earth to set one slip of them;
> No more than were I painted I would wish
> This youth should say 'twere well, and only therefore
> Desire to breed by me.

The introduction of the familiar Elizabethan horror of being "painted,"
together with the force of "breed," which once more stresses the relevance
of consummation in marriage, shatters pretty thoroughly any suggestion
that this scene is exclusively concerned with the maintenance of a state of
idyllic make-believe. Clearly, the innocent poetry so far given to Florizel and
Perdita—itself, as we have seen, full of half-suspected undercurrents—is no
sufficient resolution of the great disunities developed in the early part of
the play, and the brief moment of pastoral felicity is, in fact, shortly to be
broken by the open intervention of Polixenes. Only when the action has been
decisively raised from the pastoral level will a final integration become
conceivable.

The further list of flowers now presented by Perdita to Polixenes indeed,
confirms this. It indicates at once her sense of the connection that she feels
to exist between his person and the operations of "blood," and her repudiation of the latter. "*Hot* lavender," by the significant choice of adjective,
stresses the importunity of passion, and the marigold,

> that goes to bed wi' the sun
> And with him rises, weeping,

indicates the disillusion that follows on the self-sufficient pursuit of desire.
Perdita, in short, is at once repudiating excess, which her innocence rightly
finds incompatible with the development of the "gracious" life, and showing
that this same innocence is still unprepared to come to terms with certain
necessary aspects of mature experience. Her youth rejects an attitude that

is essentially that of "men of middle age," and indeed her own marriage will eventually and naturally be with youth, from which the stresses and egoisms present in Polixenes will be excluded; but it also, at this stage, suggests an exclusion of passion, "blood," which is itself incompatible with maturity.

The impression conveyed in this exchange is confirmed by the presence of a certain pathetic weakness, a kind of wilting from life, in the great list of flowers presented to Florizel which immediately follows. The emphasis on "virgin branches" and "maidenheads" is full of meaning in the light of the intense reaction against passion which preceded it; still more so is the contrast with "hot lavender," already referred to, and the other flowers given to men of middle age. Above all, there is the feeling behind such lines as:

> . . . pale primroses,
> That die unmarried, ere they can behold
> Bright Phoebus in his strength, a malady
> Most incident to maids.

The beauty of these lines is devoid of strength, even clings pathetically to its own lack of vigor. The final reconciliation will be far less precarious. The spring-like beauty of this episode will have to be intensified by being joined, in due course, to the deep note of penitence in Leontes. Only thus can the idyllic pastoral be given sufficient substance to balance the harshness of the early scenes; and only so can a feeling for innocent beauty be raised to the level of Shakespeare's unique sensation of the fertility and maturity of "grace."

Meanwhile the vitality which, in spite of what we have said about her flower speech, underlies Perdita's love for Florizel is indicated by the reference to the royal flowers—"bold oxlips" and "the crown imperial"—with which she rounds off her apostrophe, and by the intense feeling for life which emerges from her final turning to her lover:

> *Perdita.*   O, these I lack,
> To make you garlands of; and my sweet friend,
> To strew him o'er and o'er.
> *Florizel.*   What, like a corse?
> *Perdita.* No, like a bank for love to lie and play on;
> Not like a corse; or if, not to be buried,
> But quick and in mine arms.

The previous references to "maladies" and unconsummated fading find their natural climax in Florizel's pathetically romantic evocation of the idea of death; but equally natural, equally a part of the beautifully balanced effect, is the spontaneous warmth of Perdita's reply. The consummation of their mutual love is *not* to lie in death, but in a reaction towards life. Florizel is

not to be "buried" by the flowers which she will bestow on him, but these
are to be a sign of the vitality which is to deliver him "quick" into her arms.
The powerful strength of Perdita's youthful emotion has already, at this
moment, laid the foundations for the final consummation, and the reference,
which follows, to "Whitsun pastorals" is far more than a piece of decorative
folklore. It introduces, deliberately and at this most fitting moment, the
theme of the Holy Spirit to stress the note of "grace" (for Whitsun is, in the
Christian cycle which conditions, however indirectly, the deeper purposes
of *The Winter's Tale*, the feast of the descent of the Holy Spirit, harbinger
of grace) as a crown to that of spring and love with which this scene is
concerned.

These utterances of Perdita are balanced, immediately below, by the
quality of Florizel's reply, which can be said to gather up in a most immediate
form the basic sensation of the play:

> What you do
> Still betters what is done. When you speak, sweet,
> I'ld have you do it ever: when you sing,
> I'ld have you buy and sell so, so give alms.
> Pray so; and for the ordering your affairs,
> To sing them too: when you do dance, I wish you
> A wave o' the sea, that you might ever do
> Nothing but that; move still, still so,
> And own no other function; each your doing,
> So singular in each particular,
> Crowns what you are doing in the present deeds,
> That all your acts are queens.   (IV. iv.)

The most striking quality of this passage is the sensation it conveys of balance,
of a continual relationship between motion and stillness. The verse is carefully constructed to reproduce this sensation, this balance, in terms of the rise
and fall of the speaking voice. Consider the effect of the double "so" in the
fourth line, the first bringing the movement of the speech to its height and
the second deliberately leading from that height, whilst a third "so" in the
next line binds the central idea to those which follow; a little further on,
there is still another "so," again associated with two balanced phrases,
bringing out still further the relationship of motion to stillness, the unity of
experience to the incessant flow of its material. The same effect is obtained
by the choice of echoing sounds in "singular" and "particular." Still more
important is the final association of "*present* deeds" with "*all* your acts";
every act of Perdita's involves all her perfections and is a complete expression
of her natural queenliness. And this, in turn, connects her with the central
image of the whole speech—that of the wave which is always in motion,
and yet is ever the same. This image, like the speech of which it forms a part,

is, of course, much more than a beautiful piece of decorative poetry. It is rather the particular expression of a vital theme of the play, and indeed of all Shakespeare's mature plays—the relation between the values of human life which postulate timelessness, and the impersonal "devouring" action of time which wears these values ceaselessly away. The wave image conveys perfectly the necessary relation between the mutability of life and the infinite value of human experience which it conditions, but which is finally incommensurate with it. When this intuition, and that of Perdita in the expression of her love, has been gathered up into the wider symbolic framework of penitence and reconciliation the full scope of *The Winter's Tale* will be finally clear.

The Tempest

by Bonamy Dobrée

So much has been written in the last few years about the plays of Shakespeare's final phase, in a general re-interpretation which amounts almost to rediscovery, that we are in danger of having a veil interposed between us and whatever it is that Shakespeare may have to show. I confess that after studying some of these, and feeling myself more and more bewildered and inadequate, I comfort myself by reading that admirable Dialogue of the Dead in which Fontenelle makes Æsop and Homer talk together. You will remember that when Homer congratulates Æsop upon artfully packing so much morality into his fables, Æsop says:

> Il m'est bien doux d'être loué sur cet art, par vous qui l'avez si bien entendu.
>
> *Homère.* Moi? je ne m'en suis jamais piqué.
> *Ésope.* Quoi! n'avez-vous pas prétendu cacher de grands mistères dans vos Ouvrages?
> *Homère.* Hélas! point du tout.

and so on, in entertaining elaboration. But, of course, the great work of a great master, besides being an object in itself, is also a receptacle for what each individual person can put into it, and will be reinterpreted by every age. But recent essays upon these later dramas have made it extremely difficult for us to be absolutely honest in our own approach: because these plays, being, it is fairly safe to say, Shakespeare's deepest and perhaps final religious statement—using religion in its broadest sense as an apprehension of what life is about—that many writers have sought, and found, their own beliefs about Shakespeare in them, even their own religious beliefs, and used them to propagate their own gospels. Thus it is extremely hard for us to see the object as it really is—for ourselves. Only too often with these plays, the criticism of others, instead of removing barriers as it should, merely interposes fresh ones.

Nevertheless there are certain broad statements we can make, and the

"*The Tempest.*" From *Essays and Studies* (London: John Murray, 1952), pp. 13-25. Reprinted by permission of the author, the English Association, and the publishers.

first is that *The Tempest* cannot be considered apart from the other three of this phase, *Pericles*, *Cymbeline*, and, to my mind the greatest of all these miracles, *The Winter's Tale*. To state their scope briefly I cannot do better than quote Professor Kenneth Muir:

> It is impossible to doubt that the form of the last plays was determined by [I would prefer to say adapted to] the new vision which Shakespeare wished to express. The center of this vision was a belief in the necessity for forgiveness, the conviction that "the rarer action is in virtue than in vengeance." As Murry suggests, Shakespeare had realized, as Tchekov was later to do, that "since we are forgiven it would be strange not to forgive." The other characteristics of the plays of the last period arise from this necessity of forgiveness. Without love forgiveness is meaningless: and with forgiveness must come the reconciliation of the estranged, the restoration of the lost, the regeneration of the natural and sinful man, the birth that is a symbol of rebirth, and the conquest of death by the acceptance of the fact of death.

This is an excellent compaction of the themes, but you will have noticed that it doesn't quite fit *The Tempest*, especially as he adds "These things take time." And it does not quite fit because also—and this is the thesis I would like later to develop tentatively—Shakespeare was moving on from those themes to others, which might perhaps tacitly include these, but would be different from them. There can be no doubt, however, that *The Tempest* is closely linked with this group which is concerned with a loss or losses which seem to be death, with repentance, followed by reconciliation (after a "recognition" scene), and by forgiveness, with, as Mr. Muir also says, the sins of the fathers being healed by the children. Besides containing a very unusual number of ideas adumbrated in other plays, its structure shows more plainly than any other of Shakespeare's dramas, the storm or tempest as a symbol of turmoil with music as the healing, harmonizing influence, a structure which Mr. Wilson Knight[1] pointed out so convincingly and so long ago, that we tend to accept it, unacknowledged, as a commonplace.

But though the play belongs to this group, and is sometimes hailed as the most perfect of them all, I for one do not feel that the old intuitions have the old force. It seems to me that the poignancy of loss, and repentance, reconciliation, or forgiveness—call it grace if you like—were more convincingly brought home in the other plays, certainly in *The Winter's Tale*. I would like to suggest that the treatment of the old themes of this group is a little perfunctory. For instance, is there not a somewhat nasty taste about the quality of Prospero's forgiveness? Is it not Senecan, rather than Christian? "It is the part of a great mind to despise injuries," Seneca says in his essay on anger, "and it is one kind of revenge to neglect a man as not worth it." This seems to me exactly Prospero's sentiment with regard to Alonso. It is

---

[1] *The Shakespearian Tempest.*

Ariel who has to remind him of pity and tenderness, and even then Prospero appeals to his "nobler reason," and rather priggishly performs what he thinks is a "rarer" action. And after all, it is easy enough to forgive your enemies when you have triumphed over them. When he speaks to Antonio, he may use the *word* forgiveness, but does he feel the emotion?

> For you, most wicked sir, whom to call brother
> Would even infect my mouth, I do forgive
> Thy rankest faults—all of them; and require
> My dukedom of thee, which perforce I know,
> Thou must restore.

Does that sound like forgiveness? Is that how you would speak to a man whom you love as you forgive him? Nor can it be said that any of the three men of sin—Alonso, Sebastian, and Antonio—repent. What happens to them is that they are frightened out of their wits by Ariel's speech at the banquet. The most that Gonzalo can say is:

> All three of them are desperate: their great guilt
> Like poison given to work a great time after,
> Now 'gins to bite the spirits:

and even that is only words. For Alonso feels not repentance, but regret, because his action has lost him his son. As for Sebastian, he says he'll fight hard—one fiend at a time—and Antonio says he'll second him. There is only stubbornness there. Repentance and forgiveness seem to remain as fossils in the play, rather than as active principles. Loss and recovery certainly are there in Alonso's and Ferdinand's loss of each other; the sins of the fathers are redeemed by the children: those themes are fully stated, especially the last. But yet, with how much less power than in the other plays, with less rapturous poetry! I would ask you to compare the love speeches which Ferdinand addresses to Miranda with those which burst from Florizel as he woos Perdita. The former have amazement, but they lack warmth.

Or take one more difference between this play and the others, which if this were really of the same sort, would make it a much weaker play. I mean the great flower pieces, such a marked feature in the other three. Let me remind you just of the one in *The Winter's Tale:*

> . . . Daffodils
> That come before the swallow dares, and take
> The winds of March with beauty; violets dim
> But sweeter than the lids of Juno's eyes
> Or Cytherea's breath; pale primroses
> That die unmarried ere they can behold
> Bright Phoebus in his strength,—a malady

> Most incident to maids; bold oxlips and
> The Crown imperial; lilies of all kinds,
> The flower de luce being one. . . .

What do we get in *The Tempest*? All we find in the body of the play
is Prospero's remark to the elves:

> you demi-puppets, that
> By moonshine do the green-sour ringlets make,
> Whereof the ewe not bites: and you whose pastime
> Is to make midnight mushrumps . . .

a somewhat grim and sterile vision. And in the Masque all we get is a strictly
utilitarian catalogue—wheat, rye, barley, vetches, oats, and pease—from
Iris; and from Ceres some lines about barns and garners, and plants with
goodly burden bowing; all very proper for a fertility rite, such as the Masque
was, but this is not the passionate adoration of the loveliness of nature.
Unless we accept the postulate of a bored and wearied Shakespeare—and
therefore think the play a failure (and it is emphatically not a failure)—
we must assume that Shakespeare was not writing about the sort of thing
he had embodied in the other plays of the group.

And if this group has also as one of its themes the regeneration of natural
and sinful man, what are we to make of Caliban whom those who think
in this way regard as the only too sinful and natural man? For the moral of
the story—if the story must have a moral—is that he cannot be regenerated;
he is

> A devil, a born devil, on whose nature
> Nurture can never stick.

He must be kept in order by being hunted, pinched, tortured with cramps.
True, he says at the end, when ordered to tidy up Prospero's bedroom—
"I will be wise hereafter and seek for grace"—because he realizes he was a
fool to follow a god with a bottle. We are not impressed. Again, the natural
man in Ferdinand, apparently, can be kept in check only by threats: Prospero
warns him against pre-nuptial love in words which suggest Lear's curse of
sterility upon Goneril. This may have been to please James I; but what
Shakespeare seems to be suggesting—or at least Prospero suggests here and
in other places—is that the natural instincts have constantly to be disciplined,
scourged, whipped; they cannot be integral to regenerated man. It is true
that Ferdinand brings in a somewhat sweeter atmosphere by saying that
nothing will ever turn his honor into lust, but that does little to freshen the
general impression made by Prospero's scolding.

If I have taken you with me so far, you will conclude that though *The
Tempest* is closely related to the other three plays—*Pericles, Cymbeline, The*

Winter's Tale—it cannot be grouped with them; it is not a symbol of the same sort of attitude, of sentiment about life, which infuses and informs the other plays. What I would like to suggest is, that though to a large extent Shakespeare felt the mood of those other plays, he was no longer dominated by it, and was moving on to other things. He is not denying the intuitions of the other plays, but having expressed them he was not, as artist, interested in them so wholly as before. They are there, but perfunctorily stated, and a little flatly, as the background from which something else is emerging, to modify what he said earlier. But the play is so extraordinarily complex, and exists on so many levels, that what may seem important on one level scarcely exists on another.

But—and I would like to stress this—we must not forget that we are, after all, judging a stage play to which an audience could not be expected to come with their minds stored with the author's previous work. And it seems to me, that together with so much richness, certain themes are emerging which had not previously been very evident, and that these tend to thrust into the background the themes common to the group of late plays; and these are, destiny, the nature of reality, and, as Mr. Muir stresses, freedom. I, for my part, do not want to lay too much stress on these elements, especially the first, that of destiny. All I want to affirm is that they are parts of a very complex whole, and that by treating them a little separately we may be able to account for certain aspects of the play which if it is considered as one of the same sort as, shall we say, *The Winter's Tale*, appear as blemishes.

But before going on to discuss the themes themselves, I would like to touch upon the problem of stage illusion which all this group of plays offer in an acute form. They are, of course, utterly unrealistic poetic drama; the suspension of our disbelief must be practised constantly and whole-heartedly. In this play particularly, we have to accept, to live in, so to speak, another dimension of time. Let me give one instance. I read in an article the other day (Mr. Traversi in *Scrutiny*, June 1949) that, by the beginning of Act III, the sufferings of Ferdinand and Miranda had cemented their devotion. Now devotion implies a certain length of time, so that realistically that is absurd. They had known each other for about an hour and a half, and their suffering had been of the slightest; even Ferdinand's grief for his father had been promptly put aside. Yet we may find that the statement fits in with out notion of what the play, at least to some extent, is about. We accept the fresh reality. But Shakespeare knew that you cannot stretch fantasy too far, so from the very beginning gave his audience the security of an intellectual setting they were familiar with—nothing so strange as ancient Tyre or Roman Britain or Illyria—but, on an island such as was being discovered every day, a sort of Bermuda, the familiar figure of the magus. As the late Professor Kittredge wrote:

Prospero, to the Elizabethan audience, was as comprehensible in his feats of magic as a chemist or an electrical engineer is to us moderns . . . . [Prospero] belonged not only to a conceivable category among men, but to an established category.

Just as Marlowe in Faustus had presented a necromancer who dealt in black magic, a being his audience perfectly understood, so here in Prospero is one dealing in white magic, as did in actual life Shakespeare's contemporary, Dr. John Dee. Prospero was, in the manner of Dr. John Dee—but, we imagine, far more effectively—controlling certain forces of nature.

In this setting, with this magus, nothing that can happen on this island is incomprehensible; even Ariel is a natural force—his name is common in charms and invocations of the time. This then is a realistic story, not a fairy tale such as *Midsummer Night's Dream*. It is not on such obvious ground as that that Shakespeare is to discuss reality and unreality. Caliban, again, is not the sort of monster the Jacobeans would regard as an invented or fantastic figure: travellers' tales of wild men of this sort went on down to well into the eighteenth century. Thus in a sense this play would be easier to "believe"—as one believes stage plays—than any of the other three. What I am trying to suggest is, that here Shakespeare was giving himself as solid a framework as he could so as to have within it the maximum of freedom possible.

And with what amazing nimbleness he moves from one plane of reality to another (I am adopting Dr. Tillyard's expression), first of all, from one set of people to the opposite one, from the upper classes to the lower (to put it that way), which, seeing what they are, is no small feat. For the upper classes—especially Ferdinand, Miranda, Gonzalo and Alonso (more about Prospero soon) correspond with what Mr. T. S. Eliot has said about the characters in the romances, as being "the work of a writer who has finally seen through the dramatic action of men into a spiritual action which transcends it"; but the more materialistic people, Caliban, Stephano, Trinculo and the sailors have all the outward dramatic solidity of Shakespeare's usual figures, while Antonio and Sebastian form a link between. There is a delightful and rich earthiness about the lower group—the poet among them being Caliban—and base as they are, they are drawn with the loving realism which makes all Shakespeare's children of the lower nature so immensely likeable. Antonio and Sebastian are too puppet-like to be of any interest, as they had to be lest they should become too interesting: but when we move to the upper group the figures, as realistic figures, are pallid in the extreme. They are the dullest *jeune premier* and *jeune première*. Ferdinand is a very ordinary nice young man; the insipid young chit of fifteen that Miranda is can hardly interest us on the page (however much she might stir us in life or in the theatre). Even Prospero cannot let pass her remark "Oh brave new world that has such people in it," seeing that the people she is mainly referring to are the three men of sin. He has to say a little acidly " 'Tis new to thee"—which, incidentally, shows how far Prospero believed in "regeneration"! The "upper" characters, in short, live on an utterly different plane of reality from the "lower" ones; but this is only a sort of outer case in which the theme of the real and unreal is contained.

For the one which Shakespeare is toying with—I don't think it is more than that at this stage—is "What is reality? Is it something that we can judge of by the evidence of our senses?" The ultimate form of this question, which is touched upon only in Prospero's "cloud cap'd towers" speech, may be "Is there a quite different reality behind experience?" But short of that question, Shakespeare seems to be inducing in us this sense of the unreal to give a shimmering effect to this curious and delightful object he offers us. It gives us that peculiar sense of detachment which it seems to be one of his objects to achieve—if an effect on his audience was, as he wrote, at all in his mind. Every now and again the people in the play are deluded as to what they see, or see only what they wish to see, or even see what is not there. All the time there is a suggestion of unreality, of living in a dream world. Miranda, for example, saw the ship sink—and so, it turns out later, did the rest of the fleet. The garments of the shipwrecked people are fresher than before, in spite of their drenching in the sea (it is true there had to be some explanation on the realistic plane!); there is constantly a mysterious music— Ferdinand cannot tell whether it be in the air or the earth, and soon his spirits "as in a dream are all bound up", spell-bound by Prospero. Or take the little passage near the beginning of the second act:

> *Adrian.*   The air breathes upon us here most sweetly.
> *Sebastian.* As if it had lungs, and rotten ones.
> *Antonio.*   Or, as 'twere perfumed by a fan.
> *Gonzalo.*   How lush and lusty the grass looks! how green!
> *Antonio.*   The ground, indeed, is tawny.
> *Sebastian.* With an eye of green in't.

Which is right in their sense of reality? Is not each making his own according to his temperament? "The quality o' the climate" makes some drowsy and the spirit of others more active. Caliban lives in a world inhabited by spirits, and for him the island is full of noises, some of them ravishing, while Ariel causes the utmost confusion in the conversation of Caliban with Stephano and Trinculo. At the end Gonzalo is utterly astray between the real and the unreal, as Prospero tells him

> You do yet taste
> Some subtilties o' th' isle, that will not let you
> Believe things certain,

while Alonso fears that the Ferdinand whom he sees may prove "a vision of the island."

All the while the shimmer is there, quite apart from the scenes of magic, the banquet which vanishes, the appearance of Ariel as a harpy, the masque, with all the attendant bewilderments, out of which arises Prospero's great philosophic speech. It is true that in the Earl of Stirling's *Tragedy of Darius* Shakespeare had read

> . . . let this worldly pomp our wits inchant
> All fades and scarcely leaves behind a token . . .
> Those stately Courts, those sky-encountering walls
> Evanish all like vapours in the air

but if Shakespeare borrowed a little of the imagery, the thought is a commonplace made actual and vivid, a truth imaginatively grasped by the power of the poetry of a man who for the moment at least felt it all with the assent of an intuition. The whole sense of insubstantiality is there, one that all of us have probably felt at some time or another with varying keenness. All of us feel sometimes, perhaps hope, that we are such stuff as dreams are made on, and welcome the relief of thinking that our little lives are rounded with a sleep. Thus for a certain part of our apprehension the play gathers momentum up to this point, and after that flows away from it.

But for a certain part only, for interwoven with the theme is one almost contrary, since Fate and destiny can hardly be said to apply to shadows; yet the theme is there. In the very first scene Gonzalo says of the boatswain: "Stand fast, good Fate, to his hanging, make the rope of his destiny our cable," a jesting reference, yes, but the words are there to make an impact on our consciousness. This is somewhat waveringly supported in the next scene. It was "Providence divine"—which we may equate with destiny—that had brought Prospero and Miranda ashore; and then we learn that "bountiful Fortune" (not of course chance, in our sense, but the inescapable Wheel of Fortune familiar to the medieval mind) had brought Prospero's enemies to the island; and Prospero tells Miranda that

> by my prescience
> I find my zenith doth depend upon
> A most auspicious star, whose influence
> If now I court not, but omit, my fortunes
> Will ever after droop.

Antonio next, when egging Sebastian on to murder, appeals somewhat confusedly to destiny. But of course, the grand statement comes in the speech Ariel makes when as a harpy he sweeps away the feast offered to the bewildered travelers. It is phrased with very special power, placed so that we cannot but notice it:

> You are three men of sin, whom destiny,
> That hath to instrument this lower world
> And what is in't, the never-surfeited sea
> Hath caused to belch up . . . .

It is curious, by the way, that Ariel uses some of the coarsest imagery in the play, Caliban some of the most etherial; but that is another issue. Ariel goes on:

> . . . You fools! I and my fellows
> Are ministers of fate,

and later he informs the men of sin that

> The powers delaying, not forgetting, have
> Incensed the seas and shores—yea, all the creatures
> Against your peace.

So the idea is stated—not indeed very emphatically, since we, the audience, know that Ariel is pretending, play-acting, speaking the part Prospero told him to. Nevertheless something has happened in our minds; and perhaps when Ferdinand a little later says that Miranda is his "by immortal Providence," we may be a little inclined to believe him, though we know that it came about largely by Prospero's contrivance. The element must not, I think, be stressed; but it is there.

The last thread, that of freedom, is more insistent. It runs through the whole of the Ariel part, as I need not remind you. Again and again he asks when he shall be free; again and again Prospero promises him his freedom. We are never allowed to forget it. At first, with Caliban, we hear of the opposite: he is "slave Caliban." But he has his aspirations. One of the notes in the play that everyone remembers is his

> 'Ban 'Ban, Ca-Caliban.
> Has a new master—get a new man.
> Freedom, high-day! high-day, freedom! freedom, high-day, freedom!

as he leads Stephano and Trinculo to a happier state of life. Poor wretch, prototype here, perhaps, of the wretchedest mob, incapable of scepticism and so always deluded, believing ever that a change of masters will mean greater freedom for the man, and ever disillusioned. That interpretation need not detain us. Ferdinand, who tells us early (a romantic commonplace)

> Might I but through my prison once a day
> Behold this maid, all corners else o' th' earth
> Let liberty make use of, space enough
> Have I in such a prison,

later finds freedom in the service of Miranda. The play ends with the idea
of freedom, of release (the opposite, we note, of Fate or Destiny), with
Prospero saying to Ariel, "Be free and fare thou well"—the last line of the
epilogue which cannot but ring in our ears, being

> Let your indulgence set me free.

That then ends the play, composed throughout so musically, with a lovely
diaphaneity of verse scarcely distinguishable from the beautifully flexible
prose, itself almost verse, that gives a kind of iridescent effect to this gracious
object; and what I want to suggest is that in it Shakespeare was using for
fundamental material, not so much the moral intuitions of repentance,
forgiveness, reconciliation and so on, but the metaphysical intuitions of fate
and freedom, of appearance and reality. Perhaps that is what Mr. Eliot
meant. And out of these he spun the enchanting fable, a kind of transparent
object which, if we will let it, may set, us also, a little more free.

But is there not more? the question will be asked. Have we not here in
Prospero, Shakespeare himself taking his farewell of the stage? I fear that
some confusion has been caused by this ingenious conjecture, born some two
hundred years after the play was acted. Perhaps as he wrote some of the
passages a certain metaphorical resemblance between him and Prospero
struck him whimsically, and he developed it a little, especially in the notorious farewell passage, which was a piece of common material about magi-
cians he took almost verbatim from some lines in Golding's Ovid,[2] and, as
usual transformed. Surely he would not have wished the likeness pushed
too closely, in view of what Prospero is—a philosopher King, who like his
prototype in *Measure for Measure* was a disastrous ruler; a somewhat cruel,
uncertain-tempered man, who far from renouncing anything, was going
back to the enjoyment of worldly greatness; so we should not be pressed
to regard the play as a kind of last will and testament, especially as Shakespeare did not break his wand or drown his book (*Henry VIII* followed, at
least largely his, and portions of *Two Noble Kinsmen*). I admit it is possible
that he had solved his problems on the plane of ordinary living, that he no
longer wanted to write as he had done, and that he was moving into realms
where he was finding, as Rimbaud was to find, that *paroles païennes* would
not express what now he had to say. However all that may be, I do not
believe he was writing a kind of valedictory sermon; but that he was doing
what every artist does in every work, exploring reality, here, in some ways,
almost directly, and expressing the inapprehensible in symbols which he
hoped might bring him illumination.

Nothing more definite? Alas! I hear once more the voice of Æsop, speaking
to Homer:

[2] VII. 192-219.

Tous les savants de mon temps . . . soutenaient que tous les secrets de la théologie, de la physique, de la morale, et des mathématiques même, étaient renfermés dans ce que vous aviez écrit. Véritablement il y avait quelque difficulté à les développer: où l'un trouvait un sens moral, l'autre en trouvait un physique: mais après cela ils convenaient que vous aviez tout su, et tout dit à qui le comprenait bien.

And indeed there have not been lacking those (*qui le comprenaient bien*) to tell us what *The Tempest* is really about—from those who would have it that Shakespeare was writing so rigid a thing as an allegory, to those whose delicacy of perception delights us, helps our own imagination, leads us to follow threads which promise to lead us excitedly to the center of the maze. It may be, as Mr. Robert Graves tells us,[3] that

in one aspect *The Tempest* is a play of revenge on [Shakespeare's] personal enemies, that in another it is his farewell to the stage, in another a political satire, in another a religious mystery, in another a spectacle to please the common people, in another a celebration of a royal wedding, in another a piece of rhythmic music—all these are legitimate aspects, but. . . .

Indeed yes, but . . . . Let us pull ourselves up, even perhaps a little sharply, and desist from pursuing these threads. I do not think that in dissecting a work of art we murder it, but it is possible that we may not be such skilful anatomists as we would like to think. We may, of course, extract such morals as we see fit from any work of art, but I cannot regard *The Tempest* as a sermon, nor believe that Shakespeare was engaged in delivering what M. de Norpois would describe as "*un véritable prêchis-prêchas.*" And if in the deliciously neat, humorous and perhaps deeply felt epilogue Prospero really is Shakespeare, what was it from which he was praying to be set free? May it not have been from what Lamb called the everlasting coxcombry of our moral pretensions? It is, certainly, always a difficult point to determine how far a great artist is conscious of what he is doing until he has done it; like the rest of us (indeed more so) he must say to himself in the now common phrase which I think M. André Gide invented: "How can I know what I mean till I see what I say?" What, as I believe, the poet does, is, by giving us a thing of delight, to release our spirits into a world of conjecture, freed of any immediate necessity for action. His materials are the thoughts, impulses, velleities which at the moment most occupy him; his symbols are the people he offers to our view, what happens to them, and the music of his utterance. The difference between works of art, in their importance, is the difference in the kind of realm into which we are released, to ponder and to muse, the degree of sensitive awareness induced in us. If we allow "the meddling intellect," as Wordsworth called it, to meddle too curiously,

[3] *Poetic Unreason.*

we prevent the work of art from giving us what it might. We are forcing it, submitting it to our lesser purposes. Surely we should apply Blake's warning:

> He who binds to himself a joy
> Does the wingèd life destroy:
> But he who kisses the joy as it flies
> Lives in eternity's sunrise.

So let us be a little delicate with this lovely thing which Shakespeare gave us, a thing composed of the impulses of love and forgiveness, of fear, of the sense of destiny, of the immateriality of our existence, of the brutality of matter; composed with grace of movement to the sound of entrancing music, a music sometimes terrible, sometimes miraculously sweet, but which brings the whole into a harmony which lies beyond contradiction. The lesson? Well, perhaps there is a lesson, but art, as De Quincey said,[4] "can teach only as nature teaches, as forests teach, as the sea teaches, as infancy teaches, namely by deep impulse, by hieroglyphic suggestion." Maybe we do it wrong to offer it a show of violence in trying to extract secrets from it, the secrets it might reveal if we fitted it less into our preconceptions, and let it quietly do its work upon us. For

> . . . Who in his own backyard
> Has not opened his heart to the smiling
> Secret he cannot quote?
> Which goes to show that the Bard
> Was sober when he wrote
> That this world of fact we love
> Is unsubstantial stuff!
> All the rest is silence
> On the other side of the wall;
> And the silence ripeness,
> And the ripeness all.[5]

[4] Speaking of Pope and didacticism.
[5] W. H. Auden, "Preface" to *The Sea and the Mirror*. Copyright 1944 by W. H. Auden. Quoted by kind permission of Messrs. Faber and Faber, Ltd. and Random House, Inc.

Chronology of Important Dates

1564	*April 26*	Christening at Stratford-on-Avon.
1582	*November 27*	License for Shakespeare's marriage with Anne Hathaway.
1583	*May 26*	Christening of daughter, Susanna.
1585	*February 2*	Christening of Hamnet and Judith.
1588-94		Performance of *The Comedy of Errors, The Two Gentlemen of Verona, The Taming of the Shrew.*
1592		Reference to Shakespeare as an actor and dramatist in Greene's *Groatsworth of Wit.*
1590-99		Performance of nine English histories.
1593		Publication of *Venus and Adonis.*
1594		Publication of *The Rape of Lucrece.*
1594		Shakespeare becomes a sharer in the Lord Chamberlain's company.
1594		Publication of *Titus Andronicus.*
1594-96		Performance of *Love's Labour's Lost, A Midsummer-Night's Dream, The Merchant of Venice.*
1596		Hamnet dies. Grant of arms to Shakespeare's father.
1597	*May 4*	Purchase of New Place, Stratford.
1598-1601		Performance of *Much Ado about Nothing, As You Like it, Twelfth Night.*
1599		Opening of Globe Theatre.
1600-08		Performance of great tragedies.
1601	*September 8*	Burial of Shakespeare's father.
1601-04		Performance of *Troilus and Cressida, Measure for Measure, All's Well that Ends Well.*
1607	*June 5*	Susanna marries Dr. John Hall.
1608	*September 9*	Burial of Shakespeare's mother.
1608-13		Performance of *Pericles, Cymbeline, The Winter's Tale, The Tempest.*
1609		Publication of *Sonnets.*
1616	*February 10*	Judith marries Thomas Quiney.
1616	*March 25*	Shakespeare's will.
1616	*April 23*	Shakespeare dies at Stratford.
1623		Publication of First Folio.

Notes on the Editor and Authors

KENNETH MUIR (b.1907), the editor, is King Alfred Professor of English Literature in the University of Liverpool. He has edited three of Shakespeare's plays, three anthologies, and Sir Thomas Wyatt's poems; he has written *Shakespeare's Sources* (1957), *Shakespeare as Collaborator* (1960), *Shakespeare: Hamlet* (1963), books on Milton and Wyatt, and translations of Racine.

MURIEL C. BRADBROOK (b.1909) is Reader in English Literature, University of Cambridge, Vice Mistress of Girton College. Her many publications include *Themes and Conventions of Elizabethan Tragedy* (1934), *Shakespeare and Elizabethan Poetry* (1951), *The Growth and Structure of Elizabethan Comedy* (1955), and *The Rise of the Common Player* (1962).

HAROLD F. BROOKS (b.1907) is Reader in English in Birkbeck College, London, Joint General Editor of the Arden Shakespeare, and author of *Chaucer's Pilgrims*.

R. W. CHAMBERS (1874-1942) was Professor of English, University College, London (1922-41). His publications include *Beowulf* (1912), *Thomas More* (1935), and *Man's Unconquerable Mind* (1939).

BONAMY DOBRÉE (b.1891) was Professor of English Literature, University of Leeds (1936-55). His publications include *Restoration Comedy* (1924), *Modern Prose Style* (1934), *The Early Eighteenth Century* (*Oxford History of English Literature*, 1959), and editions of Congreve and Vanbrugh.

HELEN GARDNER (b.1908) is Fellow of St. Hilda's College, Oxford. Her publications include *The Art of T. S. Eliot* (1949), *The Divine Poems of Donne* (1952), and *The Business of Criticism* (1960).

HAROLD JENKINS (b.1909) is Professor of English Literature, Westfield College, London and General Editor of the Arden Shakespeare. His publications include *Henry Chettle* (1934) and *Edward Benlowes* (1952).

G. WILSON KNIGHT (b.1897) was Professor of English, Toronto, and at Leeds (1956-62). His books on Shakespeare include *The Wheel of Fire* (1930), *The Imperial Theme* (1931), *The Crown of Life* (1947), and *The Sovereign Flower* (1958).

CLIFFORD LEECH (b.1909) is Professor of English Literature, University of Toronto and General Editor of the Revels Plays. His publications include *Shakespeare's Tragedies* (1950), *John Webster* (1951), *John Ford* (1957), and *The John Fletcher Plays* (1962).

JOHN MIDDLETON MURRY (1889-1957) was Editor of *The Adelphi*. His books include *Countries of the Mind* (1922), *Keats and Shakespeare* (1925), *William Blake* (1933), *Shakespeare* (1936), and *Jonathan Swift* (1954).

A. P. ROSSITER (1905-57) was Lecturer at Durham and Cambridge. His publications include *English Drama* (1950) and *Angel with Horns* (1961).

ERNEST SCHANZER (b.1922) is Associate Professor at the University of Munich. His publications include *Shakespeare's Appian* (1956) and *The Problem Plays of Shakespeare* (1963).

DEREK TRAVERSI (b.1912). His publications include *Approach to Shakespeare* (1938), *Shakespeare: The Last Phase* (1954), *Shakespeare from Richard II to Henry V* (1958), and *Shakespeare: The Roman Plays* (1963).

Selected Bibliography

I. General Studies

Barber, C. L. *Shakespeare's Festive Comedy*. Princeton, 1959.

Brown, J. R. *Shakespeare and his Comedies*. London, 1957 (2nd ed. 1962).

Campbell, O. J. *Shakespeare's Satire*. New York, 1943.

Charlton, H. B. *Shakespearian Comedy*. London, 1938.

Coghill, N. "The Basis of Shakespearian Comedy" in *Essays and Studies of the English Association* (1950), 1-28.

Frye, N. "The Argument of Comedy" in *English Institute Essays* (1948). New York, 1949, 58-73.

Frye, N. "Characterization in Shakespearian Comedy" in *Shakespeare Quarterly*, IV (1953), 271-7.

Evans, B. *Shakespeare's Comedies*. Oxford, 1960.

Gordon, G. *Shakespearian Comedy and other studies*. Oxford, 1944.

Granville-Barker, H. *Prefaces to Shakespeare*. London, 1927-47.
[Contain essays on several of the comedies]

Nicoll, A., ed. *Shakespeare Survey*, VIII (1955).
[Contains several articles on the comedies]

Parrott, T. M. *Shakespearean Comedy*. New York, 1949.

Pettet, E. C. *Shakespeare and the Romance Tradition*. London, 1949.

Sen Gupta, S. C. *Shakespearian Comedy*. Calcutta, 1951.

Wilson, J. D. *Shakespeare's Happy Comedies*. London, 1962.

II. Early Comedies

Bradbrook, M. C. "Dramatic Role as a Social Image: a study of *The Taming of the Shrew*" in *Shakespeare Jahrbuch*, XCIV (1958), 132-50.

Bradbrook, M. C. *The School of Night*. Cambridge, 1936.
[Contains a chapter on *Love's Labour's Lost*]

Brooks, H. "Themes and Structure in *The Comedy of Errors*" in *Early Shakespeare*, ed. Brown and Harris. London, 1961.

Danby, J. F. "Shakespeare Criticism and *Two Gentlemen of Verona*" in *Critical Quarterly*, II (1960), 309-21.

Kirschbaum, L. *Character and Characterization in Shakespeare*. Detroit, 1962.
[Contains a chapter on Shylock]

Knight, G. W. *The Shakespearian Tempest*. London, 1932.
[Contains a section on *The Merchant of Venice*]

Merchant, W. M. *"A Midsummer-Night's Dream:* A Visual Re-creation" in *Early Shakespeare*, ed. Brown and Harris. London, 1961.

Murry, J. M. *Shakespeare*. London, 1936.
[Contains a chapter on *The Merchant of Venice*]

Pettet, E. C. *"The Merchant of Venice* and the Problem of Usury" in *Essays and Studies of the English Association*, XXXI (1945), 19-33.

Roesen, B. *"Love's Labour's Lost"* in *Shakespeare Quarterly*, IV (1953), 411-26.

Schanzer, E. "The Central Theme of *A Midsummer-Night's Dream*" in *University of Toronto Quarterly*, XX (1951) 233-8.
[Revised version in *Oeuvres completes de Shakespeare*, III (1956), pp. 1-17]

Seronsy, C. C. " 'Supposes' as the Unifying Theme in *The Taming of the Shrew*" in *Shakespeare Quarterly*, XIV (1963), 15-30.

Yates, F. A. *A Study of Love's Labour's Lost*. Cambridge, 1936.

III. *Mature Comedies*

Clark, T. W. *"Much Ado about Nothing"* in *Scrutiny*, XIX (1953), 297-316.

Fergusson, F. *"The Comedy of Errors* and *Much Ado about Nothing"* in *The Human Image in Dramatic Literature*. New York, 1957.

Gardner, H. *"As You Like It"* in *More Talking of Shakespeare*, ed. J. Garrett. London, 1959.

Jenkins, H. *"As You Like It"* in *Shakespeare Survey*, VIII (1955), 40-51.

Jenkins, H. "Shakespeare's *Twelfth Night*" in *Rice Institute Pamphlet* XLV (1959), 19-42.

Prouty, C. T. *The Sources of "Much Ado about Nothing."* New Haven, 1950.

Rossiter, A. P. *Angel with Horns*. London, 1961.
[Contains an essay on *Much Ado*]

Salinger, L. G. "The Design of *Twelfth Night*" in *Shakespeare Quarterly*, IX (1958), 117-39.

Smith, J. *"As You Like It"* in *Scrutiny*, IX (1940), 9-32.

Smith, J. *"Much Ado about Nothing"* in *Scrutiny*, XIII (1946), 242-57.

IV. *Problem Comedies*

Bradbrook, M. C. "Authority, Truth and Justice in *Measure for Measure*" in *Review of English Studies*, XVII (1941), 385-99.

Bradbrook, M. C. "Virtue is the True Nobility: a Study of the Structure of *All's Well*" in *Review of English Studies*, XXVI (1950), 298-301.

Chambers, R. W. *Man's Unconquerable Mind*. London, 1939.
[Contains an essay on *Measure for Measure*]

Coghill, N. *Shakespeare's Professional Skills*. Cambridge, 1964.
[Contains two chapters on *Troilus and Cressida*]

Knight, G. W. *The Sovereign Flower*. London, 1958.
[Contains an essay on *All's Well*]

Knight, G. W. *The Wheel of Fire*. London, 1930.
[Contains essays on *Measure for Measure* and *Troilus and Cressida*]

Lascelles, M. *Shakespeare's 'Measure for Measure'*. London, 1953.

Lawrence, N. W. *Shakespeare's Problem Comedies*. New York, 1931.

Leavis, F. R. *The Common Pursuit*. London, 1952.
[Contains an essay on *Measure for Measure*]

Leech, C. "The 'Meaning' of *Measure for Measure*" in *Shakespeare Survey*, III (1950), 66-73.

Leech, C. "The Theme of Ambition in *All's Well*" in ELH, XXI (1954), 17-29.

Maxwell, J. C. "*Measure for Measure*. A Footnote to Recent Criticism" in *The Downside Review* (1947).

Merchant, W. M. *Shakespeare and the Artist*. London, 1959.
[Contains a chapter on *Measure for Measure*]

Schanzer, E. *The Problem Plays of Shakespeare*. London, 1963.
[Contains an essay on *Measure for Measure*]

Tillyard, E. M. W. *Shakespeare's Problem Plays*. London, 1950.

Traversi, D. "*Troilus and Cressida*" in *Scrutiny*, VIII (1938), 301-19.

Wilson, H. S. "Dramatic Emphasis in *All's Well*" in *Huntington Library Quarterly*, XIII (1949-50), 217-40.

V. *Last Plays*

Auden, W. H. *For the Time Being*. London, 1954.
[Contains an interpretation of *The Tempest*]

Bethell, S. L. *The Winter's Tale: A Study*. London, 1947.

Curry, W. C. *Shakespeare's Philosophical Patterns*. Baton Rouge, 1936.
[Contains an essay on *The Tempest*]

Dobrée, B. "The Tempest" in *Essays and Studies of the English Association* (1952), 13-25.

James, D. G. *Scepticism and Poetry*. London, 1937.
[Contains a chapter on the last plays]

Knight, G. W. *The Crown of Life*. London, 1947.

Muir, K. *Last Periods of Shakespeare, Racine and Ibsen*. Detroit.

Muir, K. *Shakespeare as Collaborator*. London, 1960.
[Contains chapters on *Pericles* and *The Two Noble Kinsmen*]

Stephenson, A. A. "The Significance of *Cymbeline*" in *Scrutiny*, X (1942), 329-38.

Strachey, L. "Shakespeare's Final Period" in *Books and Characters*. London, 1906.

Tillyard, E. M. W. *Shakespeare's Last Plays*. London, 1938.

Tinkler, F. C. *"Cymbeline"* in *Scrutiny*, VII (1938), 5-20.

Tinkler, F. C. "The Winter's Tale" in *Scrutiny*, V (1937), 344-64.

Traversi, D. *Shakespeare: The Last Phase*. London, 1954.